The New Heroines in Film and Television

This thought-provoking volume offers an overview of contemporary representations of prominent female characters as they appear in an array of moving-image narratives from a Jungian and post-Jungian perspective.

Applying a theoretical frame that is richly informed by the Jungian and post-Jungian concepts of persona, individuation, and archetypes, works including *Fleabag* (2016–2019), *Ladybird* (2017), and *The Queen's Gambit* (2020) as well as Disney productions such as *Brave* (2012), *Moana* (2016), and *Frozen* (2013), are contextualized and discussed alongside their non-screen precedents and contemporaries, including myths, fairy tales, and works of literature, to closely examine new patterns of the female journey. This book identifies how young female characters rebel against the female persona of previous eras through the trickster, the shadow, and other archetypes, comparing the contemporary female protagonist with her predecessors to assess the new paths, roles, and milestones available to her. Examining the construction of the female persona across time periods and mediums in an accessibly written yet academic style, this book is the first of its kind.

With a fulsome account of the progressive developments in entertainment media and Jungian thought, this book is essential reading for students and scholars of film, as well as anyone with an interest in analytical psychology and wider feminist issues in contemporary culture.

Helena Bassil-Morozow is a senior lecturer in Media and Journalism at Glasgow Caledonian University. Her many publications include *Tim Burton: The Monster and the Crowd* (Routledge, 2010), *The Trickster in Contemporary Film* (Routledge, 2011), *The Trickster and the System: Identity and Agency in Contemporary Society* (Routledge, 2014), *Jungian Film Studies: The Essential Guide* (Routledge, 2016; co-authored with Luke Hockley), and *Jungian Theory for Storytelling: The Essential Guide* (Routledge, 2018).

'In this fascinating book, Helena Bassil-Morozow challenges and revises Jungian concepts in order to offer fresh insights into the evolution of the female persona. Drawing on a rich range of material, from folk tales through to fictions, contemporary films and tv programmes, she argues that the cultural templates for women are rapidly changing in response to their need to break free of the mask of femininity. Deftly analysing representations of defiant heroines, "liminal" mothers and female tricksters, she concludes that women are carving out new paths towards individuation and a fairer society.'

Avril Horner, *emeritus professor of English Literature, Kingston University*

'This is an important book for studies of gender in twenty-first century television and film, and also for those wanting to see Jungian theory grow up. Bassil-Morozow transforms Jungian notions of the persona and individuation to reveal the gender bias in traditional uses. For as *The New Heroines in Film and Television* demonstrates, the female persona is ubiquitous in filmed narratives, the feminine used to give meaning to male-oriented stories, or, in other words, the anima. Moreover, individuation in the Jungian sense occurs too often in its stunted masculinist form of the hero's journey. While critiquing these conservative aspects of mainstream media, Bassil-Morozow brilliantly weaves together post-Jungian and post-Freudian ideas to show the emergence of resistant and transgressive female-centered stories. If you care about gender or film or TV, this book is a must.'

Susan Rowland, *author of* Jung: A Feminist Revision (*2002*)

'A fiercely original account of the female protagonist in contemporary film and TV narratives. Bassil-Morozow continues the explorations of female individuation that have attracted a wide and enthusiastic readership. She traces the changes in the way recent heroines function as agents, rather than as passive characters. This is a timely book as female leads are emerging in roles which, previously, would have been unavailable to them. The book is a significant blend of Jungian and psychoanalytic film criticism.'

Andrew Samuels, *author of* A New Therapy for Politics? *and former professor of analytical psychology, University of Essex*

The New Heroines in Film and Television

Post-Jungian Perspectives on Contemporary Female Characters

Helena Bassil-Morozow

Routledge
Taylor & Francis Group

LONDON AND NEW YORK

Designed cover image: timoph © Getty Images

First published 2023
by Routledge
4 Park Square, Milton Park, Abingdon, Oxon OX14 4RN

and by Routledge
605 Third Avenue, New York, NY 10158

Routledge is an imprint of the Taylor & Francis Group, an informa business

British Library Cataloguing-in-Publication Data
A catalogue record for this book is available from the British Library

Library of Congress Cataloging-in-Publication Data
Names: Bassil-Morozow, Helena Victor, 1978- author.
Title: The new heroines in film and television : post-Jungian perspectives on contemporary female characters / Helena Bassil-Morozow.
Description: Abingdon, Oxon ; New York, NY : Routledge, 2023. | Includes bibliographical references and index.
Identifiers: LCCN 2022058353 (print) | LCCN 2022058354 (ebook) | ISBN 9781032181400 (paperback) | ISBN 9781032181417 (hardback) | ISBN 9781003253044 (ebook)
Subjects: LCSH: Women heroes in motion pictures. | Women heroes on television. | Women in motion pictures. | Women on television. | Jungian psychology. | Storytelling--Psychological aspects. | LCGFT: Film criticism. | Television criticism.
Classification: LCC PN1995.9.W6 B37 2023 (print) | LCC PN1995.9.W6 (ebook) | DDC 791.43/6522--dc23/eng/20221219
LC record available at https://lccn.loc.gov/2022058353
LC ebook record available at https://lccn.loc.gov/2022058354

ISBN: 978-1-032-18141-7 (hbk)
ISBN: 978-1-032-18140-0 (pbk)
ISBN: 978-1-003-25304-4 (ebk)

DOI: 10.4324/9781003253044

Typeset in Times New Roman
by Taylor & Francis Books

For Freya Muse

Contents

Acknowledgements

Firstly, I am very grateful to Kaspars and Freya for their appreciation and understanding of my multiple roles, one of which is a writer. Without this understanding this book would not have been completed.

I would also like to thank my colleagues at Glasgow Caledonian University, Julie Roberts, Katy Proctor, and Nancy Lombard, for their inspirational activities and their tireless work to promote the female agency as a right for everyone.

I am also extremely grateful to my mentors who have given me their time and wisdom. Their advice proved invaluable on the bumpy journey.

Finally, I would like to thank Routledge for their patience with my chaotic and unpredictable schedule.

Analysis of the BBC's show *Fleabag* used in Chapter 7 was initially published in 2020 in as part of an article for *Persona Studies* journal. Full reference:

Bassil-Morozow, H. (2020). Persona and rebellion in Trickster narratives. Case study: Fleabag (BBC 2016–2019). *Persona Studies, 6*(1), 30–42. https://doi.org/10.21153/psj2020vol6no1art998.

Introduction

What is the female journey? Mythology has little to say about it, and contemporary narratives – particularly on-screen ones – are just beginning to explore it. The future generations of girls need new mythology, new stories, new role models, new paths, and new possibilities. They need opportunities to break through the essentialism of societal norms and definitions, through what can be termed 'the female persona' – the mask of femininity made up of visual and behavioural cues. Women are socialized into the female persona, and stories surrounding us, these identity-structuring narratives, play a significant role in this influence. Simone de Beauvoir writes in *The Second Sex* (1949):

> [The girl's] historical and literary culture, the songs and legends she is raised on, are an exaltation of the man. Men made Greece, the Roman Empire, France and all countries, they discovered the earth and invented the tools to develop it, they governed it, peopled it with statues, paintings and books. Children's literature, mythology, tales and stories reflect the myths created by men's pride and desires: the little girl discovers the world and reads her destiny through the eyes of men. [...] Nothing is more boring than book retracing the lives of famous women: they are very pale figures next to those of the great men ...
>
> (De Beauvoir, 1949/2011: 312)

The New Heroines in Film and Television: Post-Jungian Perspectives on Contemporary Female Characters examines the new patterns of female journey in contemporary film and television as well as traces their emergence out of the more traditional representations of female characters. It does so through the Jungian and post-Jungian concepts of persona, individuation, and archetypes, examining the female individuation in the context of female persona and cultural-archetypal conditioning. At the centre of the book's theoretical framework is the concept of the female persona – a derivation of the Jungian concept of persona, or the social mask which has its roots in the collective, or rather, in the intersection of the unconscious collective and its external manifestations.

DOI: 10.4324/9781003253044-1

The book mentions an array of other conceptual frameworks and methodologies, including Freudian and post-Freudian ideas, psychoanalytic feminism, and discourse analysis amongst many others, occasionally filling an odd theoretical gap where a Jungian approach may be missing a piece, needs to be re-thought or modernized, has a comparable element in other frameworks, or can benefit from being combined with other theories.

While exploring the new avenues for female characters, it is important to acknowledge the material, environmental, and economic conditions that may prevent women from self-expression and self-fulfilment. After all, on-screen narratives belong to different genres, many of which offer unrealistic or fantastical prospects of exploring alternatives in life. Disney's latest host of heroines like Elsa in the *Frozen* franchise (2013), Mulan (*Mulan*, 2020) and Raya (*Raya and the Last Dragon*, 2021) possess magical skills, objects, or animals, and one cannot in all seriousness apply 'solutions' for inequality presented by fairy tales to real life material obstacles faced by women and girls around the world. The best we can do is interpret these special powers as metaphors which can be translated into discovering one's own special skills and unique abilities, and to motivate one to change and challenge one's circumstances. It is also important to acknowledge that introducing narratives with proactive, independent female protagonists exercising their choice in life, whatever the genre, is already an important first step in influencing the social reality with its traditions and expectations of what a woman is and how she should behave. Whether she fights alongside dragons or attempts to establish herself as a scientist, the very fact that she chooses to act instead of patiently waiting for things to appear, or relying on someone else – that she attempts to challenge the socially-accepted mask of femininity – is already an important first step in discussing the changing role of women in contemporary life.

This book does not focus on a single format or genre but casts a wide net, instead paying attention to the stories, themes, and structures, and their links with the female persona. Analyses include both film and television narratives although television predominates simply because the rise of on-demand services have made the market more competitive, offering platforms to screenwriters, directors, and actors who would have been otherwise neglected by Hollywood. These narratives are discussed alongside their non-screen precedents and contemporaries, including myths, fairy tales, and works of literature, often tracing the same themes throughout centuries and examining the construction of the female persona in different stories. In terms of the timeframe, films and TV series released over the past 20 years or so have been the primary focus of analysis. However, older screen narratives are also occasionally mentioned for contextual and comparative purposes.

Chapter 1, 'The Female Journey', explains the individuation concept in general before moving on to discuss the female individuation in particular. It looks at a range of possibilities for a female journey while also providing definitions and critique of major Jungian concepts. It also contains my 'taxonomy of archetypes' – a guide to using Jungian archetypes in screenwriting and textual analysis, previously published in *Jungian Theory for Storytelling* (Routledge, 2018).

Chapter 2, 'The Female Persona', offers an overview of the Jungian concept of persona and similar ideas in other frameworks. It brings together a range of views on the mask of femininity before combining them with the persona. It uses examples from film and television to demonstrate this amalgamated concept.

Chapter 3, 'The Red Woman and the Blue Woman' concerns the boundaries of the female persona. It explores traditional narrative clusters, which I termed 'Red Woman' and 'Blue Woman', featuring female rebels, usually punished for their disobedience. Their most prominent examples are the tales 'Little Red Riding Hood', Charles Perrault's 'Bluebeard', and Hans Christian Andersen's 'Red Shoes', and works of literature such as Nathaniel Hawthorne's *The Scarlet Letter* (1850) and Leo Tolstoy's *Anna Karenina* (1873–1877).

While Chapter 3 explores the literary and cinematic history of rebellion against the constraints of the female persona, Chapter 4, 'Buldingsroman: Rejection of the Mask' looks at the current influx of young heroines breaking the mould and rejecting societal standards. Examples include the new generation of Disney heroines and princesses (Merida in *Brave* (Disney/Pixar, 2012), Elsa in *Frozen* (2013), Moana (*Moana*, 2016), etc.), and confident young characters in *Ladybird* (Greta Gerwig, 2017), *Sex Education* (Netflix, 2019), *The Queen's Gambit* (Netflix, 2020) and many more.

New representations of motherhood are covered in Chapter 5 which examines a new host of comedic depictions of this traditionally static role. Chapter 6 discusses the changing roles of the female fighter and pursuer of knowledge. It looks at general trends in depictions of heroines, occasionally zooming in on particular narratives, and assesses the recent changes in representations of agentic elements in the female journey.

Finally, Chapter 7, 'The Female Trickster', traces the emergence and development of female trickster characters in recent film and television narratives. It looks at rebellious and outrageous characters intent on breaking societal taboos and boundaries, and ultimately eliminating the female persona. It also gives an overview of trickster theory in general, previously covered in my monographs *The Trickster in Contemporary Film* (Routledge, 2012) and *The Trickster and the System: Identity and Agency in Contemporary Society* (Routledge, 2015).

Importantly, the monograph gives an overview of the recent developments in the field rather than offers detailed analyses of particular narratives. This bird's-eye view maps out new conversations around the nature of the female journey and explores new roles and identity options currently offered to the heroine.

We Need New Stories

Comic book writer and feminist Kelly Sue DeConnick told the online community Comics Alliance back in 2012 that if a female character in a draft can be replaced with a 'sexy lamp', the creator needs another draft. A female character needs to be a protagonist, not a 'device' (Lynskey, *The Guardian*, 25 March 2015). New characters and narratives are desperately needed to shift old screenwriting conventions regarding female representation.

This book focuses on the emerging new mythology as well as on the narrative and stylistic gaps that are still left uncovered. Myths, as Frances Gray notes, are preserves of collective history that hint at 'stories of the subordinated which may also secretly exist in their own right. Together, the forgotten, the misremembered, the repressed and the remembered all inform the identity of a collective' (Gray, 2019: 71). Challenging, changing and updating myths as well as writing new ones are all slow processes involving a change of culture in the entertainment industry.

Despite the recent improvements in gender representation on screen (including, importantly, Disney which caters to the future generation of world citizens), some areas of the entertainment industry are slow to change. As Lucy Bolton notes, mainstream cinema still maintains sexual stereotypes which 'can be fitted into the patriarchal-apparatus model theorized by Laura Mulvey' (Bolton, 2011: 9). This often happens by stealth, in a fetishistic fashion, when a seemingly powerful female characters display gratuitous nudity, for example (Bolton, 2011: 9). Some of the contemporary female warrior representations, such as Wonder Woman (played by Gal Gadot, *Wonder Woman*, 2017) certainly incorporate this traditional (and safe, from the commercial point of view) over-reliance on the abundant display of the female body even when the character herself is presented as strong and independent.

This monograph uses a broad definition of myth – as a cultural construct and as a narrative deeply rooted in social structures. In turn, it structures and manages the life of an individual. Myth is an effective (and affective) tool of shaping human beings. As Darren Kelsey writes,

> Mythology plays an affective role in our lives – across the historical, cultural, and psychological complexities of individuals and societies. It is not merely the case that stories affect us because they communicate ideas that arouse thoughts and emotions. Stories often mean much more than this, since they are produced and understood from the depths of our psyche through to the archetypal expressions of language, representation, experience and ideology.
>
> (Kelsey, 2017: 1)

Female actors are still unhappy at the choice of roles available to them. For instance, actor and singer Zendaya Coleman explains in an interview with *GQ* that she has turned down multiple roles because they could have been the same one-dimensional person whose only task was to assist the male protagonist in realizing his potential (Harris, *GQ*, January 11, 2021). Similarly, in a *Vogue* interview actor Margot Robbie reveals that she is so excited to play

Harley Quinn – a DC comics character, 'professional psychopath', the dark version of the female trickster, and Joker's former lover – because 'girls never get' epic scenes with explosions and 'hero runs'(Wiseman, *Vogue*, August 2021).

Not that screen narratives completely lacked a proactive protagonist willing to challenge her passive role, her rigid mask, or her victim status until now – agentic female characters have been slowly introduced into mainstream entertainment industry and mainstream thinking. Ridley Scott has created an array of confident female characters, including Ellen Ripley (*Alien* films), Thelma Dickinson and Louise Sawyer (*Thelma and Louise*, 1991), and Lieutenant Jordan O'Neill (*G.I Jane*, 1997). Carol Clover stresses in *Men, Women and Chainsaws: Gender in the Modern Horror Film* (1992) that the horror genre was already carefully subverting the 'traditional disposition of sex roles on screen' over a decade before *Thelma and Louise* (1991) introduced female protagonists who refused to be victims of their habitus in general and of men managing this habitus in particular. This film, Clover writes, 'has been a turning point on this score' (Clover, 1992: 235). Clover also draws the reader's attention to the fact that the 'rape and revenge' motif had been a prominent feature of horror narratives such as *Carrie* (1976) and *I Spit on Your Grave* (1978) since the middle of the 1970s. The narrative element, Clover notes, has now been absorbed by the mainstream cinema (Clover, 1992: 235–236).

Indeed it has been, and quite spectacularly. *Carrie* was remade in 2013 with a host of Hollywood celebrities, and Quentin Tarantino has blatantly capitalized on formerly liminal genres, including blaxploitation and rape/revenge in the *Kill Bill* duology and *Jackie Brown* (1997) which features the *Foxy Brown* actress Pam Grier. The angry, avenging woman who no longer wants to tolerate being controlled, stalked or raped by a guy is surely a good thing to happen to moving image narratives.

Yet, a brief look at gender statistics in the film industry shows that, indeed, men still very much determine representation in moving image narratives. 'Inequality Across 1,600 Popular Films: Examining Gender, Race/Ethnicity & Age of Leads/Co Leads From 2007 to 2022' report found that while there is an upward trend in terms of female protagonists (44% in 2022 as opposed to just 2007), it still 'falls short of the US Census benchmark, where women and girls comprise over 50% of the population' (USC Annenberg, 2023: 1–2). Meanwhile, despite the palpable gender representation progress, only ten films released in 2022 had a female actor aged forty five or older as a lead or co-lead compared to 35 movies featuring a male actor in the same age bracket (USC Annenberg, 2023: 2). In other words, the stories created for the entire population, the stories transmitted across the world, the films discussed by critics as being worthy or unworthy of our attention, the narratives we project onto ourselves and introject into our lives, the characters we model ourselves on – they are predominantly thought up by men.

Action is linked to agency and self-expression. As Margo Robbie points out, the film industry, much like classic narrative traditions criticized by Simone de Beauvoir, has not been particularly prolific in creating proactive female protagonists. A girl looking for self-expression, De Beauvoir argues, can only find passive or controversial role models: fairies, mermaids, nymphs, and evil mother figures (de Beauvoir, 1949/2011: 314). Even when female characters are humanized, like Hans Christian Andersen's little mermaid, they assume the role of the suffering victim rather than an agentic character (de Beauvoir, 1949/2011: 314).

The problem is – and perhaps, naturally – that people tend to create narratives and characters based on their own feelings and experiences; out of their own vision of the world. Special effort is required to reconstruct the life and problems of the other; to imagine their journey. To this day, we do not know exactly what a female journey is because there have not been enough female creators to map it out.

As Callie Khouri, the writer of *Thelma and Louise* admits, the industry is very slow to change even though no one openly calls women incapable of doing men's work (and the situation is strikingly similar in many other industries). The only way out of this situation for women is to work harder, and eventually hope that you would be noticed and appreciated: (Donnelly, *Forbes*, 26 February 2014)

In fact, men in charge of narratives, from folkloric to critical, television and cinematic, has led to the default situation of men judging other men on the quality and social relevance of the stories produced by them. There is no surprise, therefore, that for many years the film industry had been churning out superhero films in which agency is invariably awarded to a white male protagonist. The recent improvements discussed in this book have emerged under the growing pressure to compete with on-demand services. Meanwhile, television (BBC, Netflix, Amazon, Nordic Noir, HBO, the CW) has so far been faring much better in terms of representation, with Netflix alone producing a wave of change with shows either created specifically for the service, or taken over from other content providers: *Orange is the New Black* (2013-), Jessica Jones (Krysten Ritter) from the Marvel spinoff of the same name (2015-); *Glow* (2016-), *Stranger Things* (2016-), *Crazy Ex-Girlfriend* (2015–2019), *Fargo* (2017), *Sex Education* (2019-), and many more. In 2022 Amazon Prime Video launched *Lord of the Rings: The Rings of Power* which features an elven warrior, Galadriel (Morfydd Clark), hunting the evil Sauron. Meanwhile, by creating *Game Of Thrones* with its host of female characters ranging from toughest fighters to hyper-feminine seductresses, HBO has opened up a continuing public and academic discussion about the journey of the female protagonist.

Prime Video also came up with a semiotic inversion of the male gaze, *I Love Dick* (2016–17), and BBC has an array of series, mini-series and short films exploring the destiny of the female protagonist in contemporary world, including *Top of the Lake* (2013-), *Happy Valley* (2014-), *Apple Tree Yard* (2017), *The*

Replacement (2017), *Requiem* (2018), *Doctor Foster* (2018), *Press* (2018-), *Care* (2018), *Fleabag* (2016–2019), *Killing Eve* (2018–2022), *Gentleman Jack* (2019-), *Vigil* (2021) to name but a few. Suranne Jones's confident system fighters – Doctor Foster, Anne Lister (*Gentleman Jack*) and Detective Chief Inspector Amy Silva (*Vigil*) – insist on their right to act even when they are monstered and silenced. *Care*, the story of a daughter left to care for her disabled mother, a stroke survivor, is particularly unusual as it depicts a woman with a disability – a rare candid representation on screen. Importantly, the 13th Doctor in BBC's *Doctor Who* (series 11) is female (Jodie Whittaker). Finally, Nordic Noir has introduced us to strong and obstinate female leaders, including Sarah Lund in *The Killing* (2007–12), Saga Noren in *The Bridge* (2012–15), and Birgitte Nyborg in *Borgen* (2010–2013).

Hollywood is desperately trying to catch up, particularly after the establishment of Disney+, and Disney's acquisition of Marvel and 21st Century Fox. It has new heroines – Rey (Daisy Ridley) in *Star Wars: the Force Awakens* (2015), Imperator Furiosa (Charlize Theron) in *Mad Max: Fury Road* (2015), and Alice (Mia Wasikowska) in Tim Burton's *Alice in Wonderland* (2010) and *Wonder Woman* (2017) to name but a few. Once groundbreakingly rare, Ridley Scott's strong female characters such as Ripley from the *Alien* films (Sigourney Weaver), Jordan O'Neill from *G.I Jane* (1997), and Thelma and Louise (*Thelma and Louise,* 1991) are now in good company.

These are all recent narratives, and their abundance across different countries, channels and streaming services is a testament to the gradual change in attitude towards the female protagonist as someone who has interests outside the world of makeup, fashion, and men (in contrast with the four ladies in the *Sex and the City* franchise the protagonist of which has been chasing the same uncatchable prize man for decades, or Bridget Jones and her dating dilemmas).

The Female Journey

This book looks at the female journey and its components from a post-Jungian perspective while feminist film criticism has been traditionally dominated by Freudian and Lacanian analyses of both women on screen and female spectatorship. Occasional attempts to introduce Jungian ideas into film criticism (by Susan Rowland, Terrie Waddell, Greg Singh, Catriona Miller, Helena Bassil-Morozow, and Luke Hockley) have not been substantial enough to challenge the domination of Lacanian thought in feminist analyses of screen media. This book aims to redress this imbalance and to produce a comprehensive framework for discussing the representation of female characters on screen in general, and the narrative path of female protagonists in particular. Now more than ever film criticism needs a Jungian view on the heroine.

Lacanian theory, so preoccupied with phalluses as social and political symbols, and equating the female with the unknowable, the caring, and the 'lacking', is not fit for exploring a woman who is keen to shake off the rigid persona and move away from her position as a victim of patriarchy. While acknowledging the importance of Freudian and post-Freudian theory for screen studies in general and for feminist analysis of screen narratives in particular, it is necessary to move on to less restrictive frameworks. Freud cannot not offer genuine freedom to the female heroine, pinned to the wall by the male gaze or trapped in the narrow confines of male projection.

Theorists like Laura Mulvey, Mary Ann Doane, Theresa de Lauretis, Barbara Creed, Kaja Silverman, and others have all employed the Lacanian theoretical framework in their discussion of women as characters and spectators. When used in feminist film analysis, Lacanian theory, which presents women as 'the other' and identifies masculine symbols as the seat of power, turns against itself, creating theoretical gaps.

This does not mean, however, that Freudian theory can be completely dispensed with when building a Jungian film feminist framework. It is still used throughout this monograph, albeit sparingly, for its influence on cultural studies is indisputable, and some of the terms it utilizes have become part of the cultural canon because of their precision and meaningfulness. Among them are, for instance, the Oedipus Complex, the Lacanian Symbolic, object relations, phantasy, the male gaze, and scopophilia to name but a few. Whereas post-Jungian theory can offer alternative terms to describe these phenomena, sometimes the use of Freudian concepts is unavoidable. The important thing is not to become too over-reliant on them.

Thanks to Laura Mulvey (1975) perhaps, the focus of feminist film studies has been on the gaze to which the female character (and the actress) is subject. This kind of focus makes the female character – especially a protagonist – look powerless while the overall perspective puts the male in charge of the process of interaction. My argument has been that the framing which the 'gaze' theory provides (as well as Freudian theory on the whole) does not account for proactive female qualities - agency, integrity, creativity and self-expression. In other words, what the 'gaze' analytical framework is lacking is an acknowledgement of the woman's proactive behaviour, of both her right and her ability to create, to do things, to make decisions, and to move forward. Jungian Analytical Psychology, although a problematic and biased tool in its own right, at least has space for discussing and fostering these qualities.

While Freudian theory centres on the penis, literal or symbolic, its presence or absence defining a position of the individual in society, for Jung, gender differences are more symbolic than social (the same cannot be said of Jung the man which will be discussed in later in the book). Susan Rowland writes:

> where a Freudian interpretation reduces visual pleasure to a sexuality organised around the phallus as the significant organ of pleasure and

meaning, Jung regarded psychic energy as essentially neutral and *hence not privileging one gender.* Where Freud (and Lacan after him) considers the Oedipus myth to possess an originating role in the structuring of the psyche, Jung makes room for many potential myths of being. Some of them can even emphasise the feminine!

(Hauke and Hockley, 2011: 148–149)

This theoretical neutrality is certainly helpful, and offers space for the development of the female journey. Although it does not eliminate Jung's own biases (often expressed in his work), it nevertheless maps out potentialities on the journey towards the heroine's selfhood.

Jungian discussion of women as actresses and spectators would differ significantly from the one employed by the Freudian and post-Freudian theorists. Firstly, Jungian feminist analysis is not as politicized as its Freudian counterpart. Andrew Samuels rightly notes that Jungian discourse on the feminine is 'directed away from political and social action' (Samuels, 2015: 102). This is also generally true of Jung's writings, for he was more interested in the spiritual than in the socio-political applications of psychological phenomena although he was also concerned with the relationship of the individual to society at large. As all Jung-influenced analyses, a Jungian feminist approach to women on screen is bound to be mildly spiritualized and discussed in terms of the woman's transcendental journey instead of being a closely focused examination of the social and political conditions that oppress her.

This, however, does not mean that Jungian concepts are completely apolitical or could not be used to discuss social issues such as the position of women in society or transgressing gender expectations. Jung's concepts of the anima, the animus and the mother are certainly useful in the discussion of cinematic representation of women as well as female spectatorship. Moreover, with Jung's emphasis on the feminine, his psychology may even be more relevant for the study of women on screen. Unlike Freud's psychology, which is explicitly patriarchal and father-centred, Samuels argues, Jung provided 'a mother-based psychology in which influence is often traced back much earlier, even to pre-natal events' (Samuels, 2015: 213). Moreover, Jungian thought has never stressed the difference in gendered journeys in the way in which the Oedipus Complex prescribes, namely, that men join society through the threat of castration and in turn become enforcers of the order while women never fully enter the order. Why should they: they have babies and emotions, and just don't have time for intellectual pursuits or agency outwith the family.

This also applies to Lacan, who poeticized Freudian ideas and made them more palatable for textual analysis. He projects all kinds of male perceptions and fantasies onto women, designating the woman as a 'signifier' (the vessel as opposed to the signified, or meaning) which, apparently, 'grounds woman's status in the fact that she is not-whole' (Lacan, 1999: 73). Importantly, Lacan, as Stephen Heath rightly points out, reads the symbolic and the metaphorical through the physical; he 'instates the visible as the condition of symbolic functioning, with the phallus the standard of the visibility required' which, ultimately, means that those who 'lack' a penis and those who 'possess' one are so fundamentally different that their psychological and social experiences are inherently incomparable (Merck, 1992: 50). Automatically in this cage of the social order, the woman becomes 'the hysteric', fighting the very definition of identity through the physical possession of a penis (Merck, 1992: 50–52). Because she is 'not whole', she is 'excluded from the nature of things', and subsequently her jouissance is complementary 'compared to what the phallic function designates by way of jouissance' (Lacan, 1999: 73). His core ideas are so steeped in poeticized prejudice that the feminists' continuous insistence on using his theory as a valid critical framework is all the more surprising.

Conversely, rather than emphasizing the 'lack', sexed or sexless, Jung writes about masculinity and femininity lacking something on their own, without each other. Hence his extensive use of the gnostic idea of syzygy – the divine unity, the double-gendered nature of God. Psychological wholeness is a matter of equality and enlightenment, not a retrospective exercise in eliminating difference or an immature search for similarity and perfect mirroring.

The Oedipus Complex is effectively a theoretical prison. Laura Mulvey notes in her essay 'Changes: Thoughts on Myth, Narrative and Historical Experience' that, as a journey, the Oedipus complex does have a variety of paths for a questing female:

> In this scheme, any attempt at an exploration of the maternal relationship and its fantasies must appear as a retreat into the body, as a rejection of the symbolic and the Word, into a Utopian quest for a natural femininity, outside the "tragic and beneficial" experience of castration.
>
> (Mulvey, 1989: 172)

This defining presence of the concept of castration in the Freudian/Lacanian theoretical framework effectively limits the range of paths a heroine could undertake as well as the number of possible interpretations of her journey. For Jung, myth is not limited to a single narrative scheme.

Where the post-Freudians (including Lacanian feminists) stress the importance of the all-encompassing Oedipal metaphor claiming that the whole of society is built on it, the principal focus of Jungian thought is the journey of self-discovery and change – the so-called individuation process. However, individuation is not only a personal process, it is also very much about society. The idea is to strike a certain balance between personal interests and the interests of the family, community, and society. Human beings cannot develop in isolation, without any external influences: they form themselves in relation to, and in conflict with, their environment. Only by interacting with others does the individual see the difference between self and environment, and only by building oneself into the social structure does one become fully human. As Jung puts it:

> In general, [individuation] is the process by which individual beings are formed and differentiated; in particular, it is the development of the psychological *individual* as a being distinct from the general, collective psychology. Individuation, therefore, is a process of *differentiation*, having for its goal the development of the individual personality.
>
> (Jung, CW6: para. 757 – emphasis as original)

The individual in society is also required to wear a mask in line with their role in this particular society. This mask, explored in detail in the next chapter, is shaped by cultural mythologies, and in contemporary societies often reflected in screen narratives. In fact, screen narratives often become more than a mirror in which inequalities, biases, silences and assumptions are reflected – it is a repository of possibilities for action, a library of possible activities and outcomes. These mythologies are reflected in storylines, in paradigmatic and editing choices, in cinematic codes and subcodes, in punctuation and in enunciation. More often than not, however, women in myths and fairy tales were mere props in the male hero's journey: princesses and hags, mothers and daughters, dragons and water spirits, sirens and beautiful sorceresses. They were various incarnations of two archetypes – the anima and the great mother.

Terrie Waddell writes that Analytical Psychology offers a good set of tools for the analysis of visual images: 'The three major concepts integral to Jung's 'analytical psychology' provide an obvious framework for analysing the visual media: first, images common in dreams, myth and creative art are often projections of unconscious archetypal patterns; second, there is a 'collective unconscious' where these patterns are constellated; and third, the gradual conscious unravelling of these structures promotes the development of a more aware sense of self' (Jung, 2006: 1).

The social mask and the screen are in a constant dialogue, sharing content and influencing each other. In the case of the female persona, the mask of femininity, the screen had long been helping to shape the mask, to keep it in place, to control its wearer, to dictate her behaviour, and to transmit and solidify the message about the normative elements in female behaviour to the masses.

The opposite of the female persona is action as well as self-expression via agency and voice. In classic Hollywood the (metaphorically) silent woman is the one who attracts projections from males, the one who generates her individuality and controls the contents of her identity and personality instead of passively relying on 'fillers' from societal projections. The new heroine is not the passive receptor of other people's fantasies and desires. Neither is she a victim (as she is in exploitation genres) or a monster of the horror narratives. She refuses to be either. Going beyond the usual choice of archetypal images and situations suitable for a 'traditional' female persona, this book explores new female identities, possibilities and paths as well as the roots of the rebellion against the mask in pre-existing on and off-screen narratives.

References

Bassil-Morozow, Helena (2013) *The Trickster in Contemporary Film*, London: Routledge.

Bassil-Morozow, Helena (2015) *The Trickster and the System: Identity and Agency in Contemporary Society*, London: Routledge.

Bassil-Morozow, Helena (2018) *Jungian Theory for Storytellers: a Toolkit*, London: Routledge.

Beauvour, Simone de (1949/2011) *The Second Sex*, London: Vintage Books.

Bolton, Lucy (2011) *Film and Female Consciousness: Irigaray, Cinema and Thinking Women*. London: Palgrave Macmillan.

Clover, Carol J (1992) *Men, Women, and Chain Saws: Gender in the Modern Horror Film*, Princeton, N.J: Princeton University Press.

Donnelly, Lisa (2014) 'Pop Culture And Feminism: An Interview With Hollywood's Callie Khouri', *Forbes*, 26 February.

Gray, Frances (2019) *Jung, Irigaray, Individuation*, London: Routledge.

Hauke, C. and Hockley, L. (2011). *Jung & Film 11: The Return, Further Post-Jungian Takes on the Moving Image*. London & New York: Routledge.

Heath, Stephen (1992) 'Difference', in Mandy Merck (ed.) *The Sexual Subject: Screen Reader in Sexuality*, London: Routledge, pp. 47–107.

Izod, John (2006) *Screen, Culture, Psyche: A Post Jungian Approach to Working with the Audience*, Hove: Routledge.

Jung, C.G. (n.d.) *The Collected Works*, Herbert Read, Michael Fordham and Gerhardt Adler, (eds.) R.F.C. Hull, (trans.), London: Routledge. (Except where a different publication was used, all references are to this hardback edition.)

Kelsey, Darren (2017) *Media and Affective Mythologies: Discourse, Archetype and Ideology in Contemporary Politics*, London: Palgrave Macmillan.

Lacan, Jacques (1999) *The Seminar of Jacques Lacan: Bk. 20: On Feminine Sexuality, the Limits of Love and Knowledge: On Feminine Sexuality, the Limits of Love and Knowledge*, New York: W.W. Norton and Company.

Lynskey, Dorian (2015) 'Kapow! Attack of the Feminist Superheroes', in *The Guardian*, 25 March.

Merck, Mandy (1992) *The Sexual Subject: Screen Reader in Sexuality*, London: Routledge.

Mulvey, Laura (1975) 'Visual Pleasure and Narrative Cinema', *Screen*, Autumn (16) 3, pp. 6–18.

Mulvey, Laura (1989) *Visual and Other Pleasures*, Basingstoke and New York: Palgrave Macmillan.

Samuels, Andrew (2015) *Passions, Persons, Psychotherapy, Politics: the Selected Works of Andrew Samuels*, London: Routledge.

Wiseman, Eva (2021) 'Margot Robbie Refuses to be Put in a Box', *Vogue*, August.

Websites

Annenberg Foundation (2023) 'Inequality Across 1,600 Popular Films: Examining Gender, Race/Ethnicity & Age of Leads/Co Leads From 2007 to 2022', available at: https://assets.uscannenberg.org/docs/aii-inequality-1600-films-20230216.pdf (accessed 24 February 2023).

Chapter 1

The Female Persona

This chapter concerns the female persona in its traditional guise on screen as well as the gradual emergence of the more pronounced agentic patterns in narratives for the past four decades. Traditionally, screen storytelling presents the female protagonist as fragile and sensitive, embedded in the family structure and dependent on other people. When the female character plays a secondary role – a princess, for example – she is often a valuable possession, a boon for the hero to win at the end of his journey. Whenever the female character is the protagonist, like Beauty in *The Beauty and the Beast* in its many regional variations, or Scheherazade, whose narrative frames the *One Thousand and One Nights* cycle, it is expected that the main aim of her journey will be finding a suitable husband – and appeasing him with her charm, patience, subtlety, and wisdom.

The 'masked woman' is passive and subordinated to the masculine, she is contained within the context of Mulvey's 'phallocentrism' (Mulvey, 1975: 833) or stuck in Neumann's 'patriarchal marriage' (further discussed in Chapter 2). In a narrative, she is 'an unknowing and unwilling victim' of 'surreptitious observation' (Mulvey, 1975: 835), observed and followed (Madeleine (Kim Novak) in *Vertigo*, 1958), admired and abused (Rita Hayworth's character in *Gelda*, 1946) or sexualized, displayed, and keen to please (Marilyn Monroe's characters in pretty much any of her works).

She is wearing the female persona, the mask of femininity – the very essence of modesty and compliance. This kind of narrative structure aims to show that a female cannot survive on her own in the world, and that she needs a male or/and community to protect and support her, or sometimes prod her into life. Characters emerging out of the female persona, and out of the 'patriarchal marriage', have more fulfilling and varied journeys in which they are allowed to make their own mistakes and decisions. Contemporary characters explored throughout this book, including the new generation of Disney princesses, Saoirse Ronan's character in *Lady Bird*, or Beth Harmon (Anya Taylor-Joy) in Netflix's mini-series *The Queen's Gambit* (2020), are aware of the restrictions that come with wearing the female persona, and reject them in their own ways.

DOI: 10.4324/9781003253044-2

The 'traditional' passive heroine with her mask of femininity and drafted as an archetypal sketch to assist the hero on his path, is still present in Hollywood. In September 2020 the Academy of Motion Picture Arts and Sciences published a list of inclusion standards for eligibility in the best picture category. The standards aim to achieve a greater gender, race, sexual orientation, and disability diversity in the industry as well as off-screen. In the words of Academy President David Rubin and Academy CEO Dawn Hudson:

> The aperture must widen to reflect our diverse global population in both the creation of motion pictures and in the audiences who connect with them. The Academy is committed to playing a vital role in helping make this a reality. We believe these inclusion standards will be a catalyst for long-lasting, essential change in our industry.
>
> (Oscars, September 8, 2020)

While traditional cinema has been making very slow progress towards inclusion, television has been leading the revolution in representation and creating narratives with varied paradigmatic choices at all levels – not just the choice of actors (e, g., simply replacing a male protagonist with a female one), but also of genres, plotlines, and subjects. Some of the genres – such as coming-of-age narratives – have finally shifted from being male-only clubs to spaces in which the story of entering the adult world and finding yourself through trial-and-error is finally seen as something a young woman can do without becoming hopelessly attached to a guy or ending up dependent on a sponsor.

The Public Mask

Persona, or the public self, has been defined by theorists in a variety of ways yet all of them focus on the presence of a metaphorical mask which covers up (and protects) the contents of one's 'real' personality. This hidden or veiled personality can be less presentable, or more authentic, but in any case it is less socially acceptable. The mask is an important liminal formation protecting both the public and oneself from the consequences of miscommunication. As Marshall et al put it, as human beings, we are constantly engaged in production of this public self as we negotiate ourselves through life (Marshall et al., 2019: 1). Even though the persona has 'the appearances of being an individual', it is, in fact, 'the way an individual can organize themselves publicly' (Marshall et al., 2019: 3). Persona is thus a 'performance of individuality' and not in any way the authentic individual self.

In Jungian Analytical psychology, the persona is a social mask whose appearance and contents depends on social requirements and rules. It has an indispensable socio-psychological function – that of adaptation to external circumstances. As Frieda Fordham remarks, the persona is a necessity because it makes our communication with other human beings smoother as it cloaks the raw feelings and reactions into polite phrases and socially acceptable responses. People who reject the idea of a persona (perhaps because it feels like a false construct to them), tend to be 'gauche, to offend others, and to have difficulty establishing themselves in the world' (Fordham, 1991: 49). For instance, instead of punching someone when we feel like it because they jumped a queue, or bumping into people because they don't give way on a busy street, we tend to politely extract ourselves from potential conflict. Meanwhile, society views people who engage in open (and particularly physical) conflicts as being unable to develop and display a persona, and therefore keeps such an individual from advancing on the social ladder.

Persona can take the form of a personal image, a career, a profession, or an official role. For instance, people may want to be seen as a model mother, a benevolent boss, a cultured person, a successful scientist, an elegant dresser, or a high earner. Despite its obvious usefulness and importance for adaptation, there are dangers associated with it; mainly because the desire for acceptance by the outer world often gets out of control, and turns into an obsession. The desire for success and status can be so powerful that the mask outgrows the individual and a set of artificial traits take over the ego. Jung writes:

> When we analyse the persona we strip off the mask, and discover that what seemed to be individual is at bottom collective; in other words, that the persona was only a mask of the collective psyche. Fundamentally the persona is nothing real: it is a compromise between individual and society as to what a man should appear to be. He takes a name, earns a title, exercises a function, he is this or that. In a certain sense all this is real, yet in relation to the essential individuality of the person concerned it is only a secondary reality, a compromise formation, in making which others often have a greater share than he. The persona is a semblance, a two-dimensional reality, to give it a nickname.
>
> (Jung, CW7: para. 246)

In his writings Jung repeatedly emphasises the artificial nature of persona and the fact that this artificiality comes from a social necessity. Society is a system of relationships and roles, and it needs to assign all individuals a purpose and a place. How valuable we are to other members of the system – in other words, our social status – depends on our ability to wear the mask well, and to ensure the consistently high quality of performance in the roles we have been nominated to perform (Jung, CW7: para. 305).

Other authors who explored the masks worn in public have also emphasized the fairly inflexible, yet deceptive in its subtlety, nature of the production process of the public face. For instance, the American sociologist Erving Goffman's vision of personal interaction consists of observations on rituals of communicative exchange. He employs terms such as facework, deference, demeanour, embarrassment, stigma, alienation from interaction, communication boundaries, situational proprieties, and other terms to describe the intricacies of the interaction ritual and public behaviour.

Unlike the psychoanalytic tradition, Goffman is not interested in the authentic self vs public self-dichotomy, but only in the ritual interactions between people, which he calls 'the ritual roles of the self' (Goffman, 2005: 31). Neither is he interested in origins and development of the authentic personality like Freud, Jung, Kohut, or Winnicott. Instead, he defines the self as 'an image pieced together from the expressive indications of the full flow of events in an undertaking; and the self as a kind of player in a ritual game who copes honourably or dishonourably, diplomatically or undiplomatically, with the judgemental contingencies of the situation' (Goffman, 2005: 31). In other words, to the outside world which, in most cases, has no time for exploring personalities and individualities, what really matters is one's ability to participate in the 'game'. Anyone unable or unwilling to participate in it is sidelined as only compliance is rewarded. The interaction ritual is what really matters. Thus, the interaction between the individuals in their official capacity is symbolic, and does not have to contain any elements of a genuine sentiment.

Components of the Female Persona

Applied to female characters on screen, the female persona results in a narrow vision of the heroine as well as limited paths available to her. The woman behind the mask is invisible. For the outside world, she does not exist as someone with a quest of her own. Moreover, the person behind the mask is also interchangeable. In a narrative, such characters can only perform supportive functions, remaining purely archetypal, barely fleshed, mostly sketchy. Even compared to schematically written male superhero characters, women in supportive roles are mere props, with a role but without an aim; disembodied and directionless.

Freud, Jung and Goffman do not actually explore the social mask, or persona, from a gendered point of view. Expectations of propriety are different for women and men, and the female persona has its own dimensions defined by societal expectations and reflected in traditional narratives. It has connotations of modesty, kindness, dependency, silence, and fragility. The female persona, the mask of femininity, is an inactive woman who voluntarily renounces her agency in order to be accepted by society. To transpose Goffman's analytical framework onto gendered interaction, women are participants in the interaction ritual who 'accept definitional claims made by others present' (Goffman, 1990: 21–22). Human beings would normally aim to keep definitional disruptions to a minimum, and take precautions to avoid them. For instance, one would typically employ 'defensive practices' to save the definition of the situation, including 'to save the definition of the situation projected by another' (Goffman, 1990: 24–25). Women are socialized into gender descriptions, into what women look like and how they should behave, and perform according to societal rules for the rest of their lives.

Do women enjoy this performance? Are they willing to conform to the defined part in the interaction ritual? Here Goffman presents several options (albeit applied to the generic social performance which can be extrapolated onto the female persona): a performer may be fully believing in the act, they may be cynical of the act, or, more likely, they will move back and forth between cynicism and belief (Goffman, 1990: 28–32). Thus in gender performance, women sustain 'self-illusion' (Goffman, 1990: 32) in order to be accepted by society. The 'front' (the performed self), Goffman notes, is closely connected with appearance (Goffman, 1990: 34). Even more so, one might add, the female version of the 'front' (which we will label the female persona for our purposes) whose socially prescribed front-creating activities involve the use of cosmetics and clothes emphasizing the female form. Despite not discussing the female persona directly, Goffman nevertheless cites Simone de Beauvoir's *The Second Sex* (1949) as part of the analysis of the artifice of social performance (Goffman, 1990: 65). Characters like Holly Golightly and Sugar Kane (Marilyn Monroe in Billy Wilder's *Some Like It Hot,* 1959) are acutely aware of their personas, managing them successfully and moulding them into traps for rich men.

Freud, Jung, and 'the Essence of Femininity'.

Freud and Jung do comment on the 'essence' of femininity without theorizing it as a mask but rather presenting it as set of unfortunate traits shaped by a combination of nature and nurture.

On the one hand, in his lecture on femininity, Freud admits that conflation of biological sex with innate behavioural traits cannot be not justified, particularly if one looks at other species in which female passivity is not prevalent (Freud, 1960/2001: 115). Therefore, he concludes, 'even in the sphere of human sexual life you see how inadequate it is to make masculine behaviour coincide with activity and feminine with passivity' (Freud, 1960/2001: 115). He also emphasizes the influence of social conditioning; the 'social customs' that 'force women into passive situations' (Freud, 1960/2001: 116). As a result, the 'suppression of women's aggressiveness' which is 'imposed on them socially' leads to the 'development of powerful masochistic impulses' (Freud, 1960/2001: 116).

On the other, Freud's critique of the social, shaping women into passive objects, does not sound particularly resolute, nor does it last throughout the lecture. In fact, it is soon replaced by basic stereotypical binary thinking based on anatomical features: Freud appeals to the 'riddle' of femininity which is 'worrying' to men but not to women since they are the problem (Freud, 1960/2001: 113). Thus, the masochism he mentions becomes part of the 'riddle', as does the castration complex which in women takes the form of 'penis envy' (Freud, 1960/2001: 125). The 'envy' doctrine is essentially based on a physical attribute, but Freud extends it onto a whole range of activities traditionally perceived as 'masculine'. For instance, a woman's ambition to join an 'intellectual profession' is a 'sublimated modification' of repressed penis envy (Freud, 1960/2001: 125). Naturally, the woman without a penis would ideally like a metaphoric replacement, and eventually her envy transforms into a wish for what Freud bizarrely terms a 'penis-baby' (Freud, 1960/2001: 129). At this point it becomes clear that, having started the lecture with a reluctant acknowledgement of the impact of social conditioning on women, Freud moved on to a full-on conflation of anatomy and gendered behaviour: women's desire for a child stems from their lack of a physical penis. So, for Freud, femininity could be summarized as passivity, envy, and masochism.

This kind of assumed, projected 'masochism' often finds itself on screen in scenes of violence and harassment, such as the one in *Blade Runner* (1982) in which Deckard (Harrison Ford) manhandles and then forcibly kisses Rachael, a replicant (Sean Young). Deckard's behaviour follows the macho logic which assumes that women enjoy sexual violence, that they like being chased and 'taken', and that it is all part of the sexual game. Rachel's 'otherness', which can be extrapolated onto Deckard's sexism, in the scene is also reflected in her non-humanity. Being a replicant she can be treated as an object which does not have the same ability to feel or the right to be valued as someone with a soul and a will. While the replicant male must be killed, the replicant female is still useful and can be subjugated – unless she is strong like Pris (Daryl Hannah) and therefore not fit for the role of a faceless yet masked, pliable, masochistic, fragile female.

In a way, masochism becomes synonymous with the female persona as the female character is expected to experience agency and wholeness through their partners, children, or male members of their family. The myth of female masochism persists even though this is actually just part of the persona in its many renditions. Narratives such as *Cinderella* and *The Beauty and the Beast* emphasize the imagined masochistic nature of female attachment with its endless ability to tolerate abuse and control. With this *a priori* masochistic stance, female protagonists focused on 'finding the right man' in their quests while female secondary characters have served as attachments or mirrors for the male protagonist on his quest. Whole chunks of popular mythology were dedicated to the male action hero, omitting female agency altogether. In other words, patriarchal cinema expected a female character to exist, but not to act.

Like Freud, Jung directly links these chimeric qualities to biological sex. Demeris Wehr notes that 'androcentrism and misogyny distort Jung's discussions of women, the anima and the animus, and the feminine. As a result, Jung's individuation process may be skewed for women' (Wehr, 1988: 99). Jung stresses that it is unnatural for women to enter masculine professions or adopt proactive behavioural patterns for it interferes with their innate psychology and they become overwhelmed with by their judgemental, screaming animus. A masculine woman

> develops a kind of rigid intellectuality based on so-called principles, and backs them up with a whole host of arguments which always miss the mark in the most irritating way, and always inject a little something into the problem that is not really there. *Unconscious assumptions and opinions are the worst enemy of woman; they can even grow into a positively demonic passion that exasperates and disgusts men, and does the woman herself the greatest injury by gradually smothering the charm and meaning of her femininity and driving it into the background.* Such a development naturally ends in profound psychological disunion, in short, in a neurosis.
> (Jung, CW10: para. 245; emphasis is mine)

Having written rather aggressively and condescendingly about the dangers of 'mental masculinization', he nevertheless admits that the real female identity remains invisible in the patriarchal culture, overshadowed by men's fantasies and projections: 'Woman always stands just where the man's shadow falls, so that he is only too liable to confuse the two' (Jung, 1982: 55).

Jungian feminist critics and therapists have generally been on the same page as their Freudian/Lacanian colleagues, criticising society which puts physical, moral and intellectual restraints on women's activities, with the only exception that the Jungians actually have a solution on offer which is not limited by the Oedipal metaphor: the individuation process. In the individuation metaphor, the heroine's initial position before the start of the journey is the process of incompleteness, the feeling of not being fulfilled. This, however, has nothing to do with the idea of 'the woman as not-all' because male protagonists embark on their journeys for the exact same reason as women – the desire for self-discovery. In this sense, it is not just women who are 'not-all' – it's everyone. Moreover, the state of being incomplete is not permanent or determined by biology and enforced by social structures. It can be challenged and changed by the persistence and willpower of the individual. Although the forces of society are still at play (and often decisively so) in the individuation process, they do not fully determine the place of the female individual in the social structure.

Jung, too, dwells on the inactive stance of women although he does avoid the typically Freudian terms such as 'masochism' or 'envy'. As previously mentioned, Jung was ambivalent regarding the female persona, sometimes lamenting its loss to gender equality, other times feeling empathetic with women's struggle to find their way in the complex modern world with voting rights, labour equality, and changing domestic life. For instance in 'Woman in Europe' he discusses the increasing ambition, enabled by the changing environments of modernity, to enter 'masculine professions' ('become active in politics', 'sit on committees') and exhibit 'masculine' behaviours (Jung, CW10: para. 243). This, according to Jung, is problematic:

> This step towards social independence is a necessary response to economic and other factors... [...]. Certainly the courage and capacity for self-sacrifice of such women is admirable ... [...] But no one can get round the fact that by taking up a masculine profession, studying and working like a man, woman is doing something not wholly in accord with, if not directly injurious to, her feminine nature.
>
> (Jung, CW10: para. 243)

What does this feminine nature entail, though? Its ingredients are 'a purely feminine sexual pattern of unconsciousness', 'passivity', and 'the principle of Eros'. The woman also 'allows herself to be convinced by the man's projected feelings' (Jung, CW10: paras. 240–255), in a sense, willingly taking on the mask of femininity. Thus, Jung appears to be confused and conflicted in his analysis of the feminine, conflating the social and the biological, psychological, and physical; admiring the woman's assumed fragile passivity, while simultaneously lashing out at the animus-dominated woman who 'has lost her charm' because of the 'demonic passion' brought about by 'intellectuality'. Meanwhile, Freud's patronizing attitude towards the presumed female masochism and 'penis envy' leaves no space for equal opportunities or varied life options.

Similarly, Lacan writes in *On Jouissance* that the woman's 'sexual organ is of no interest' and she is defined as 'not whole' in respect to *jouissance*. Regarding her sexual characteristics, 'it is those of the mother that take precedence in her' (Lacan, 1999: 7). His famous controversial proposition, repeated in many of his essays, that 'the woman does not exist' (Lacan, 1999: 57) can be interpreted in a number of contradictory ways, including the refusal to objectify the feminine, and the insistence that women are of no importance because of their 'castrated' sexual organs. In any case, in this phrase Lacan emphasizes 'the absence', the 'lack', the incompleteness inherent in female nature and determined by her body. The woman is excluded from the nature of things for being not-whole, and even her *jouissance* has a 'supplementary function' (Lacan, 1999: 72–73).

Freudian and Lacanian film feminists emphasize that women are banned from participating in male activities – i.e., activities that involve investigating and discovering, speaking one's mind, fighting and conquering, and pursuing the 'holy grail' awaiting at the end of the journey. Their discussion of women's positions both on screen and in society is also deeply politicized, and their psychological analysis of the situation is linked to social and political issues.

The female persona is shaped by this exclusion from the order. As Tong and Botts point out, the female image is largely determined by the linguistic structuring of the Symbolic order: 'lacking feminine words, women must either babble outside the Symbolic order or remain silent within it' (Tong and Botts, 2018: 173).

To his credit, Lacan admits that his assessment of female sexuality as passive may in reality simply stem from a lack of 'insider' knowledge:

> The plausibility of what I am claiming here – namely, that woman knows nothing of this jouissance – is underscored by the fact that in all the time people have been begging them – I spoke last time of women psychoanalysts - to try to tell us, not a word! [...] If she simply experienced it, and I knew nothing about it, that would allow us to cast myriad doubts on that notorious (*fameuse*) frigidity.
>
> (Lacan, 1999: 75)

As such, the Freudian-Lacanian framework clearly indicates that there is no place for a woman in the Symbolic order - the 'order of things', the male-orientated system of rituals and signs that determine the hierarchy and define the rules of conduct.

Ultimately, any nuances in attitude between the Jungian and the (post) Freudian positions do not matter as the overall picture of the female persona painted by them is bleak: the woman is fragile, passive, masochistic, charming, 'a riddle', 'a problem', and dominated by hormones and penis envy. Her role in society is: 'to perform invaluable social tasks' (Freud, 1960/2001: 134). She must not: adopt masculine behaviours for fear that she will become undesirable, or even 'exasperate and disgust' (Jung) and 'frighten' men (Freud) with her 'rigidity' (his description of a woman of 'about thirty') (Freud, 1960/ 2001: 134). There is a clear warning in the language used by both: the woman who oversteps the confines of the female persona is frightening and disgusting. She becomes the 'other', the abject when she is no longer prepared to wear the artificial mask which serves as a mirror to the entitled masculinity. The expressions they use demarcate the reaction to women's stepping out of the female persona, or refusing to conform to its conventions. The desire for control is reflected linguistically in these essays: it shifts from admiration for the fine and delicate female persona (the 'carer and provider' projection) to a warning that men will be terrified in the presence of a female who possesses motivation, determination, or expresses strong opinions.

The Anima and the Mask

The female persona is closely linked with the anima archetype. The anima is one of the two archetypes (the other being the animus) delineating the romantic/sexual other residing in one's psyche and determining one's romantic relationships. The anima is often shaped by the mother (which links it with the Mother archetype) (Jung, 1964: 186–187). Jung defines the anima as 'a magical feminine being' (Jung, CW9/I: para. 53). Everything she touches 'becomes numinous – unconditional, dangerous, taboo, magical' (Jung, CW9/I: para. 59). In traditional narratives she is depicted as a serpent, a nixie, a wood-nymph or classical seductresses like Helen of Troy (Jung, CW9/I paras. 53–60). Jolande Jacobi's description of the anima is more prosaic: the anima is the 'solidly constituted functional technical complex' and a 'complementary part of the psyche' which, when undifferentiated, is projected onto others (Jacobi, 1973: 114–115). Marie-Louise von Franz calls the anima 'a female personification of [a man's] unconscious' (Jung, 1964: 186).

Definitions and perceptions of the anima, however, go beyond looking for a potential mate: she is the inspiratrice, the muse, the silent companion, the man's inner voice, she shows the way and is the boon at the end of the journey. Yet, because of her duality, she can also be treacherous and seductive, and, much like the mythological Circe or the sirens, ensnare the man and hold him captive against his will (which is, obviously, an excellent ploy for laying the blame on women for men's sexuality).

In Jung's own words, man cannot influence the anima:

> on the contrary, it is always the *a priori* element in his moods, reactions, impulses … […] It is something that lives of itself, that makes us live; it is a life behind consciousness that cannot be completely integrated with it, but from which, on the contrary, consciousness arises.
>
> (Jung, CW9/I: para. 57)

Obviously, Jung writes of the anima from the male, and contrasexual, point of view, not taking into consideration how it might be perceived by women, or how women might feel once the weighty expectation of being 'life behind consciousness' is projected onto them.

Like the other archetypes, the anima is dual: in narratives and dreams she can appear to be good or bad. According to von Franz, 'negative' anima in narratives appears as a *femme fatale,* or a murderous water spirit, bewitching and killing passing men (Jung, 1964: 188). In her 'soul' manifestation, however, she becomes the man's inner voice, 'waspish or poisonous', or taking the individual away from reality (Jung, 1964: 190–191). Or she can be a positive guide on the individuation journey, a source of wisdom, 'a mediator between the ego and the Self'; Virgin Mary, or Mona Lisa (Jung, 1964: 195).

Whether positive or negative, being a complex, the anima is ripe for projections – for being transposed on to real people and mistaken for the inner image. As von Franz puts it, 'women who are of "fairy-like" character especially attract such anima projections, because men can attribute almost anything to a creature who is so fascinatingly vague, and thus proceed to weave fantasies around her' (Jung, 1964: 191).

The 'fascinatingly vague' creature is, of course, not the real woman because the 'fairy-like' character is a mask, a fantasy, an artificial construct worn to reflect societal standards, for the purposes of acceptance and integration, or even with manipulative intentions. Cinematic and television narratives – as more traditional narratives before them – tend to reflect the current state of society in which they are created. As Susan Rowland notes, 'where the woman incarnates the anima she has unconscious powers denied to her independent self. It may be possible to justify this psychologically, but the sense remains of the woman *getting lost* in the writing of the anima' (Rowland, 2005: 67). Importantly, Rowland argues, had Jung acknowledged his own personal biases, 'then his descriptions of independent women would be less likely to be taken as either pure prejudice ... or as deep insights into the true path of contented women' (Rowland, 2005: 67).

Meanwhile, Jungian feminists have been exploring the dynamic aspect of the feminine experience – the individuation process and its relation to agentic behaviour. In her book, *Jung and Feminism: Liberating Archetypes* (1988), Wehr highlights that patriarchal structures discourage women from seeking agency and from 'gratifying their own needs or seeking fulfilment of their own desires. In the face of such deprivation – furthered by psychologies and theologies that have defined women's fulfilment in terms of their service to others – many women in patriarchy lack a sense of themselves as persons, or agents, in their own right' (Wehr, 1988: 101).

Neumann emphasises that male relationship to the female counterpart is constellated as 'the anima figure' which is seen as 'transformative' yet 'foreign' (Neumann, 1994: 252). In this sense, the anima coincides with the mask, the female persona, and hides the genuine personality of the individual. The unity of the patriarchal family is dependent on this mask as its stability 'is guaranteed in the patriarchal marriage precisely by the fact that it ensures the unequivocal masculinity of the man and the unequivocal femininity of the woman' (Neumann, 1994: 261). In the same way, Kim Novak's character in *Vertigo* is forever elusive, mysterious, and disembodied. She is an eternal enigma which Scottie (James Stewart) is resolved to solve. Scottie's gaze, in whose beam the anima becomes alive, is reproduced by Hitchcock using a wide range of cinematic means such as subjective focalisation including close-ups and camera angles. There is no question of 'enigma's' personality or her real intentions; only the requirement that the male protagonist sets on a journey of self-discovery, and is later 'transformed' by her secret. She is perpetually teasing the protagonist, luring him into dangerous places like a seductive water spirit. In this sense, she us unreal – a fantasy version of a woman, specific to his psyche, and possibly just a figment of Scottie's wild, voyeuristic imagination.

Feminist Approaches to the Mask of Femininity

The mask of femininity has been explored by feminist authors like Simone de Beauvoir, Luce Irigaray, Laura Mulvey, and Mary Ann Doane. All of them have drawn attention to the artificial, exaggerated, and socially-determined nature of the mask women have to wear in public. Appearance is a big part of this performance, as the costume and make-up are seen as an inherent part of being a woman. Simone de Beauvoir notes that 'costumes and styles are often devoted to cutting off the feminine body from any activity [...] She paints her mouth and her cheeks to give them the solid fixity of a mask; her glance she imprisons deep in kohl and mascara [...]' (De Beauvoir, 1997: 190). Often metonymically conflated with nature via her connection with 'natural rhythms', the woman has to enhance her body and face because 'in woman dressed and adorned, nature is present but under restraint, by human will remoulded nearer to a man's desire' (De Beauvoir, 1997: 191).

The traits associated with the female persona, according to the post-Freudian feminist scholars, are formed by several societal requirements: to be silent, to conceal her real identity and desires, being pliable (masquerade), and to hide the pain from mistreatment while being discouraged from fighting back. Mulvey famously speaks of the 'determining male gaze' projecting its phantasies onto the silent, 'castrated' female (Mulvey, 1975: 837). The woman becomes the spectacle whose presence needs to be managed as it works against the male-focused narrative by infusing it with distracting eroticism (Mulvey, 1975: 837). Or, to use Jungian terminology, the woman distracts (positively or negatively) the hero on his journey simply by her existence, by making an appearance on the hero's path. Her entire personality and purpose in the narrative are, of course, shown through the prism of the hero's vision and purpose. She does not have a motive of her own, for it would be 'unfeminine'.

Meanwhile, Luce Irigaray emphasizes the fact that the mask does not form a natural part of the woman's personality, and is instead worn to please others. The mask and the mirror serve the purpose of confirming one's own otherness to oneself while, paradoxically, being the author of this otherness. It is a voluntary act yet one is also coerced by society and its definitions of femininity to participate in it. It is also an act of self-alienation, of creating a distance between one's genuine self and the mask presented to the public:

> Female beauty is always considered a garment ultimately designed to attract the other into the self. It is almost never perceived as a manifestation of, an appearance by a phenomenon expressive of inferiority – whether of love, of thought, of flesh. We look at ourselves in the mirror to *please someone*, rarely to interrogate the state of our body or our spirit, rarely for ourselves and in search of our own becoming. The mirror almost always serves to reduce us to a pure exteriority – of a very particular kind. [...] The mirror signifies the constitution of a (fabricated) female other that I shall put forward as an instrument of seduction in my place. I seek to be seductive and to be content with images of which I theoretically remain the artisan, the artist.
>
> (Irigaray, 2007: 65)

The act of mask-wearing, although the result of societal coercion, can nevertheless be transformed into creative-revolutionary activity, as Mary Doane points out: 'the masquerade, in flaunting femininity, holds it at a distance' (Doane, 1982: 81). In her view, wearing a mask of femininity is a 'form of resistance' to 'patriarchal positioning' – to the patriarchal manipulation of the social order. It is also a form of self-protection, Doane highlights, by quoting Joan Riviere that womanliness can be worn 'both to hide the possession of masculinity and to avert the reprisals expected if she was found to possess it' (Riviere, quoted in Doane, 1982: 81).

Appropriating the mask of femininity to mock the social order is certainly something recent on-screen female tricksters do with pleasure. For instance, Fleabag wears make-up, sexy lingerie, and revealing clothes yet she also farts in lifts, impersonates Norman Bates from *Psycho* (1960) to terrify her unsuspecting boyfriend in the shower, openly discusses bodily functions with strangers, and is forthcoming to the point of being rude. If anything, the make-up and nice clothes, suggestive of social compliance, sharply contrast with her disdain for the bland neurotic middle-classness displayed by her sister Claire (Sian Clifford). Similarly, Margot Robbie's Harley Quinn in *Birds of Prey* (2021) and *The Suicide Squad* (2021) enjoys a good semiotic mismatch: although she spends most of her on-screen time wearing 'girly', provocative, or ultra-feminine clothes, she is also a brutal killer and is completely unpredictable. In other words, the female trickster performs gender in order to destabilize the referent, and to make the chain of signification as fluid as possible.

The performative nature of gender is also highlighted by Judith Butler in her book *Gender Trouble* (1990). She emphasizes the social nature of 'doing' the gender, of wearing a socially acceptable face. Similar to the writers on persona and social front, Butler pays attention to the fact that the person wearing the mask is aware of the requirements of being accepted by society, and is constructing the outward behaviour as part of social adaptation:

> If gender is a kind of a doing, an incessant activity performed, without one's knowing and without one's willing, it is not for that reason automatic or mechanical. On the contrary, it is a practice of improvisation within a scene of constraint. Moreover, one does not 'do' one's gender alone, even if the other is only imaginary. What I call my 'own' gender appears at times perhaps as something that I author or, indeed, own. But the terms that make up one's gender are, from the start, outside oneself, beyond oneself in a sociality that has no single author [...].
>
> (Butler, 1990: 1)

Dressing, De Beauvoir argues, has twofold significance: to express social status, and to express agentic elements:

it is her uniform and her attire; the woman who suffers from not doing *anything* thinks she is expressing her *being* through her dress. [...] She thus believes that she is choosing and re-creating her own self. And social customs encourage her to alienate herself in her image.

(De Beauvoir, 1997: 585)

The traditional Hollywood heroines – Ilsa Lund (Ingrid Bergman) in *Casablanca* (Michael Curtiz, 1942), Gilda (Charles Vidor, 1946), Lorelei Lee (Marilyn Monroe) in *Gentlemen Prefer Blondes* (Howard Hawkes, 1953), or Holly Golightly (Audrey Hepburn) in *Breakfast at Tiffany's* (Blake Edwards, 1961), display this mixture of mystery and unpredictability, randomly labelled as charming or hysterical, and contrasted with the masculine persona.

Perhaps one of the most prominent social behaviours befitting a woman is 'being seen but not heard', for the act of speaking may disrupt the mask and associated illusion of ownership and control of the female object. On the subject of the silent woman, Kaja Silverman writes that, as a castrated object, women are not allowed to speak because they represent 'an alien and unwanted quality' (Silverman, 1988: 17). They are desired, but from a distance, in a fetishist way so as to prevent the fearful male subject from being affected by 'castration'. A castrated object who speaks is a male nightmare personified. It is important that women remain silent, which proves to be difficult in real life. The screen therefore provides an ideal safe distance for such consumption of the silent object, for it is a fantasy life in which the male can look but not be looked at; in which he can consume females without having to deal with the actual woman; and in which the woman is guaranteed to be silenced without any chance of her being out of control. The mask suppresses the voice. Speaking, a decidedly agentic activity is more difficult to control than the static elements of an image.

In her article 'Remembering Women: Psychical and Historical Constructions in Film Theory' (1988), Mary Ann Doane emphasises that objectification of women in classic cinema (read: cinema produced by men) has resulted in them being turned into cultural abstractions. A generalized cinematic woman, 'Everybody's Lady', emerges from 'the combination of a disembodied voice and a mechanical image' and becomes 'the product of the apparatus' (Doane, 1982: 1). Although, presumably, this attractive abstraction has power over the male viewer, she has no agency as this power is constructed and objectified: 'But the woman is also like the cinematic apparatus insofar as she constitutes a lure for the male subject – more dangerous even than the cinema since she frequently leads him to his doom. Yet without knowledge of her effect, she has no access to subjectivity' (Doane, 1982: 1).

Somewhere underneath these layers of projections is the female voice. 'Everybody's Lady', Doane reminds us, is no one:

The refusal of the apparatus as fully adequate to its object is a refusal of its totalising force and the concept of Woman which it produces. The task must be not that of remembering women, remembering real women, immediately accessible – but of producing remembering women. Women with memories and hence histories.

(Doane, 1982: 1)

As Simone de Beauvoir notes, the myth of the 'feminine mystery' – the building block of the female persona – offers an invaluable opportunity for lazy inter-personal communication in patriarchal contexts. For, trying to understand the other person is harder than to project some kind of aura of inexplicability onto them. This illusion is infinitely comfortable and profitable:

> ... first it allows for an easy explanation for anything that is inexplicable; the man who does not 'understand' a woman is happy to replace his subjective deficiency with an objective resistance; instead of admitting his ignorance, he recognises the presence of a mystery exterior to himself: here is an excuse that flatters his laziness and vanity at the same time. An infatuated heart thus avoids many disappointments: if the loved one's behaviour is capricious, her remarks stupid, the mystery serves as an excuse. [...] faced with a living enigma, the man remains alone: alone with his dreams, hopes, fears, love, vanity; this subjective game that can range from vice to mystical ecstasy is for many a more attractive than an authentic relation with a human being.

(De Beauvoir, 2011: 278)

Raised with the myth of the female mystery, women learn to imitate its fundamental aspects, and 'dissimulate their objective image', adopt 'enigmatic impassivity' and 'carefully hide their real feelings and behaviour' (De Beauvoir, 2011: 280). They take on the roles of 'Harmony, Repose, Mother Earth' (De Beauvoir, 2011: 281). In other words, they are taught to fake the persona, to replicate its stock features, to lie about its authenticity. Andrea Dworkin writes in *Life and Death* (1997) that half-measures and fear of confronting male power have kept the female gender in the subordinate position: '... we internalize [hatred of women] and we settle for second-best because we know we can't have day-to-day real equality. And we try to cut our losses, and we cut our deals, and we do the best that we can ...' (Dworkin, 1997: 164). Narratives contextualise these processes, and provide templates for girls and young women to be easily replicated.

The Mask Slips Off

The mask is a rigid structure and maintaining its coherence every day is a difficult task. What happens if it can no longer be kept on or its coherence cannot be maintained? Without the mask, the beautifully frail creature, the clean slate for male projections, becomes an alien, the other, the terrifying (rigid, inflexible, disgusting) witch. The turning of the woman into the other in the absence of the mask has been referred in feminist analysis using Kristeva's concept of *abjection*. The abject is an object mis-recognized, or not recognized; it is characterized by the failure of transference and withdrawal of a projection. It is also characterized by terror and shame associated with the disappearance or loss of an imagined and projected upon object. Kristeva describes it as 'what neither subject, nor object but increasingly returns, disgusts, rejects, fascinates. It is near but not able to be assimilated. Different from the uncanny, "abjection is elaborated through a failure to recognize its kin"' (Kristeva, 2018: 88).

Importantly, Kristeva reminds us in *Powers of Horror,* the abject's central quality is its being 'opposed to I' (Kristeva, 1982: 1), which in case of the female persona would mean being opposed to the mask, the inversion of the mask, the radical act of rejecting it. The mis-recognition, the loss of the mirrored image, the withdrawal of projection – the abject describes the patriarchal denial of proprietary loss that comes with the disappearance of the mirroring, meek, passive female persona. Openly flaunting this loss, and the fear that comes with it, the female horror protagonists and antagonists in the 1970s and 1980s foreground the abject and its attributes, the abject that is terrifying and grotesque in its refusal to show the prettily artificial female body. Instead, the viewer is confronted with rage and menstrual blood (*Carrie,* 1976), unspeakable, inhuman loss of control (*The Exorcist,* 1973), or the image of reproduction, of what used to be 'warm' and 'maternal' imagery, turned on its head and presented as a bloody alien, 'the perfect organism' with admirable survival skills (Ridley Scott's *Alien* (1979) and *Aliens* (1986).

Impropriety is incompatible with the female persona, and therefore defilement, as Kristeva points out, is 'jettisoned out of the Symbolic system' (Kristeva 1982: 65). Similarly, Erich Neumann notes that fear of the feminine is born out of splitting it into 'a higher and lower femaleness', out of the inability to relate to women in all their totality – i.e., as actual people, as human beings, and as people with real (rather than imagined, or projected upon) bodies (Neumann, 1994: 259). Barbara Creed traces female monsters all the way back to Greek mythology – Medea, Medusa the Gorgon, the Sirens (Creed, 1993: 2). The woman, or female character, without a mask can look (owns the gaze – like the Gorgon) and has a voice (like the Sirens). Ownership of the self-expression is regarded as deeply transgressive. The woman who has dropped her persona, or refuses to wear one, like Medea, is categorized as a monster simply because there is no life for her outside male projections.

Until representatives of various feminist movements started openly questioning the patriarchal positioning of women in society, mainstream filmmakers assumed that a female character, reflecting real women in Western societies, has no need for proactive behaviour or independent thinking. Freudian film feminists, starting with Laura Mulvey, have demonstrated that agency and action had been reserved exclusively for male characters. For decades, iconic characters such as James Bond, Indiana Jones, and the screen versions of DC and Marvel superheroes enjoyed dominant position in narratives while using female characters as a foil to enhance their power, skill, ingenuity, intellect, and attractiveness.

Many of the traditional moving image heroines reflect the anima qualities whose 'fuzziness' aims to be attractive and non-threatening. The breathy voice of Monroe's protagonists and the seductive dancing skills exhibited by Rita Hayworth's heroines can count as the typical traps exhibited by anima-like characters. Cinematic techniques such as soft focus make the appearance emphasize the ethereal, superhuman quality of the anima by concealing the realistic appearance of the actress who may have physical flaws. In *Casablanca,* for instance, Elsa's skin appears to be smooth and glowing as if she is surrounded by an aura, or exuding warmth. The same cannot be said about other characters, including Humphrey Bogart's protagonist who is allowed to have wrinkles because he has other redeeming qualities – for instance, he can stand up to injustice or kill traitors. Despite being 'fateful' and 'bad' for Rick, Elsa nevertheless makes him display his best features – courage and generosity of heart. Meanwhile, she remains capricious and unpredictable until the end of the film as much of the romantic part of the plot is based on her fluid, ever-changing, treacherous, manipulative 'feminine nature'. Narratives such as *Casablanca* do not require a heroine to be anything beyond the projection, or to possess any truly agentic element as this would take the focus off the hero's journey, or somehow compromise its integrity. The woman 'has nowhere to go' precisely because the persona she wears is a convenient combination of a mirror and a narrative prop.

The anima is not about action – it is about the action (or actions) whose journey she complements with her caprices, her femininity, her dancing, her high heels, her pretty face, and her perfect complexion. She is the 'soul-image', the muse, the damsel in distress, guiding the male character on his journey of becoming his true self, helping him discover and develop his best qualities.

Classical Hollywood is not the only one to blame for the countless examples, savagely criticized in the 1970s and 1980s by Freudian-Lacanian feminists, of animas, 'fairy-like' creatures, ripe for male projections; created by men for male consumption. Challenge to the mask – to the very concept of the female persona – has been a gradual process in filmmaking. Many of the iconic films made in the last couple of decades of the twentieth century – *Groundhog Day* (1993), *The Mask* (1994), *The Matrix* (1999) – have female characters sexualized and sidelined to showcase the development of the male character. Even co-protagonists and feminist icons like Sarah Connor of *The Terminator* franchise are drafted into the narrative as an inspiration, as someone who needs to be worshipped because she is the One Who Created the Hero. The female persona, in all her incarnations and cultural implications (attractiveness, motherhood, caring personality) is a tough feature to challenge when it comes to moving image narratives.

The Trailblazer: Ridley Scott

When it comes to challenging the validity of the female persona, Ridley Scott has repeatedly offered radical narratives questioning its very necessity. From *Alien* to *G.I. Jane* (1997), his films dismantle the persona, revealing its artificiality, and particularly the societal insecurities behind its existence: fear of the feminine, of the female biology, and of gender equality. Although more known for his work with sci-fi and horror genres, Scott also confronted the female persona in his more realistic narratives, such as *Thelma and Louise* (1991) which is in many ways a pioneering film – a narrative that was utilizing but also revising exploitation elements such as rape/trauma/revenge and victim/avenger to deliver a message about deeper societal issues instead of simply presenting the viewer with a cheap morality tale achieved by a straightforward reversal of roles.

Two friends, Thelma Dickinson (Geena Davis) and Louise Sawyer (Susan Sarandon), go on a weekend break to escape their tedious and prospectless everyday existence: Thelma is a housewife stuck in a controlling relationship, and Louise is a waitress dating a musician who is often on the road. Things start to go seriously wrong when Thelma is raped by a stranger in a roadside bar, and Louise shoots him. They both flee the scene knowing that no one would believe that they are telling the truth. Their subsequent adventures include meeting and seducing J.D, a handsome young thief (young Brad Pitt), robbing a convenience store, and locking a policeman who stops them for speeding, in the boot of his car. They also punish a catcalling truck driver by setting his truck on fire. The film ends with them deliberately driving their convertible over the edge of the Grand Canyon after being trapped by police officers who demand their surrender.

Ridley Scott admits that it was hard to get the screenplay approved by the executives because they had 'a problem with women' (Lewis, *The Guardian,* 7 May 2017). Scott is certainly no stranger to dealing with gender bias in Hollywood; he remembers how the original *Alien* script included an all-male crew, but eventually two of the characters were switched to women, including Sigourney Weaver's Ellen Ripley (Lewis, *The Guardian,* 7 May 2017). The result was one of the most memorable survivor female protagonists, and the first in the line of his iconic heroines.

Tasker notes that the female protagonists in *Thelma and Louise* achieve their temporary freedom thanks to the ownership of traditional symbols of masculine power: a car and guns (Tasker, 1993: 139). Two women taking justice into their own hands was an unusual choice of narrative for a mainstream Hollywood film because most of the decisions concerning paradigmatic choices (which inevitably form syntagmatic canvasses of the cultural discourse of which Hollywood is such a big part), are made by men – producers, directors, investors, and screenwriters. It is only natural to suggest that male makers of discursive practices are predominantly interested in male issues, male obsessions, and male journeys. Without more fundamental changes, such as introducing into the Hollywood machine more female creative workers, the state of things and the structures accompanying it will not change.

Genre is crucial in challenging the female persona, and particularly in bringing the issue closer to the existing social order. Sci-fi, being a non-realistic genre, can have a strong female lead which in a more realistic film representation becomes more problematic – simply because realistic films reflect the social reality. Ripley can win the battle with an extra-terrestrial monster, but Thelma and Louise cannot win a battle with society; mainly because it is controlled by men (including men in executive positions in the entertainment industry). The protagonists of the film attempt to liberate themselves from societal expectations (and particularly from the patriarchal pressures of their immediate habitus, the rural America), by doing everything a pretty woman is not supposed to do: choosing a partner instead of being taken by force and punishing men who verbally or physically assault them.

The tragic finale of *Thelma and Louise* is dictated by the genre: society is still built in such a way that if a woman wants to escape her fate and exercise her agency, she has to be forceful, and in the protagonists' case this forcefulness results in a range of blunders. Narrative outcomes showing women protagonists as victors allowed to punish their tormentors without any legal or social consequences, belong to different genres. The final scene interweaves close-ups of Thelma and Louise's simultaneously confused and excited faces with images of cartridges being loaded into rifles. Semiotically, this is a very interesting scene as the expressiveness of a human face is contrasted with the coldness of the murdering steel. Two metonymies, the face and the faceless weapon, placed next to each other, emphasize the women's defencelessness before the social and legal systems. The policeman's voice from a loudspeaker in the last scene sums up the women's experience with men – the control, the projections, the violence, the objectification; it is the women who are presented as the problem, not the men who victimize them.

Conclusion

The persona (as described by authors from a variety of disciplines) is a social mask aimed at creating a threshold between the personal and the social, and is therefore necessary for the individual's successful integration into society. It eases social interactions by curtailing authentic expressions which otherwise might be perceived by others as strange, offensive, or inappropriate. By so doing, it standardizes social interaction, makes it somewhat bland, and plays an important role in the communication economy by reducing the time spent on working out the status of others. A persona has therefore to be fairly rigid in order to be reliable because others should be able to predict one's behaviour in repeated interactions.

Interpolated on to women's social status and position in social hierarchy, the female persona becomes the inflexible, and generalizing, mask aimed at defining, predicting, and controlling a whole group of diverse individuals. The female persona is a collection of gender markers, including those related to appearance (clothes, make-up), behaviour, and roles. These elements defer responsibility for female individuation by replacing the very need to think for oneself with ready-made formulaic projections. One just has to accept them without doubting their validity or integrity. Yet, women (and their on-screen counterparts) have an acute need to individuate outside the societal projections, and to choose their own paths. This need to individuate, as well as constituents of the individuation process (both female and generic), will be further explored in the next chapter.

References

Beauvour, Simonede (1949/2011) *The Second Sex*, London: Vintage Books.

Butler, Judith (1990) *Gender Trouble: Feminism and the Subversion of Identity*, London: Routledge.

Creed, Barbara (1993) *The Monstrous Feminine: Film, Feminism, Psychoanalysis*, London: Routledge.

Doane, Mary Ann (1982) 'Film and Masquerade: Theorising the Female Spectator', *Screen*, 23 (3–4), pp. 74–88.

Dworkin, Andrea (1997) *Life and Death: Unapologetic Writing on the Continuing War Against Women*, Boston: Little, Brown and Co.

Freud, Sigmund (1960/2001) 'Femininity', in J. Strachey (ed. & trans.), *The Standard Edition of the Complete Psychological Works of Sigmund Freud* (Vol. 22), London: Vintage.

Fordham, Frieda (1991) *An Introduction to Jung*, London: Penguin.

Gray, Frances (2007/2019) *Jung, Irigaray, Individuation: Philosophy, Analytical Psychology, and the Question of the Feminine*. London: Routledge.

Goffman, Erving (1990) *The Presentation of Self in Everyday Life*, London: Penguin.

Goffman, Erving (2005) *Interaction Ritual: Essays in Face-to Face Communication*, New Brunswick and London: AldineTransaction.

Harris, Hunter (2021) 'Welcome to Zollywood', *GQ*, January 11.

Irigaray, Luce (2007) *Je, Tu, Nous*, New York and London: Routledge.

Jacobi, Jolande (1942/1973) *The Psychology of C. G. Jung* (8th Edition), trans. Ralph Manheim, New Haven and London: Yale University Press.

Jung C.G. (n.d.) *The Collected Works*, Herbert Read, Michael Fordham and Gerhardt Adler, (eds.) R.F.C. Hull, (trans.), London: Routledge. (Except where a different publication was used, all references are to this hardback edition.)

Jung, Carl Gustav and von Franz, M.-L. (eds.) (1964/1978) *Man and His Symbols*, London: Picador.

Kristeva, Julia (1982) *Powers of Horror: an Essay on Abjection*, New York: Columbia University Press.

Kristeva, Julia (2018) 'The Psychic Life: a Life in Time', *The Journal of French and Francophone Philosophy*, XXVI (2), pp. 81–90.

Lacan, Jacques (1999) *The Seminar of Jacques Lacan: Bk. 20: On Feminine Sexuality, the Limits of Love and Knowledge: On Feminine Sexuality, the Limits of Love and Knowledge*, New York: W,W Norton and Company.

Marshall, P. David; Moore, Christopher and Barbour, Kim (2019) *Persona Studies: An Introduction*, Hoboken, NJ: Wiley and Sons.

Mulvey, Laura (1975) 'Visual Pleasure and Narrative Cinema', *Screen*, Autumn (16) 3, pp. 6–18.

Neumann, Erich (1994) *The Fear of the Feminine and Other Essays on Feminine Psychology*, Princeton, NJ: Princeton University Press.

Rowland, Susan (1964) 'The Process of Individuation', in Carl Gustav Jung and Marie-Louise von Franz (eds.) *Man and His Symbols*, London: Picador, pp. 159–254.

Rowland, Susan (2005) *Jung as a Writer*, London: Routledge.

Silverman, Kaja (1988) *The Acoustic Mirror: the Female Voice in Psychoanalysis and Cinema*, Bloomington, IN: Indiana University Press.

Strachey, J. (ed. and trans.) (1960/2001) *The Standard Edition of the Complete Psychological Works of Sigmund Freud*, London: Vintage.

Tasker, Yvonne (1993) *Spectacular Bodies: Gender, Genre and the Action Cinema*, London: Routledge.

Tong, Rosemarie and Botts, Tina Fernandes (2018) *Feminist Thought: a More Comprehensive Introduction*, London: Routledge.

Wehr, Demaris (1988) *Jung and Feminism: Liberating Archetypes*, London: Routledge.

Chapter 2

The Female Journey

This chapter looks at the concept of individuation in general before exploring the female journey in particular. It discusses the female questor, the stages of her journey, and her developmental aims. It also investigates whether there is such a thing as a specifically 'female' individuation process. Finally, it looks at some examples of journeys of the new generation of television and film heroines.

Individuation: Definitions

Analytical psychology has two major concepts linked to agency and its role in the individual's life: individuation and archetypes. These concepts have been extensively applied to analyse all kinds of narratives. Importantly, unlike another beloved tool of film theorists, the Oedipus Complex, the individuation process in itself does not position the man as the centre of the universe. Jung did not define individuation in terms of gender, although many of the examples he used to illustrate it are, indeed, examples of male hero myth. In other words, it is not how the concept is conceived but how it is used that may pose potential problems.

In analytical psychology, individuation is a journey the aim of which is to find oneself. Importantly, such a journey can only happen in context of one's society or culture; it does not take place in detachment from the needs of the family, community, or social structures. In this sense, the individuation process does not imply being self-centred – rather, it translates into a balance between the personal and the social. Its idea is that the individual learns to make personal choices while also taking others into consideration. In other words, one cannot be an independent person at the expense of society – one can only become an individual *within* society, with its rules and regulations. Individuation, Jung explains, 'does not shut one out from the world, but gathers the world to oneself' (Jung, CW8: para. 432).

Individuation is also mostly a creative, spontaneous process, a 'natural process within the psyche' that is 'potentially present in every man, although most men are unaware of it' (Jacobi, 1973: 107). We are all protagonists in

DOI: 10.4324/9781003253044-3

our own individuation narrative, and the fact that our paths are unique makes our existence meaningful and worth exploring: all life, Jung writes, 'is bound to individual carriers who realize it, and it is simply inconceivable without them. But every carrier is charged with an individual destiny and destination, and the realization of these alone makes sense of life' (Jung, CW15: para. 330).

The individuation process is driven by what Jung called the centre of personality – the Self which stands for psychological wholeness (not perfection) and a freedom from all worldly conflicts and peace with oneself. This centre is more of a guideline and a phantom rather than something that can be really achieved. One can dream of achieving wholeness, but this may never happen. There is nothing tragic in this state of things, however. Having inner conflicts is only human, and while it is possible to integrate some of these issues, it is not possible to get rid of them completely. Arguably, nor is it entirely desirable as the resolution of psychological conflict is one of the spurs to creativity. Meanwhile, narratives show us our unique problems while, at the same time, making us realize that we do not suffer alone, and that our problems are as personal as they are universal.

Essentially a metaphor for the contemporaneous experience of being human, individuation consists of elements, or archetypes, each referring to a universal experience and its metaphorical representations. The word *archetype* means 'very typical example', 'an original model' and 'a recurrent motif in literature or art', *arkhe* meaning 'primitive' and *tupos* 'a model' (Soanes, et al., 2001). The archetype, Jung writes, 'is essentially an unconscious content that is altered by becoming conscious and by being perceived, and it takes its colour from the individual consciousness in which it happens to appear' (Jung, CW9/I: para. 5). In other words, consciousness, or rather, 'conscious elaboration', as Jung calls it, transforms the psychological phenomena arising from the depths of the unconscious. Archetypes, representing issues, questions, and problems, work alongside agency, or the force that motivates the individual to start and to continue on the journey.

What Exactly is a Female Journey?

The Oxford dictionary defines agency as 'action or intervention to produce a particular result' (Soanes at al., 2001). As such, it implies a motivation and a willingness to be in control of one's environment. Yet, female characters placed within the broad concept of the 'patriarchal marriage' are denied both agency and control except within the narrow sphere of 'female mysteries' or 'rituals' such as childbearing or homemaking (although sometimes they are not even afforded this luxury).

The woman on a journey is such a seemingly simple concept, and yet it is also unorthodox. Psychotherapist Maureen Murdock, the author of *The Heroine's Journey: A Woman's Quest for Wholeness* (1990) recalls an excerpt from an interview with Joseph Campbell she conducted as part of her research for the book:

> My desire to understand how the woman's journey relates to the journey of the hero first led me to talk with Joseph Campbell in 1981. I knew that the stages of the heroine's journey incorporated aspects of the journey of the hero, but I felt that the focus of the female spiritual development was to heal the internal split between woman and her feminine nature. I wanted to hear Campbell's views. I was surprised when he responded that women don't need to make the journey. 'In the whole mythological tradition the woman is there. All she has to do is to realise that she's the place that people are trying to get to. When a woman realises what her wonderful character is, she's not going to get messed up with the notion of being pseudo-male'.
>
> (Murdock, 2020: 7)

What Campbell implies here is that the woman is already at one with the Self, and therefore does not need to individuate. If she does not need to individuate, she also does not need an agency, an independent identity and a motivation to go on a journey. Campbell is confusing the woman as an individual with the public persona of a woman; with the white screen upon which male fantasies can be projected. Campbell's woman does not need to 'begin' anything because she embodies the passive treasure the male character is seeking. The most obvious problem is that, despite being a gender-neutral concept, individuation has often been used to create or discuss male-centered narratives – mainly because they have been readily available. It has been hijacked by the male hero-mythologists.

Not surprisingly, the same approach has been lingering in screenwriting for decades, resulting in female characters who either have nowhere to go, and expected to accept their fate (or even desire it - like Marilyn Monroe's seductresses); or rebel against this bleak, boring (and often painful) destiny, only to be branded 'hysterical', their rage presented as monstrous or grotesque. Gilda's drunken 'Put the Blame on Me' performance in *Gilda* (Charles Vidor, 1946) is one such cry for help, mistaken by Johnny (Glen Ford) for dangerous volatility. As Mulvey famously puts it, 'films reflects, reveals and even plays on the straight, socially established interpretation of sexual difference which controls images, erotic ways of looking and spectacle' (Mulvey, 1975: 6). Mulvey is, of course, using the Oedipus complex and Freud's vision of sexuality to critique representation of women in cinema. Quite apart (and beyond) the issue of sexuality, however, it is clear that these socially established interpretations have been robbing female characters (including in moving image narratives) of agency and of meaningful, diverse journeys. Deeply ingrained within 'warning' narratives such as 'Bluebeard' and 'Little Riding Hood' (and their numerous remakes and adaptations), these cultural directives threatened disobedient women with repercussions should they display any proclivity towards proactive behaviour, curiosity or decision-making. Better remain inactive and protected than be eaten by a wolf or end up hanging from a hook in the bloody chamber. The 'Red' and 'Blue' Woman narratives and their evolution in cinema and television will be discussed in Chapter 3.

Campbell is not alone in his insistence on the passivity of the female narrative. Jacques Lacan assumes, for instance, that the woman is the signifier - the outer shell of the sign rather than its meaning. It echoes Campbell's assertion that the woman is 'already there' – after all, the signifier is also 'already there', waiting to be filled with content, the permanent fixture, lacking direction unless she is filled with a signified. Woman, Lacan writes, cannot signify anything because of her status of being not-whole (Lacan, 1998: 73). Also, 'being not-whole, she has a supplementary jouissance compared to the to what the phallic function designates by way of jouissance' (Lacan, 1998: 73). Yet, even though she 'does not exist and does not signify anything', she nevertheless (magically) possesses men, Lacan insists (Lacan, 1998: 73–74). Or, to translate it into Campbell's language, men want to be where women already are. Or where their fixed abode is, to be precise.

Depth psychology theorists and scholars of narratives have consistently propagated the idea that the woman 'has nowhere to go'; that her function is to procreate, to nurse and to look after others. In this sense, she should stay put as she has to be available to those dependent on her at home. From Freud's 'heads in hieroglyphic bonnets' (a synecdoche he borrowed from a poem by Heine) to Lacan's view that women 'do not exist' (at worst) and are not 'whole' (at best) and Jung's assertion that women with opinions are annoying because their masculine side is overwhelming them, the woman is reduced to parts, to fragments, to synecdoches. She is deliberately fragmented and told that 'this is a natural state of things', meaning that a quest would not help her restore herself from the fragments. She would never be whole because her body and mind are 'naturally' flawed. So why even try? She already has everything she needs.

Screenwriter Christopher Vogler's attempts to address what he calls the 'gender' problems do little to improve the situation. Whereas Vogler admits that the Hero's Journey [as it was envisaged by Joseph Campbell] 'is sometimes critiqued as a masculine theory' and 'there may be some masculine bias', he also writes, bizarrely, that men's journeys are more linear, 'proceeding from one outward goal to the next' compared to women's journeys which 'may spin or spiral inward or outward' (Vogler, 2007: xxi–xxii). He also admits that there has been 'some masculine bias built into the description of the hero cycle since many of its theoreticians have been male', because after all, 'I'm a man and can't help seeing the world through the filter of my gender' (Vogler, 2007: xxi). He suggests that a woman's path 'may spin or spiral inward and outward' while 'male journeys may be in some sense more linear, proceeding from one outward goal to the next' (Vogler, 2007: xxi–xxii). Vogler defends the spiral analogy:

> The spiral may be a more accurate analogue for a woman's journey than a straight line or a simple circle. Another possible model may be a series of concentric rings, with the woman making a journey inward towards the center and then expanding it again. The masculine need to go out and overcome obstacles, to achieve, conquer, and possess, may be replaced in the woman's journey by the drives to preserve the family and the species, make a home, grapple with emotions, come to accord, or cultivate beauty.
>
> (Vogler, 2007: xxi–xxii)

It is unclear what precisely he means by the specific female journey structure, but juxtaposing a universal male journey with a universal female journey does bring this kind of thinking in line with other proponents of gender essentialism. Vogler does use some female characters as examples in the book, including *Dorothy from Wizard of Oz*, to illustrate his theory, although it is still unclear whether the 'spiral' journey shape is still applicable to her, or whether she follows the 'standard' hero's journey.

Susan Rowland highlights the tension at the heart of Analytical Psychology's treatment of the feminine. On the one hand, 'it contains a gender politics in a drive to displace the feminine into the position of 'other' (anima) to the masculine psyche' (Rowland, 2002: 19). On the other, archetypes are androgynous (Rowland, 2002: 40) and, unlike Campbell's visions of the journey, the individuation process is not described by either Jung or his disciples in specifically gendered terms - although most of the examples they use, inevitably, come from traditional narratives led by a male protagonist. Importantly, Rowland emphasizes, 'the mind can never be of one fixed gender and archetypes will work with and produce contrasting notions of the femininity and masculinity witnessed in material culture' (Rowland, 2002: 40).

Still, as Christopher Hauke points out in his book *Jung and the Postmodern* (2000): although the individuation process and most of the archetypes are gender neutral, some of the archetypes are still gender-specific, such as the pairs anima-animus and mother-father (old man/woman). Jung's own explanations of the anima and the mother archetype do not make it any easier for feminists to reclaim his theory for the benefit of female characters.

The Mother Goddess Trajectory

A predictable, and seemingly empowering, direction of the female journey has been mapped out by what Susan Rowland calls 'the Goddess movement' (Rowland, 2002: 49). This movement, Rowland writes, 'bestows upon women a metaphysical "home" quite outside the restrictions of Christian monotheism' (Rowland, 2002: 49). References to (and reverence of) the Goddess are informed by Jung and Neumann's analysis of the great mother, her dual nature, and her chthonic powers. Jung describes the great mother as possessing ambivalent chthonic powers, 'the magic authority of the female', 'wisdom and spiritual exaltation that transcend reason', 'helpful instinct' and 'all that cherishes and sustains, that fosters growth and fertility' (Jung, CW9/I: para. 158). On the other hand, she also presides over the underworld, and represents everything that 'devours, seduces and poisons, that is terrifying and inescapable like fate' (Jung, CW 9/I: para. 158). For instance, in her book *Descent to the Goddess: a Way of Initiation for Women* (1981), Sylvia Brinton Perera, a Jungian analyst and author, advocates a 'return to the goddess' if the modern woman is to regain her energy and spirit:

> The return to the goddess, for renewal in a feminine source-ground and spirit, is a vitally important aspect of modern woman's quest for wholeness. We women who have succeeded in the world are usually 'daughters of the father' - that is, well adapted to a masculine-oriented society - and have repudiated our own feminine instincts and energy patterns, just as culture has maimed or derogated most of them. We need to return to and redeem what the patriarchy has often seen only as a dangerous threat and called terrible mother, dragon or witch.
>
> (Perera, 1981: 7)

The patriarchal ego of both genders, the Pereira writes, had fled 'from the full-scale awe of the goddess' in order to maintain its 'instinct-disciplining, striving, progressive, and heroic stance' (Perera, 1981: 7).

A further attempt to identify the trajectory of the heroine's journey has led Valerie Estelle Frankel to conclude that the heroine's true goal is to become the 'archetypal, all-powerful mother' because 'she was worshipped as the ultimate creator, the vessel of emerging power and the source of all life. Girls emulate this path on their journeys by forming a family circle they can role as supreme nurturer and protector' (Frankel, 2010: 7). Frankel further provides examples of a combination of power, motherhood and sacrificial behaviour in folkloric and mythological female protagonists:

> Thus, many heroines set out on rescue missions in order to restore their shattered families: a shy princess knits coats of nettles to save her six brothers from a lifetime as swans, Psyche quests for her vanished lover. Demeter forces herself into the realm of the dead to reclaim her daughter, while Isis scours the world for her husband's broken body. Little Gerda in Hans Christian Andersen's tale quests all the way to Finland to rescue her playmate from the unfeeling Snow Queen. This goal does not indicate by any means that the girls are trying to 'stay at home' or 'play house'. Though they redeem beloved family members or potential husbands, these heroines work as hard as any fairytale hero. And they do it without swords.
>
> (Frankel, 2010: 7)

What this approach does not take into consideration is that 'doing it without swords' may not necessarily be a compliment or a useful skill, as some recent cinematic and television heroines attest, including Arya Stark (Maisie Williams) in *Game of Thrones* (HBO, 2011–2019), Imperator Furiosa (Charlize Theron) in *Mad Max: Fury Road* (2015), *Wonder Woman* (Gal Gadot) (2017) or the Dora Milaje of Wakanda (*Black Panther,* 2018). In fact, the peaceful/calm/patient/wise image could be doing more harm than good in terms of on-screen representation of women, feeding further into societal perceptions of women as docile and agreeable whose anger and ambition have to be hidden lest they repulse others and make themselves look 'unattractive'.

Similarly, at the end of *The Heroine's Journey* Maureen Murdoch offers an ode to mother Goddess, essentially describing the transformative potential of the mother archetype:

> Women are weavers. We intertwine with men, children and each other to protect the web of life.
> Women are creators. We can give birth to the young ones and to the children of our dreams.
> Women are healers. We know the mysteries of the body, blood and spirit because they are one and the same.
> Women are lovers; we joyfully embrace each other, men, children, animals and trees listening with our hearts to their triumphs and sorrows.
> Women are alchemists; we uncover the roots of violence, destruction and desecration of the feminine and transform cultural wounds.
> Women are the protectors of the soul of the Earth; we bring the darkness out of hiding and honor the unseen realms.
> Women are divers; we move down into the Mysteries where it is safe and wondrous and oozing with new life.
>
> (Murdock, 2020: 203)

Reiterating once more the 'Goddess narrative', Murdoch hopes that the journeying heroine will rediscover her femininity by diving into mysteries and healing the social fabric of society torn by bellicose men who enjoy war and destruction. It paints a very traditional picture of femininity, complete with expectations of being the glue of family and community. What this manifesto neglects, however, is the heroine who enjoys exercising what is traditionally regarded as masculine qualities and perhaps would like to stay away from embracing, healing, and mysteries as far as possible. While restoring respect for the community-building aspect of traditional female roles, Goddess feminism nevertheless neglects a whole host of behaviours available to women, including being a warrior or simply choosing to be alone, away from the duties of being an 'embracing lover'.

Meanwhile, Shinoda Bolen emphasizes in *Goddesses in Every Woman: New Psychology of Women* (2014) that there are women who enjoy providing nourishment to others, who see this as a meaningful activity and an important part of the journey. There are different paths, she argues, and a unified formula will not be suitable for everyone. People are guided on their journey by archetypes, and these powerful archetypes are responsible for 'major differences among women' (Bolen, 2014: 1). Some women, she argues, need

> monogamy, marriage, or children to feel fulfilled, and they grieve and rage when the goal if beyond their reach. For them, traditional roles are personally meaningful. Such women differ markedly from another type of woman who most values her independence as she focuses on achieving goals that are important to her, or from still another type who seeks emotional intensity and new experiences, and consequently moved from one relationship or one creative effort to the next. Yet another type of woman seeks solitude and finds that her spirituality means the most to her.
>
> (Bolen, 2014: 2)

Yet, all these type of journeys, Bolan argues, are still covered by the figure of the Goddess – it's just they are different Goddesses activated in every woman (Bolen, 2014: 2). While acknowledging the importance and archetypal power of the Goddess as a derivative of the mother and anima archetypes, this monograph nevertheless aims to move the female journey away from traditionally 'female' figures and archetypes to explore the ones that have usually been dominated by male characters, including the shadow, the trickster, the child, the self, and the hero.

The oxymoronic, caring yet terrifying mother Goddess with her ability to create and destroy is certainly an attractive role as it challenges cultural vision of women as physically and emotionally fragile, and the sociological contextualization of them as powerless in the world of the Symbolic. It paints the feminine as possessing different yet equal powers with the male. However, as Rowland rightly points out, the 'Goddess movement' has its biases: 'This kind of feminism can be radical in its philosophical or theological propositions, yet also conservative in its prescriptions for women's material lives' (Rowland, 2002: 50). Importantly, it is still gendered and, as such, 'allows us to unpick the binaries of theory that has dominated cultural debates on gender. Even the great Goddess is not a feminine version of monotheism, which forms a binary by casting out so much that is "other"' (Rowland, 2002: 69). Indeed, had the 'Goddess' been the only path for women (and female characters), narratives centred on female characters would have become as repetitive and reductive, as grotesque and self-parodic, as Marilyn Monroe's stories of womanhood.

Erich Neumann's Female Journey

A more interesting (and varied) version of the female individuation is presented by Erich Neumann in his 'essays on feminine psychology'. His view is often overlooked in favour of more extreme positions such as locking the woman in the anima role, or turning her into the representative of the numinous 'Great Mother'. In 'Stages of Woman's Development' Neumann outlines female developmental stepping stones, or stages. He does not always clearly separate them so it is often unclear where one stage ends and the other begins. In the absence of detailed maps of the female journey, it is important to add Neumann's conceptualizations to the library of possible options.

The first stage can be considered to be 'gender neutral' rather than explicitly feminine. At this stage, the (female) child is largely managed by the unconscious and her ego is contained in the uroboros (a serpent or dragon eating its tail; in analytical psychology this metaphor traditionally represents the unconscious) (Neumann, 1994: 4–6). There is no identity as such, and particularly no gendered identity.

The next stage somewhat echoes Campbell's assertion that the woman does not have to go anywhere to achieve her ambitions. At this next stage humans have to separate themselves from the unconscious, but it goes differently for men and women. Apparently, 'the woman does not have to leave the circle of maternal uroboros' and separate herself from the unconscious. In a female, 'self-discovery and primal relationship coincide' (Neumann, 1994: 6–9). She also has the option to 'remain in this realm', and to stay 'childish and immature', but she will not be estranged from her true nature (Neumann, 1994: 9). A man in the same situation would be regarded by culture as 'castrated' and 'robbed of his authentic being' whereas a woman would remain 'in an immature form of her authentic being' (Neumann, 1994: 9).

Interestingly, Neumann recognizes that flourishing in the 'I am a goddess' state is not the ultimate goal of female individuation, and suggests that the next step would be to deal with the 'masculine' aspect of the psyche (and culture). This is when the 'paternal uroboros' (or, rather, the 'masculine' side of the dual uroboros) arrives and overwhelms the female psyche. According to Neumann, it is a chthonic experience, often represented in traditional narratives as being overtaken by a serpent or a dragon (Neumann, 1994: 18). This is the phase when 'self-preservation' (unity with the maternal uroboros) is followed by 'self-surrender' (Neumann, 1994: 18–19). To the female individuand, the undifferentiated masculine feels 'numinous, anonymous, and transpersonal' as she is captured by the 'Spirit Father' (Neumann, 1994: 20–21). Meanwhile, she also becomes hostile to the maternal principle and 'estranged from herself' to the extent that she 'loses even her relationship to her femininity' (Neumann, 1994: 22).

At the next step of the individuation, the woman assimilates the powerful archetypal representative of the masculine (the animus, the Great Father, the Spirit Father, etc) and becomes liberated from both the matriarchal and the patriarchal uroboros (Neumann, 1994: 25). As patronizing as this sounds, what Neumann perhaps means is the necessity for self-reflection, self-awareness, and for separation from the primary relationships (be it the father or the mother) in order to progress as an individual. Interestingly, he also postulates that this crucial third stage – that of processing and assimilating the father – 'is the task of the male hero' rather than the female individuand who is still dependent 'on the help of archetypally masculine power' (Neumann, 1994: 26).

The good news is that after accomplishing this task, the heroine becomes more autonomous and independent from her male partner (Neumann, 1994: 27). The bad news is, having separated herself from the dual unconscious and achieving the precious self-awareness, she is met with the wall of patriarchal thinking in a society built for men:

> The patriarchal line of the development of consciousness leads to a con-
> dition where patriarchal-masculine values are dominant values that are
> often conceived in direct opposition to those of the archetypal feminine
> and the unconscious. This development, directed by the archetypally
> conditioned cultural canon and impressed upon the development of every
> male and female child in Western cultures, leads to the separation of
> consciousness from the unconscious, to the evolution of the independent
> conscious system with a masculine ego as the center...
>
> (Neumann, 1994: 28)

What this means is that the female journey, like any individuation, does not happen in a cultural vacuum, and is partially determined by the culture in which it happens. Unfortunately for the female individuand, this culture is geared up for the male hero and his needs, and the newly-enlightened female who may feel that she is on the way to somewhere, may find that she is, in fact, severely restricted in any further development.

Unlike Lacan, Neumann does not really delve into the intricacies of the Symbolic order, but he is aware of the negative impact of its limitations on women who want more than a husband and a baby. In a way, 'Goddess femin-ism' which celebrates the 'uniquely female' qualities of connectedness, care and love, inadvertently supports patriarchal assumptions that, indeed, women have nowhere to go and should embrace the natural unity with the unconscious – with the female uroboros.

Thus, Neumann maps out the outline of female individuation that finds itself at odds with the rigidity of highly gendered cultural canons. He then admits that the socio-political aspect of this assimilation into the patriarchal culture is unsatisfactory for women:

> regardless of whether the patriarchy is primitive or highly civilised, when
> the woman is integrated into it and subordinated to its values, the male
> becomes the representative of consciousness and the development of con-
> sciousness for woman. This grants the male a psychological preponderance
> that determines ... woman's place in life.
>
> (Neumann, 1994: 30)

The patriarchal marriage thus presents 'a not an inconsiderable danger for the woman's development' (Neumann, 1994: 30). However, as more people individuate and challenge traditional ways of doing things, there arises a challenge to 'the archetypally based collective ideal' resulting in a 'crisis in the patriarchal marriage and the patriarchal structure of culture' (Neumann, 1994: 33). Importantly, these 'individuated persons' are aware of the culturally suppressed duality of human nature; of the fact that in the original uroboros neither of the binary sides really prevails or is regarded as somehow superior (Neumann, 1994: 33).

The patriarchal crisis which Neumann mentions in his 1951 essay is now acutely felt in the television and film industry which has finally started to explore the different options a female individuand can face in her adventures. The thing is,

> ... in every case, the cultural symbiosis of the patriarchal marriage works out less favourably for the Feminine and for women than it does for the Masculine and for men. Due to the circumstance that women are compelled to embrace the unequivocal femininity while the values of consciousness in a patriarchal culture are masculine, women remain undeveloped in this domain and are continually dependent on the aid of men. But this is why men consider themselves superior and see women as inferior.
>
> (Neumann, 1994: 33)

Challenging cultural canons, fixed attitudes and structures, and gendered assumptions, is as important as ever. Patriarchal values, Neumann emphasizes, endanger women's psychological development, keeping her infantile (Neumann, 1994: 34). This is because they place the woman on the receiving end of such relationships. Being dependent on a man means being part of someone else's fantasy of you.

Creative solutions to this psychological endangerment are more important than ever. Dismantling of cultural tropes is also necessary – primarily the dissolution of millennia-old projections and ancient binaries. Another important step would be de-stereotyping of both the unconscious and consciousness, dissolving their metaphorical bond respectively with performative femininity and masculinity. Narratives discussed in this book make an effort to dissolve, and to dismantle, the old assumptions about the female journey and the 'patriarchal marriage' in all its cultural variations. From the focused hunters and stalkers that are female detectives in television series around the world, to the shameless, foul-mouthed, bumbling female characters such as BBC's Fleabag and Netflix's Princess Teabeanie from *Disenchantment*, the new heroine is rejecting these canons, either explicitly or implicitly.

The Elements of the Journey: Archetypes

Before discussing the possible elements of the female journey and their inter-action with the female persona, let us have a look at the concepts of indivi-duation and archetypes.

Jung discerns a range of archetypes (discussed in more detail later in the chapter): the anima and the animus, the shadow, the hero, the child, the trickster, the old wise woman, the old wise man, and the self. Even from this brief summary we can see that they cover a whole range of basic yet pow-erful human experiences: finding a partner (the anima, the animus), dealing with the parents (the old wise figures), being conscious of your negative traits (the shadow), maintaining the balance between being an individual and belonging to society (the trickster), keeping the creativity alive (the child) and, finally, trying to keep together the different parts of the psyche (the self).

All archetypes have a positive and negative side to them. For instance, the old wise woman/Great Mother can appear to you in a dream as a witch or as a helpful fairy godmother; and the trickster in fairy tales can be an outlaw or a culture hero. Depending on whether you take the perspective of Zeus or the people who learned to use fire, Prometheus is a criminal who deserves a tor-tuous punishment for his theft of fire, or a man who led humanity out of darkness and into progress.

Jacobi also emphasizes that archetypes can take a variety of forms, from static images to actions, processes, reactions and attitudes (Jacobi, 1942: 40). In fact, these archetypes designating processes rather than human characters are named by Jung 'the archetypes of transformation'. Their task, he writes, is to represent a transformation on the individuation path: 'Like the per-sonalities, these archetypes are true and genuine symbols that cannot be exhaustively interpreted, either as signs or as allegories' (Jung, CW 9/I: para. 80).

Jung goes on to say in his essay 'Archetypes of the Collective Uncon-scious' that archetypes are nothing less than unconscious contents fleshed out as group beliefs in accordance with a particular culture. These group beliefs take many forms: myth, fairy tale, tribal lore, dreams and fantasies (and even, I dare say, urban mythology expressed in contemporary narra-tives in film and television). Jung carefully traces this delicate process of 'fleshing out' – the moment when the archetype, a shapeless blob of unconscious material, emerges in the culture or the mind of a dreamer in the shape of a seductive female water spirit, an ugly witch, a helpful elf or an amusing fool.

Their meaning-making properties explain why archetypes are often acti-vated, and become particularly powerful, when the individual cannot see where they are going. Suddenly we may start having recurring dreams, or become drawn to certain films or start liking certain kind of books. The goal of this often difficult and overwhelming process is 'illumination of higher consciousness, by means of which the initial situation is overcome on a higher level' (Jung, CW 9/I: para. 82).

Archetypes, as Jung envisaged them, are the constituents (as well as stages) in the individuation process. Because they represent different human experiences, they more or less define what it means to be human.

Importantly, there is a distinction between archetypes as universal ideas (experiences, processes) and archetypal images that are the fleshed-out, culturally (and individually) specific versions of each archetype. Archetypes are 'invisible' for consciousness while cultural representations and individual visions have concrete impressions on societies. The archetype, Jung writes, 'is essentially an unconscious content that is altered by becoming conscious and by being perceived, and it takes its colour from the individual consciousness in which it happens to appear' (Jung, CW9/I: para. 5).

Individuation as a Narrative

Before returning to the female journey, let us have a look at the generic definition and purpose of the individuation process. Individuation of a human being is all about becoming oneself in a given environment. In a story, the individuation becomes the protagonist's path and can be regarded as a living narrative with the sole protagonist as its centre, a sort of a skeleton plot of events guided by the protagonist's motivations and goals. Screenplays and stories are about the protagonist's struggle to find themselves and to find meaning in existence. We watch films and TV shows, and read books precisely because narratives serve as mirrors for our own individuation journey. They show us the possible ways of dealing with things, the alternative turns that can be taken on our path, the various results from decisions that can be made. For instance, *The Crown* (Netflix, 2016–) depicts the journey of a woman who has to balance her official duties with her personal preferences and emotions. Despite the fact that being a monarch is the role most people will never experience, the public still feels a connection with the protagonist as she navigates her way through a range of archetypal situations, including the ever-present tension between the individual and the system. When we are watching a screen narrative, it is as if we are living our lives through someone else's failures and successes. It helps us understand ourselves, our past, present, and future.

The individuation process is driven by what Jung called the centre of personality – the self – which stands for psychological wholeness (not perfection) and a freedom from all worldly conflicts and peace with oneself. This centre is more of a guideline and a phantom rather than something that can be really achieved. The reason why we are capable of multiple journeys which link together into one long 'life journey' is this unattainability of perfection. One can dream of achieving wholeness, but it might never happen. There is nothing tragic in this state of things, however. Having inner conflicts is only human, and while it is possible to integrate some of the issues, it is not possible to get rid of them completely. Arguably, nor is it entirely desirable as the resolution of psychological conflict is one of the spurs to creativity. Meanwhile, narratives show us our unique problems while, at the same time, making us realize that we do not suffer alone, and that our problems are as personal as they are universal.

There is nothing wrong with having inner demons, though – indeed, they are unavoidable. Everyone individuates, and, since human beings share the collective unconscious, we all have similar individuation milestones. These milestones are expressed in metaphors and metaphorical situations – or archetypes and archetypal situations, as Jung preferred to call them. All human beings have issues with parents or parental figures, struggle with undesirable character traits such as envy, greed and aggression, deal with instincts and sexuality, try to find path and place in life, look for love and acceptance, and try to achieve something significant before death. In other words, individuation is the basic skeleton filled out with personal details: all parents (and the issues associated with them) are different; and the ways in which human beings experience sexual feelings are also very individual. Cinematic and television narratives provide frameworks for reflecting on a variety of individuation moments, and, as the interaction with the screen is one-way, they are pliable canvases for one's fantasies and projections. They are ideal providers of objects for one's individuation narrative.

Jung (and his disciples, including Jolande Jacobi) identify the sequence in which archetypes appear to the hero on their path: first it is the shadow, then the contrasexual element (anima or animus), then the parental archetypes (mother/father), and then, finally, the self (Jacobi, 1973: 109–130). Somewhere in between these archetypes the individual also encounters the child and the trickster. The rigidity of the individuation process which made many of Jung's fans and users of his ideas, including Vogler, view it as a continuous hero myth with a predetermined sequence of events.

The fixed order of appearance of archetypes not only determined the appearance of the individuation process as a sort of hero myth, but also – starting with Campbell – resulted in a fixed view of narratives as being centred around a (predominantly male) hero who has to go through certain stages to achieve a state of wholeness. For Campbell, the number of stages in a journey is 17, and Vogler divides the hero's journey into three acts and 12 segments. They include existing in the ordinary world, call to adventure (or 'inciting incident'), refusal of the call, meeting with the mentor, crossing the threshold, encountering tests, allies and enemies, approaching an ordeal, going through the ordeal, being rewarded, returning home, resurrection and reaching home with the 'elixir' (or treasure, or boon) (Vogler, 2007: 9).

Jung, Campbell, and Vogler offer different but still rigid and repetitive journey structures. Essentially, it is about the hero's change of status and the different stages of this process: it starts with the hero being immature and ends with him being ready to be a responsible adult capable of protecting his community and his family. All three authors focus on the male hero's journey and his achievements, and whereas it could be possible to translate it into the female journey, it would still be one of the many possibilities open to the heroine. The journeys needs to be more flexible, it has to have more options. This can only be achieved by separating the archetypes from the journey stages and exploring each of them separately, which is covered in the next section.

Taxonomy of Archetypes and Themes in the Individuation Process

'Staged individuation' resulting in a staged narrative not only obscures the importance and meaning of the particular archetypes standing for various life events but also creates a 'one size fits all' approach which offers little flexibility to the variety and wealth of human experiences. Instead, in my book *Jungian Theory for Storytellers* (Bassil-Morozow, 2018) I propose that authors, critics and other users of narratives think of the individuation process as consisting of many events, each focused on a particular archetype or a theme. I also group the nine archetypes into three themes, each covering a group of issues in an individual's life: social adaptation, reality-testing and self-actualization. My argument is that a narrative may be focused on one of the archetypes, a theme, or a combination of themes and archetypes. Moreover, in my view, this approach opens up opportunities for exploring a range of human experiences instead of focusing on the hero myth, and particularly its male version.

Table 2.1 Taxonomy of Archetypes

THEME 1 *Social adaptation*	THEME 2 *Reality-testing*	THEME 3 *Self-actualization*
Morality and rules	Parents and partners	Achievements and creativity
Two archetypes	Four archetypes	Three archetypes
the shadow	the anima	the child
the trickster	the animus	the hero
	old man/father	the self
	old woman/mother	

Theme 1: Society

Social adaptation contains two archetypes, the shadow and the trickster, and is the basic, underlying theme both in human development and in narrative storytelling. Social adaptation is the first issue a human child faces as they enter the world. Freud discusses this issue as the problem of narcissism – the child is gradually introduced to the fact that they are not the only creature in the world, and has to learn to co-exist with other family members as well as society members. In other words, the child learns to 'tame' his or her narcissistic impulses. Lacan's version of it is the 'mirror stage' – a developmental phase when this awareness of the presence of others happens, and when the child starts to realize that he or she is one of the many individuals inhabiting the same social space. Eventually, the initial (primary) narcissism is thus replaced with a healthier version, which allows the individual to successfully co-exist with others and to see them as equal human beings with feelings and rights.

Meanwhile, society has a set of moral rules, implemented in a variety of official and unofficial codes, such as religion, law, traditions, or what is known as 'common decency'. All of them are here to make sure that the individual internalizes the ways of co-existing with others without damaging either themselves or others.

Jung rarely writes about narcissism *per se*, but he uses a metaphor to describe the basic, selfish impulses in human nature: the shadow. It follows us whenever we go, and our task is to integrate it, to make sense of it – otherwise it will take over us, and we will not be able to examine our negative impulses. Stories, both visual and traditional, such as Robert Lewis Stevenson's *The Strange Case of Dr. Jekyll and Mr. Hyde* (1886), Oscar Wilde's *The Picture of Dorian Gray* (1890), or the more contemporary example of David Fincher's film *Fight Club* (1999), all show a male protagonist struggling to separate himself from his shadow, and to integrate its unpalatable contents (ranging from sexuality to greed and aggression) into his personality.

Interestingly enough, whereas there is an abundance of narratives about the male and his shadow, there are virtually none about women struggling with their evil *doppelgänger* – perhaps that's because, culturally, women are not allowed to be seen as anything but kind, nurturing, and caring. Female characters who do not fit into this stereotype are split off into villainesses, but there is no middle ground: very few narratives portray a woman trying to make sense of her dark side. Moreover, the 'dark side' is often conflated with the desire for agency and self-expression. Whenever it so much as manifests itself, like it does in Powell and Pressburger's *The Red Shoes* (1948) or Luis Buñuel's *Belle de Jour* (1967), the heroine who dares to be morally ambiguous, strives for self-expression or develops some form of agency, has to face the brutal consequences of her transgressions. The protagonist of *Red Shoes* commits suicide while *Belle de Jour's* Séverine loses her lover and becomes a carer to her disabled husband which effectively ends her transgressive activities as a part-time prostitute.

While the male hero is traditionally afforded inner conflict and is mired in moral ambiguity, complexity and dialectical tension out of which his new status gradually emerges, the heroine is static, her individuation focused on the maternal and the familial. Female characters and protagonists were more often than not depicted as one-dimensional – either wholly good or wholly bad, but not morally ambiguous. Only recently did we get to observe the acceptance and attempts at integrating the female shadow on television, with examples such as Sandra Oh's and Jodie Comer's messy rebels in *Killing Eve*, Suranne Jones' heroines fighting an inner darkness in the mini-series *Dr. Foster* (2015–) and *Vigil* (2021), Phoebe Waller-Bridge's chaotic character in *Fleabag* (2016–) as well as female prisoners, each dealing with her own doppelganger, in Netflix's *Orange is the New Black* (2013–). Season 4 of Charlie Brooker's *Black Mirror* contains an episode (*Crocodile*) in which the female protagonist (played by Andrea Riseborough) is balancing her existence as a successful architect and a family woman with the life of a murderer. Elsa from Disney's *Frozen* franchise is also allowed to have an unresolved conflict which is also a seat of inspiration, change, and the quest for the self.

Still, female shadow protagonists are fairly rare as evidently few authors consider women to be capable of going through moral struggles, or even having the capacity for moral ambivalence. It is refreshing to see that the new television era triggered a revolution in the way women are depicted in moving-image narratives.

The same pattern is observable in relation to the trickster archetype – only recently have female tricksters begun to emerge as a discernible category. A trickster story is a narrative which questions the norms of society and ascertains the power of the individual as an agent. The task of the trickster is to test the system and to find its week points. The trickster is a metaphor for change and the way it is often perceived by the system: as something dangerous and unpredictable something to be framed and controlled. The trickster and the system are locked in eternal struggle, but they cannot live without each other. The crossing of boundaries in 'pure' trickster narratives is celebrated and showed as liberating because social and systemic boundaries restrain individual agency. Cinematic trickster characters include, for instance, Jim Carrey's unruly protagonists in *The Mask* (1994) and the *Ace Ventura* series (1994–1995). Tricksters in narratives share a range of traits such as breaking boundaries and shapeshifting; they are also creative, uncontrollable, and shameless.

However, all of the traditional and most of the cinematic trickster characters are male; presumably because taboo-breaking, and chaotic and shameless behaviour is seen as being contrary to the patriarchal vision of the well-behaved woman. The arrival of the female trickster in recent television narratives signals a social shift, and shows that there is a demand for a new type of female protagonist, the one who does not conform to the traditional vision of what it means to be a woman; a protagonist who is not afraid to challenge the norms and to make change happen.

The trickster and the shadow are related, and form a continuum of character traits; sometimes they are indistinguishable from each other. A playful trickster may become a menacing shadow like it does in the characters like Joker and Harley Quinn. Chapter 6 explores the emergence of the rebellious, unruly and chaotic female protagonist in recent television narratives, including *Crazy Ex-Girlfriend* (The CW/Netflix; 2015–2018), *Disenchantment* (Netflix; 2018–), *Killing Eve* (BBC; 2018–) and *Fleabag* (BBC, 2016–2019).

Theme 2: Relationships

Theme 2 comprises four archetypes, each of which also has a significant negative aspect. If the trickster and the shadow bounce off each other, the anima, the animus, the old man (father) and the old woman (mother) have their own negative aspects to bounce off in narratives. Jung envisaged that everyone has a sort of inner inspiration figure, a 'soul-image', one that is also linked to romantic involvement and sexual attraction, often creating 'magically complicated relationships' (Jung, CW9/I: para.61). This image is often influenced by the parent of the opposite sex, creating an invisible link between parents and future partners (Jung, CW9/I: para. 61). In men this image take the form of a woman, the anima, and is often projected onto real women. Meanwhile, women have an inner man, or several of them (for the animus has the propensity to multiply into several figures), and men have an anima (or two, as they often come in the dual angel/whore package) (Jacobi, 1973: 121–123). Like all the other archetypes, the soul-image is dual, possessing a positive and a negative side; a destructive seductress or a wise guide on one's individuation path (Jacobi, 1973: 122).

Jung and his disciples' insistence on the contrasexuality of the 'soul image' does not account for the possibility that one can be equally inspired by the parent of any sex; by one or by both. He also unnecessarily ties the soul image to sexuality which may or may not be the case for different people and does not take into account individual differences. As they stand in their original conception, the anima and the animus in narratives should guide the male or female character on their individuation path. Yet, as traditionally depicted in narratives, they tend to play different roles in the male and female individuation processes: the anima is an element of the male individuation journey, facilitating his self-discovery by being supportive and accepting. For instance, Stanley Ipkiss (Jim Carrey) in *The Mask* sees the beautiful Tina Carlyle (Cameron Diaz) and imagines how his social status would improve if he could afford to go out with her. Tina is an inspiration and a prestige item; a rather sketchy character whose task is to wear the female persona well, and to occasionally become a damsel in distress impressed by Stanley's trickster-hero metamorphosis. The anima is a stepping stone on the protagonist's individuation path, and she is often a schematic and objectified character.

Meanwhile, animus appearances in film and television have not been known for more equitable representations. The animus is often portrayed as the ideal man, the prince on a white horse, a knight in shining armour, whose task is to emphasize the female character's vulnerability, beauty, lack of agency, and other prominent qualities of the female persona (this is exactly what happens in Cinderella-style narratives). Alternatively, the animus is dangerous, seductive, or hostile, initiating the female into the world of male aggression and sexual desires while the initiation itself should ideally result in the woman becoming submissive, and in strengthening the female persona (Beauty and the Beast-type narratives).

As it stands now, the 'soul-image' theory has been reflecting patriarchal assumptions about women (also reflected in traditional and contemporary narratives): gender roles are fixed, the anima is matched up with the female persona and projected onto women in society, the anima and the animus are invariably contrasexual, and also necessarily creating romantic and sexual links with the protagonist.

To turn it into a more inclusive piece of theory would be to replace literal romantic involvement with the metaphorical (perhaps leaving space for literal when necessary), to remove rigid gender assumptions from the anima and the animus, and to dissolve the obligatory and constraining contrasexual element. As Susan Rowland notes, the 'soul-image' concept can perhaps be rebranded as a *methodology* rather than 'an absolute truth about the gender identity for all time' (Rowland, 2005: 67). Rowland also notes that the stark polarity of the soul-image – the very quality that makes it a low-hanging fruit so suitable for projections onto reality – was perhaps a ghostly narrative process behind the emergence of a dialectical subject (Rowland, 2005: 69).

The fixedness of the anima and the animus to their opposites, as well as the links, identified by Jung himself, to the female and male personae, need to be challenged. After all, the individuation process was devised as a dialectical task, never truly resolved, always in a flux, always sustaining tension between the individual and the collective. Archetypes such as the shadow and the trickster are already dialectical, containing more grey areas than defined aspects. As are the child, the hero, and the self which are allowed to have features gliding across the negative-positive spectrum. It is only fair if gender (or soul-images, to use Jung's terminology) too is released from the constraints of binary thinking.

Indeed, many contemporary narratives defy both the heterosexuality and the romantic aura of the soul-image. For instance, Phoebe Waller Bridge's character, Fleabag (BBC, 2016–2019) has sex with men but is also interested in women. The same applies to Beth Harmon (Anya Taylor-Joy) in Netflix's *The Queen's Gambit* (2020) who has a date with a woman, a model called Cleo (Millie Brady). Both Fleabag and Beth are complex characters bearing a shadow and not regarding a romantic involvement as an end in itself. Both look feminine and chic, a habit that is regularly mistaken for the female persona until one realizes that the glamorous appearance is not really aimed at attracting and keeping men but is a form of self-expression, or perhaps an ironic interpretation of the mask of femininity. Hidden behind the façade is a strong individual rebuilding themselves; a long process in which encounters with the anima or the animus is merely a phase.

Theme 3: Self-actualization

Finally, self-actualization is the theme covering inspiration, ambition, and advancement as well as dealing with the tension between free will and God's omniscience and control. It contains three archetypes: the child, the hero, and the self. Theme 3 touches upon the inspiration and motivation behind the impulse to self-actualize, to find yourself, and to individuate. The 'free will versus control' conflict is not necessarily presented in Theme 3 narratives as a form of rebellion against God; often it is about exploring the balance between the two, or examining the dual nature of God (helpful versus destructive).

The self in Theme 3 narratives does not necessarily take the shape of a human god. Jung points out in his essays about the so-called UFO phenomena that in the middle of the twentieth century 'the mysteries of god' trope became more technogenic in its expressions, often taking the shape of alien arrival and abduction stories. Many contemporary narratives exploring the issue of free will vs god's discuss god in its newest forms – god as an alien and god as technology. In fact, the sci-fi genre was born simultaneously with the contemporary versions of the self: aliens, technology, and artificial intelligence. The latter was already being explored in Romantic fiction which started the dialogue about the dangers of industrialization and technology, for instance in Mary Shelley's *Frankenstein* (the monster) and E.T.A. Hoffman's *The Sandman* (Olympia).

Although the self has acquired new shapes, deep down this is still the same archetype. Or, to use proper Jungian terminology, the archetype of the self now has a new range of archetypal images which are more in line with the realities of industrial and post-industrial societies. The god portrayed is still the same complex archetype of the self – omniscient, conflicting, controversial, elusive, and full of riddles. It speaks a strange language, which human beings have to learn, or at the very least decipher. Sometimes it is inexplicably silent. It gives human beings riddles and puzzles which they have to solve; sometimes it provides advice, and at other times it completely throws people off balance. This is not a kind, benevolent god, but a tough one; the god that makes you work hard and sometimes suffer. The self in all its manifestations is the metaphor for how demanding and punishing the individuation process can be.

Different media present different sides of the self. This concerns all kinds of sci-fi lore, including aliens and artificial intelligence. For instance, in *Arrival*

(2016, directed by Denis Villeneuve), the self is presented as an alien looking like a giant octopus. Louise (Amy Adams) is a linguist who is hired to learn the language of the heptapod guests, which leads to the discovery that the aliens had come to earth to spread the message of unity and peace. Similarly, *E.T. the Extra-Terrestrial* (1982) depicts extra-terrestrial guests as benevolent and even cute.

Narratives with 'the good self', however, are outnumbered with warnings about its potentially destructive side. Films such as *Mars Attacks!* (1996), *The Day the Earth Stood Still* (1951), *Independence Day* (1996) and its sequel, and numerous other mass invasion movies warn the viewers of the power and unpredictability of god-like forces – of the dangers of the self. In video gaming the self often emerges in puzzle games in which the player is given little information about the circumstances in which they find themselves, and attempts to decipher the ways of this foreign world. Examples of this include, for instance, *Portal* (Valve) and *The Talos Principle* (Croteam). Some of the manifestations of the self in film and television are less obvious and remain vague, for instance Andrej Tarkovsky's *Stalker* (1979) and *Solaris* (1982).

Movies such as *Blade Runner* (1982) and *Blade Runner 2049* (2017), the *Terminator* and the *Matrix* franchises depict the self as a relentless and unstoppable god of technology which is a threat to humans. VOD television has also been capitalizing on the negative side of the archetype of the self. It pays special attention to the subject of artificial intelligence and the possibility that it will take over the world. To name but a few, Netflix has *Black Mirror* and *AI: Artificial Intelligence*; Amazon has *Humans* (2015–) and HBO has *Westworld* (2016-) Some of them are particularly scathing and negative in their observation of humankind and its relationship with the self/god figure. For instance, Charlie Brooker's *Black Mirror* (2017) contains vignettes about the future of humanity in the world progressively dominated by computers. All of them show human beings as being undermined by technology (*Fifteen Million Merits* (S1), *Crocodile, Metalhead* (S4), which is a remaking of the Terminator idea), while others show people as being lazy to make their own mistakes – i.e., too lazy to individuate, relying on the predictive precision of their god instead (*Hang the DJ* (S4), *Nosedive* (S3), *The Waldo Moment* (S2)).

Female protagonists and characters have been gradually included into self narratives, either as someone who deals with an externalized manifestation of the self (Louise Banks (Amy Adams) in *Arrival*) or as an agentic character finally fully allowed to explore her individuation options and led by an inner voice (Elsa in *Frozen II*, 2019).

Narratives with the hero at the centre, too, are gradually moving away from focusing solely on male characters, with heroines now given detailed individuation paths and allowed to be fighters such as Rey (Daisy Ridley) in the *Star Wars* franchise, Wonder Woman (Gal Gadot) in the eponymous superhero film, and numerous casting and narrative choices made by Netflix in the past decade, etc. However, heroines do not have to be literal fighters, as they are in the more schematic genres like sci-fi, in order to overcome a range of obstacles on their path. They can be mathematicians (*Hidden Figures*, 2016), chess players (*The Queen's Gambit*, Netflix, 2020), or just thoroughly confused, blundering individuals not knowing who they want to be in life, which, again, is absolutely fine (BBC's *Fleabag*, The CW's *Crazy Ex-Girlfriend*, (2015–2019)).

The child, the hero and the self form a continuum representing personal development. The child is at the start of the line, standing for the beginning of human motivation and self-actualization. The hero is the next step while the self is the (unachievable) goal of the individuation process acting as an invisible guide throughout the adventure or adventures in the narrative.

The archetype of the child stands for motivation and creativity, and often emerges as a secondary character or an inspirational memory when the hero protagonist is stuck or has run out of steam. Some directors, for instance, Tim Burton, build their imagery around the child archetype. The majority of Tim Burton's protagonists are either children or stuck in the childhood mode, which keeps alive their creativity and individuality. The child is pure and naïve, untouched by the corrupting influence of society, and is a source of spiritual renewal. The hero is the one who goes on a journey of discovery for their true self. Both are characterized by their ability to be motivated, brave, decisive, and to overcome obstacles. Contemporary mythology likes to present them as schematic, but the searching hero character can also possesses a lot of depth.

Up until 20 years ago, the hero archetype both in fiction and in moving image narratives has been predominantly male while female characters had been stuck in the supporting role of the 'beautiful anima' or 'the doting mother'. The very few female protagonists were mainly given Theme 2 quests, namely the quest for a partner (Monroe in *Gentlemen Prefer Blondes*). More recently, there have been attempts to steer the very few women's protagonist roles from that of the hunter for a perfect partner (the animus) and towards the hero, the old wise person (like Jodie Whittaker's *Dr. Who*), the shadow – or, in fact, anything else but the sexual object or someone searching for a perfect man. Characters such as Rey in the *Star Wars* Franchise, *Wonder Woman* (2017), and numerous TV shows (such as Netflix's *Jessica Jones*) continue to challenge the heteronormative approach of classical Hollywood.

Meanwhile, the child narrative cluster has been exploring female protagonists and secondary characters in alienated, split-off versions in the horror genre for quite a while. Female children have been depicted as terrifying, monstrous, and possessed (*The Exorcist*, 1973; *Carrie*, 1976), or the image of the child has been linked to the theme of pregnancy as a form of possession (*Rosemary's Baby*, 1968; *Alien*, 1979). The recent development of female bildungsroman, discussed in detail in Chapter 4, which follows the maturation of an ambitious, free-spirited, self-sufficient female child, is finally bringing equality to gender representation within Theme 3. The new generation of

Disney princesses (Moana, Merida in *Brave*, Elsa and Anna in *Frozen*) are given the opportunity to find their own voice and exercise their agency outside the constraints of the female persona (which, traditionally, is placed very early on the female child).

Importantly, archetypes perform educational roles, which is why it is important for female viewers to have appropriate role models. Human beings have the capacity to learn from narratives: novels, TV series, films, video games, plays, myths, and fairy tales. Every encounter that happens within a narrative is educational in two ways: on the one hand, it makes one learn about oneself (by empathizing with the protagonist, by using the story as a mirror, by examining one's reactions to the story). On the other, it allows one to learn more about one's environment and community (by testing out various solutions to problems; by testing the boundary between the personal and the social, or between one's own interests and intentions, and the intentions of others). Women need new narratives that stretch the bounds of the female persona. Female characters should use the entire spectrum of archetypes and archetypal situations.

Our goals and identities merge with the narratives as we watch narrative sequences we may encounter later on in life. We project our own issues on to the stories, and equally introject the material contained in them to form our own experiential wisdom. In other words, we learn from someone struggling, making mistakes, going through difficulties, working out successful strategies, and solving issues. We learn from seeing others try and lose; or try and win. Narratives allow us to experience struggles, obstacles and difficulties safely, engaging us while at the same time emphasizing the distance between fantasy and reality. We know that a film does not represent reality; that a game does not represent reality – it is an enhanced version of it, but it is still a game. As such, narratives are a safe way of exploring the world and its dangers; they teach by entertaining. We learn from them incessantly for we are programmed to improve our knowledge of the world by carefully observing it and optimizing our chances of surviving and succeeding.

Exploring Theme 1 and Integrating the Shadow: *Cruella* (2021)

Disney's *Cruella* delves into the previously unfamiliar theme – a female villain with a back story, and a quite detailed one at that. Instead of being shown as a one-dimensional, purely archetypal pantomime villain, Cruella (Emma Stone) has a journey from being a rejected child to a successful designer and owner of her own business empire. As a child, she witnesses her mother fall of a cliff when the Baroness, a narcissist and the owner of a fashion house (Emma Thompson), sets a pack of Dalmatian dogs on her. As an adult, Estella (her name before she turned angry and bitter) is struggling to integrate the 'evil' part of her personality into the everyday one, and is drawn to the Baroness who she sees as talented and special. She does not know that it was the Baroness who killed her mother.

The archetypal range of the character therefore expands from being an antagonist stuck in Theme 2 – a one-dimensional bad mother/death goddess – to a whole range of roles covering all three themes: the protagonist gets a developed shadow which communicates dynamically with her social mask, she has a trickster side reflected in her playful, punk fashion designs, and she is constantly going back to her 'wounded child' roots which are also the roots of her drive and talent. In an interesting twist, the characters also moves from being an invariant of the negative mother to *having* a negative mother, and dealing with the feelings of betrayal and rejection.

Jungians recommend that the shadow's owner at least attempts to integrate it – otherwise it will end up splitting into a sub-personality with its own (often tricksterish) life because of its 'autonomy' and obsessive/possessive quality (Jung, CW 9/II: para. 15). The good news is, with 'insight and good will, the shadow can to some extent be assimilated into the conscious personality' although 'there are certain features which offer the most obstinate resistance to moral control and prove almost impossible to influence' (Jung, CW9/II: para. 16). Insight and good will, however, are not the qualities associated with female antagonists often relegated to the one-dimensional roles of witches, cruel step-mothers, perfect fairy mothers, ugly sisters or lovely and suffering beauties.

By contrast, Cruella is a dynamic character struggling with her inner demons and desperately trying to keep on the social mask which is eventually dissolved by the combination of the dark child and the shadow eating her from within. Her dramatic black/white hairstyle reflects the personality/shadow split and the internal/external conflict that comes with it. Whereas the shadow (with elements of the trickster as she plays her punk tricks on her arch-rival) reflects her struggle with the inner darkness, the child motivates her and gives her endless, often explosive, creativity. The anguish, born out of the abandonment aspect of the child archetype and previously afforded to male 'dark children' such as Tim Burton's Edward Scissorhands, is reflected in Cruella's fashion sense – punky and rebellious, full of clashing dramatic colours, ironically derivative postmodern silhouettes and chaotic excess. This explosion of punky colours and shapes won the film's costume designer, Jenny Bevan, an Oscar nomination.

Apart from the child and the shadow, Cruella's individuation cocktail has a dash of a trickster as her rebellion escapes and infuses otherwise proper and decent social settings – such as the Baroness's formal gatherings and fashion shows – with chaos. For instance, she arrives at the Black and White Ball wearing a white coat which promptly burns down revealing a vintage red dress designed by the Baroness herself. After this grand entrance, which, naturally, attracts everyone's attention, Cruella's friends release rats, causing turmoil and ruining the party. Moreover, naming issues (for instance, having multiple names or no name at all) is one of trickster characters' most prominent features signifying their inability to accept social reality (Bassil-Morozow, 2012; 2015).

After all, one's name is part of the official record, and tricksters defy social norms, despise systems and reject any forms of head count. With her smeared make-up and dishevelled hair, Estella/Cruella is similar to other female trickster-shadows such as Harley Quinn (as depicted by Margot Robbie in *Suicide Squad* (2016), *Birds of Prey (and the Fantabulous Emancipation of One Harley Quinn)* (2020) and *The Suicide Squad* (2021)). Both the characters use fashion and make-up subversively, turning the mask of femininity into an exaggerated grimace. If one is forced to wear a mask, one might as well stretch the trope to its limits, make it grotesque to the point of being repulsive, and becoming abject instead of being a perfect canvas for projections.

By the end of the film, Cruella's major conflicts (with the mother and the shadow) remain unresolved, hinting at further individuation perspectives while asserting her right to keep the conflict alive. After all, conflict is the source of creativity, and Cruella will remain creative as long as the child, the trickster and the shadow are alive within her and not subdued by the mask.

Challenging the Dominance of Theme 2: *Crazy Ex-Girlfriend* (2015–2019) and *One Day at a Time* (2017–2020)

Some narratives – like the sitcoms *Crazy Ex-Girlfriend* (2015–2019) and *One Day at a Time* (2017–2020) – rather refreshingly, have dispensed with the idea that getting married is the woman's final destination altogether, and opted for an open ending in which the protagonist, despite having a choice of eligible partners, opts to stay single. In both the series, it happens more or less for the same reason: the protagonist is still figuring out who she is, or what she wants from life. Genre-wise, both combine humour with discussing serious issues such as mental health, suicide, social issues, and equality and diversity. Both defy the traditional 'animus finale' in which the girl gets together with the man of her dreams.

Throughout the four seasons, *Crazy Ex-Girlfriend*'s Rebecca Bunch (Rachel Bloom) goes full circle from wanting to fulfil the societal requirements for the female persona to realizing that none of them are at all important. The first seasons opens with her abandoning her life in New York, complete with a high-powered lawyer job, and moving to the town of West Covina where her ex-boyfriend, Josh Chan (Vincent Rodriguez III), lives. Rebecca imagines that her fantasy relationship will make her whole and will cure her very extensive range of abandonment and abuse issues: she is the child of a narcissistic mother and a neglectful father who to this day barely remembers her existence.

Throughout the show, she goes through a whole series of boyfriends and casual partners: after being rejected by Josh (who already has a girlfriend), Rebecca starts dating Greg Serrano (Santino Montana) until both realize that they do not exactly improve each other's mental health. Meanwhile, Josh Chan becomes available and Rebecca becomes engaged to him, only to be abandoned at the altar. However, even before the failed wedding she becomes attracted to her co-worker, Nathaniel Plimpton III (Scott Michael Foster), and the two even share a kiss when they get stuck in the lift. At the end of the show, she is being pursued by all three suitors, but discovers that she needs to continue on the journey of self-discovery instead of choosing a partner right now.

The show does not just centre on the 'desperate to get married' aspect of the female persona – one of its most translatable, narrative-friendly elements. Instead, it uses humour and satire to dismantle all facets of it. A sitcom-musical hybrid, it uses songs to isolate and ridicule various aspects of the mask such as the pressure to look attractive ('The Sexy Getting Ready Song'), to be adorably naïve and silly ('I'm just a Girl in Love', 'The Love of Math Triangles'), to have perfect sex without mentioning the possible side effects or consequences ('I Gave you a UTI', 'Period Sex'), and to be the pliable object of someone else's fantasies ('Love Kernels', 'Ping Pong Girl'), etc.

In the songs, the artificiality of the mask is not simply exposed and examined, but turned upside down, subverted, presented as something so grotesque that, as a social construct, it becomes meaningless. For instance, the 'Sexy Getting Ready Song' reveals the 'behind the scenes' part of the perfectly groomed female persona as Rebecca winces with pain when she is plucking her eyebrows and nose hair, or waxing her backside, with blood spluttering over the bath panel. Rebecca and her singers writhe mockingly in shapewear, the bathroom shelf is covered in products and devices that promise instagrammable perfection, and Rebecca ends up with a burn on her neck from the hair curlers. The smooth surface of the female persona is disrupted, torn, mauled, revealing an uncomfortable truth about the kind of artificial, superficial, airbrushed, soft-focus beauty standard set by the media in general and the social media in particular.

Crazy Ex-Girlfriend is really good at exposing the cogs behind the fantasy machine, be it the animus ideal with whom the heroine must settle and produce children, the victim mentality expected of the female partner, the smoothed-out sex scenes in which everyone and everything looks pretty, the perfect friendship, the cliché movie birth scene idealizing the process and making it look quick and easy, etc. Where the female persona turns mental health issues into a mystery or hysteria, Rebecca's diagnosis and treatment become an important moment of self-recognition, a pivotal moment in her journey of self-discovery.

The last season of the show features a song called 'Antidepressants are So Not a Big Deal', aimed to destigmatize mental health issues. Stigma, a form of social punishment for the one who deviated from the role and the mask, emerges automatically when the public spots a break in the 'routines of social intercourse in established settings' (Goffman, 1990: 12). Society constantly looks for uniformity, for conformity to normality, to the existing rules. Human beings lean on anticipations of 'ordinary', 'transforming them into normative expectations, into righteously presented demands' (Goffman, 1990: 12). When these demands are not fulfilled by the member of society, this person is 'reduced in our minds from a whole and usual person to a tainted, discounted one' (Goffman, 1990: 12). In relation to the female persona in particular, the woman rejecting the persona, or the woman not hiding her suffering underneath a social mask is stigmatized as 'mad', her rebellion is classed as deviant behaviour rather than the right to be a personality and she is ostracized – more so than a man displaying the signs of 'tricksterish', mask-rejecting behaviour would. A female rebel, angry and ready to act, is neither funny nor ridiculous – she is dangerous and terrifying, and needs to be brought under control. Unlike the male trickster, she cannot be integrated into the system as the abject cannot be part of the system while the 'different' and the 'creative' still can. Being an individual is intrinsically a creative process; even when creativity is limited by societal expectations. It is even truer for women whose creative selves have been culturally linked with their biology, the implication being that making babies is enough to feel fulfilled and realized.

As Lisa Appignanesi notes in the introduction to Gilbert and Gubar's classic text, *The Madwoman in the Attic*, the rage and the perceived 'madness' associated with the feeling of powerlessness, social control and the threat of stigma and ostracism, particularly for a creative person, are the result of the tension between the creative energy, the right to self-express, and the status quo (what I call the trickster-society conflict). The masks, the approved persona variations available to wear are constrictive and suffocating:

> Resignation to an allotted, conventional space as an obedient wife, mother, angel of the house, even as a good spinster aunt is desired but hard to come by side by side with that other desire for greater freedom – to roam, to learn, to write, to move freely, to challenge the status quo. […] Deep, intractable conflict, a swing between renunciation and rage can all too easily end with a toppling of self-control. Imagination and turmoil played themselves out on the canvas of their work: enter the reeling Gothic heroine immured in a great house in which all the keys to doors or escape belong to a cruel husband or father.
>
> (Gilbert and Gubar, 2020: xii)

The Gothic-abject woman is replaced in the new heroine narrative with someone who renounces the shame, the label of madness, the implication of disgust and abjection. At the end of the narrative, Rebecca realizes that none of the fantasies, whether the ones projected on to her or the ones she used to project on to others, would help her on her journey of self-discovery. She fails at the mask, but succeeds at being herself. She decides to be alone, at least for a while, as she is still working out her various archetypal issues, from the shadow (setting up or stalking female rivals, for instance) to the (wounded) child (parental issues such as trying to escape from the pressure of the narcissistic mother).

Similarly, the protagonist of Gloria Calderon Kellett's *One Day at a Time,* rejecting the perceived 'shame' of being 'incomplete' (without a man) and imperfect (because of her mental health issues). Penelope (Justina Machado) is a single mother of two teenage children. She is an ex-veteran and works as a nurse. The entire family, including Penelope's Cuban mother (Rita Moreno) lives in a small flat, with grandmother Lydia residing in an alcove separated from the kitchen by a curtain. Despite the cramped living conditions, the flat is always full of guests, including the rich and quirky landlord Pat Schneider (Todd Grindell), Penelope's boss Dr. Leslie Berkowitz (Stephen Tobolowsky) as well as numerous friends and relatives.

Penelope exists in a state of flux, battling with anxiety and PTSD and individuating in the context of social, racial, cultural, and gender restrictions. This flux of instability results in multiple liminal positions in which Penelope finds herself: she is sandwiched between two generations and two cultures, represented by her children and her mother; between the workplace and the family; between becoming herself and transforming into someone her society (in its many versions) wants to be.

Multiple cultural and societal assumptions make her defend and maintain her own position all the time. She has to fight for gender pay equality at work when she finds out that her male colleague Scott (Eric Nenninger) has a higher hourly rate just because he appeared more confident at the inter-view and managed to negotiate a better deal. She also has to deal with racism directed at her family, and specifically at her son, Alex (Marcel Ruiz). She has defended the right to take antidepressants and to attend a therapy group when both these activities are considered shameful by Lydia whose own way of dealing with mental and physical ill health is denial. Penelope also feels judged by her friends and relatives for failing to be in a permanent relationship, and this feeling intensifies at the end of Season 3 when she has to attend her ex-husband's wedding. Ultimately, Penelope rejects the various types of shame and stigma coming from both inside and outside her family by choosing to deal with her mental health issues, by not getting married simply for the sake of being with someone, and by absorb-ing the cultural extremes within her family to provide an inter-generational bridge.

In particular, the idea that the heroine does not need a partner to feel whole, or to lead a fulfilling life, is revolutionary in its frustrating effect on the viewer. After all, we are led to believe that the 'happy ending', a closure, is what a female protagonist wants. New generation narratives such as *Crazy Ex-Girlfriend* and *One Day at a Time* offer a new timeline for the heroine's journey which does not have to end in being happily married. Instead, they depict the heroine's dilemmas, problems and issues, and her fight for survival. She does not have to be protected by a man, but has friends and family who help her understand her mission in society and community. This is the individuation without the mask of femininity; the kind of individuation that presupposes being exposed and having to deal with a complex social reality.

Outside the 'Patriarchal Marriage': The Will to Individuate

What drives a woman on a journey of self-development and takes her away from the cage that is the female persona? This drive can be discussed in relation to human agency, its ultimate goals and directions, and its potential misuse and misrepresentation in certain genres (such as action movies, for examples). Additionally, it is important to explore whether agentic behaviour precludes communal activities in female characters, such as helping, caring or looking after someone. Finally, questions of sexuality and attractiveness, and who should control, own and manage them in a narrative, are also crucial.

Dan McAdams writes in *The Stories We Live By: Personal Myths And The Making Of The Self*: 'To know [my wife] well, you would need to know her *identity* – that is, you would need to know what it is about her life that provides her with meaning, unity and purpose' (McAdams, 1997: 6). So, what provides the female character with meaning, unity, and purpose (resulting, presumably, in *agency* which organically stems out of genuine and wholesome *identity*), and how can the future generations of playwrights, screenwriters and novelists create female characters in general, and importantly, female protagonists with detailed journeys reflecting a living, developing, learning personality and not a one-dimensional stereotype (wife, mother, victim, survivor, etc)?

Feminist film theory has been right to pinpoint that elements of agentic expression, namely, the voice, the gaze and control, have traditionally belonged to male characters in moving image narratives. McAdams suggests that there are two types of motivational orientation: agency (proactive, individualistic behaviour) and community-oriented behaviour. As a rule, the two are not isolated but often combined in one person, and constitute 'motivational duality':

> Agency refers to the individual's striving to separate from others, to master the environment, to assert, to protect, and to expand the self. The aim is to become a powerful and autonomous 'agent', a force to be reckoned with. By contrast, communion refers to the individual's striving to lose his or her own individuality by merging with others, participating in something that is larger than the self, and relating to others in warm, close, intimate, and loving ways.
>
> (McAdams, 1997: 71)

Agency is associated with decisiveness and force, and in its turn can be subdivided into two groups: power motivation and achievement motivation which are 'the two faces of human agency' because 'they both share an emphasis on the active assertion of the self over and against the surrounding environment' while 'agentic motives for power and achievement, and communal motives such as the intimacy motive begin to govern desires, goals, and actions' (McAdams, 1997: 72–73).

To give depth to his concept of motivational duality, McAdams recycles the altered archetypes used in the advertising and screenwriting industries: the warrior, the traveller, the sage, and the maker are agentic characters, while the lover, the caregiver, the friend, the ritualist are communal characters. Agency, McAdams maintains, is 'the path of power and achievement' because 'an agentic man or woman may describe himself or herself as especially dominant, assertive, achieving, independent, disciplined, and aggressive. These qualities are traditionally associated with sex-role stereotype of masculinity' (McAdams, 1997: 282).

An agent is an individual characterized by an ability to produce something new, something that has a unique imprint of that person. Agency thus results in 'generative action' which can be one of the three kinds: creating, maintaining, and offering:

> One meaning of generative behaviour is to generate things and people, to be creative, productive, and truthful, to 'give birth', both literally and figuratively. This is the most agentic meaning of generativity, and it ties most closely to the agentic desire for symbolic immortality. [...]
>
> A second kind of generative behaviour is to pass on something from the past and present into the future, to preserve and maintain traditions in order to improve or enhance the future. This is both an agentic and a communal generative behaviour.
>
> The third category of generative action involves the idea of giving gifts, of making offerings to the next generation, of letting go of one's own creations so that they may eventually bear their own fruit.
>
> (McAdams, 1997: 238)

The opposite of the agentic, the communal contains

> numberless characters who act, think, and feel in communal ways. Oriented toward love and intimacy, these are characters who seek to unite with others in passionate embrace, who love and care for others, who nurture, cooperate, encourage, communicate, and share with others. They work to provide settings for love and intimacy, and to cultivate the best in human intercourse. They are described by adjectives such as affectionate, charming, altruistic, enticing, gentle, kind, loyal, sensitive, sociable, sympathetic, and warm, among others.
>
> (McAdams, 1997: 148)

McAdams is careful to include examples of life narratives of both women and men when he gives examples of agentic behaviour. Yet, the section describing communal behaviour, unsurprisingly, almost exclusively mentions women as lovers, caregivers and friends. This is, in fact, a standard societal imagining of the roles of women – the roles that have woven themselves into a myriad of narratives, and structured female characters and protagonists in such a way that they do not need or do not want to engage in agentic and generative (beyond 'generating human beings') behaviour. Women are thus regarded as 'communal' rather than agency-orientated. Motivational duality, as McAdams calls it, has been denied them.

Traditionally, cinema has seen female characters, even protagonists, as more communal than agentic, as focused on their role of family builders, or carers; mothers, daughters, wives, and lovers. Agentic protagonists are the ones attempting to establish what it is they want in life as well as trying to use the self as an extrinsic, not just an intrinsic guide for motivation. This agentic motivation is not dependent on a partner, and is separable from him.

Yet, the dichotomy of the communal vs the agentic is a false one. Expressing one's right to be an agent does not mean being incapable or unwilling to exhibit communal behaviour or to be caring (without displaying the often-objectified 'goddess' qualities). Even though the heroine's first priority may be taking responsibility for her own individuation process, becoming self-aware also means being aware, and taking responsibility, for others. New heroines display a wide range of elements, both agentic and communal, in their quests. For instance, BBC's Fleabag is someone who deeply cares about her family despite the fact that she is disorganized, unpredictable and rude. Unlike Holly Golightly in Blake Edwards' adaptation (1961) of Truman Capote's novel, *Breakfast at Tiffany's*, Fleabag does not look for a man to reform her, or to address her emotional needs. Many female detective characters, such as Robin Griffin (Elizabeth Moss) in *Top of the Lake* (2013–2017), invest a lot of energy into their job because they care about others. The communal and the agentic form a continuum of behaviour instead of being mutually exclusive.

Agentic behaviour is proactive and stands in opposition not only to communal behaviour, but also to victimhood. An increasing number of female characters rejects the passive stance by opting for a more dangerous but also a certainly more rewarding path; a path that, although fraught with difficulties, will nevertheless eventually lead to a greater clarity and understanding of one's identity. It is also the ability to show compassion and strength in the most difficult of circumstances. For instance, the protagonist of *The Girl with the Dragon Tattoo* (2009), Lisbeth Salander, has to fight for her rights on her own, for instance, by punishing her sexually abusive legal guardian by tattooing the words 'I am a sadist pig and a rapist' on his abdomen. She is a hacker who can also fight off street thugs and avenge a friend. Her agency has extreme, angry and violent expressions. This does not mean, however, that she does not care for those around her – in fact, her caring is active, and proactive, and her agency takes the forms of vigilance and protection.

Suranne Jones' characters also tend to be a combination of caring and agentic, culminating in protective behaviour in the name of the search for the truth. In *Doctor Foster* her eponymous character cares deeply about her family and proceeds to destroy her cheating husband (played by Bertie Carvel) over the course of two seasons. Although her focus on pursuit is informed by anger and, at times, self-destruction, the very drive, the unstoppable energy, is admirable and livens up the narrative. Jones is the perfect actress for agentic roles of women balancing the personal and the professional while also unafraid to appear difficult and display traits that could be seen as problematic. Importantly, her characters pursue truth with passion and energy afforded to the traditionally masculine Theme 3 quests; her protagonists combine the quest for the self with the quest for the truth. Jones' characters are obsessive; and obsessions are powerful drives making it impossible to keep the mask on. Jones's characters cannot control their obsessions any more than they are able to adhere to societal standards of 'womanly' behaviour. In this sense, agency and obsession are the drives on the quest for the self, and they pretty much guarantee the impossibility of keeping the female persona intact whatever the initial intention of its wearer.

Amy Silva in the police procedural *Vigil* is a chaotic yet focused detective who cares so much that she puts her life and career on the line in her pursuit of truth. Much like Dr. Foster, Amy has a turbulent family past (her partner drowns after their car crashes and falls into a lake while Amy manages to save their daughter Poppy), is stubborn and an obsessive perfectionist. Throughout the series she is investigating a murder on board a nuclear sub-marine, and ends up discovering a large-scale spy scandal. The dim, claus-trophobic setting becomes the backdrop for detective Silva's quest for the self, reflecting the pain of the crushing survivor guilt that comes back in flashbacks of being trapped in the car underwater.

Paradoxically, she is trapped both in her mind and on the boat but still questing, still moving both in her pursuit of truth and in her search for inner peace. The submarine becomes a sort of claustrophobic Russian doll – it is full of increasingly smaller places in which detective Silva is locked by her new (male) colleagues. In fact, she is often restrained by various men on the boat on the grounds that she is 'hysterical' – mentally unstable, overreacting and unnecessarily meddling with procedures. As if locked in her quarters by Lt. Commander Prentice (Adam James) is not bad enough, she is later trap-ped in a torpedo tube filling with water by the chief villain, Chief Petty Offi-cer Matthew Doward (Lorne MacFadyen).

The physical entrapments mirror and replicate her previous trauma for-cing her to confront herself and making the journey into herself dark, claustrophobic and perilous, further emphasized by the muted, bluish col-ours of the show's mis-en-scène. Importantly, Silva is presented as a hero overcoming difficulties and negotiating the boundary between the internal and the external; a turbulent but relentless individual with a razor-sharp mind and a crystal-clear focus. Not solely a mother or a wife, she is also a professional and an individual with problems – which, paradoxically, is an important trait as a woman is not just a passive, empty slate absorbing everyone's projections – she is a fighter and an agent on a journey who has the right to explore her emotional pain.

Conclusion

Locked out of balanced representation for millennia, women are only now starting to think about what motivates them on their journeys; about what actually constitutes their development – encounters, problems, solutions, future goals. With no mirror to reflect their path – and with the path being limited by socio-economic forces – women have been stuck in the narrow set of representation through the eyes of male creators and critics, serving as muses and secondary characters; as empty vessels; as blank screens upon which fantasies can be imprinted, always ready to accept any projection, however insane or violent. There is still a lot of work to do in finding and defining the female journey, and then reflecting these emerging, new paths in media and criticism.

Divorced from Jung's occasional (sometimes dubious, sometimes insulting) comments on the female autonomy, individuation offers the female protagonist (as well as secondary characters) to survive as an independent, decision-making human being. It offers her *agency*. Narratives containing examples of the passive adaptor of the female persona are not particularly useful for providing role models for the next generation of viewers or challenging internalized stereotypes in older members of the audience.

The Goddess figure is not a valid alternative to the challenge as, far from reclaiming her archetypal power, the female protagonist would be limited by a series of stereotypes. Although the goddess narrative is a glamorous, archetypally inspiring escape into a fantasy, it does not particularly reflect the agentic features of the protagonist. This is not to say that the heroine cannot display any of the Goddess attributes at all – they can be combined with agentic elements, as embodied, for instance, in the character of Daenerys Targaryen/Mother of Dragons (Emilia Clarke) in *Game of Thrones*. What is still needed is a variety of options for the heroine; a variety of available combinations of archetypes and archetypal situations, of the agentic and the communal. Current narratives are emerging out of the rigidity of the female persona that is mostly rooted in the passive anima or the available mother, or indeed their reversals – the terrible mother and *the femme fatale*. Narratives exploring the shadow, the trickster, the self and the child – the very nuances of human nature – alongside revising some of the stereotypes associated with the anima and the mother in relation to female characters would certainly enrich the repertoire available to the female protagonist – and help the viewers (especially the young ones) looking for role models on screen.

References

Bassil-Morozow, Helena (2012) *The Trickster in Contemporary Film*, London: Routledge.
Bassil-Morozow, Helena (2015) *The Trickster and the System: Identity and Agency in Contemporary Society*, London: Routledge.
Bassil-Morozow, Helena (2018) *Jungian Theory for Storytelling*, London: Routledge.

Bolen, Shinoda (2014) *Goddess in Every Woman: Powerful Archetypes in Women's Lives*, New York: HarperCollins.

Campbell, Joseph (1968/2008) *The Hero with a Thousand Faces*, Novato, CA: New World Library.

Frankel, Valerie Estelle (2014) *From Girl to Goddess: the Heroine's Journey Through Myth and Legend*, Jefferson: McFarland.

Gilbert, Sandra M. and Gubar, Susan (2020) *The Madwoman in the Attic: The Woman Writer and the Nineteenth-Century Literary Imagination*, New Haven and London: Yale University Press.

Goffman, Erving (1990), *The Presentation of Self in Everyday Life*, London: Penguin.

Jacobi, Jolande (1942/1973) *The Psychology of C. G. Jung* (8th Edition), Ralph Manheim (trans.), New Haven and London: Yale University Press.

Jung C.G. (n.d.) *The Collected Works*, Herbert Read, Michael Fordham and Gerhardt Adler, (eds.) R.F.C. Hull (trans.), London: Routledge. (Except where a different publication was used, all references are to this hardback edition.)

Lacan, Jacques (1999) *The Seminar of Jacques Lacan: Bk. 20: On Feminine Sexuality, the Limits of Love and Knowledge: On Feminine Sexuality, the Limits of Love and Knowledge*, New York: W.W. Norton and Company.

McAdams, Dan P. (1997) *Stories We Live By: Personal Myths and the Making of the Self*, New York: Guildford Press.

Mulvey, Laura (1975) 'Visual Pleasure and Narrative Cinema', *Screen*, Autumn, 16 (3), pp. 6–18.

Murdock, Maureen (1990/2013) *The Heroine's Journey: a Woman's Quest for Wholeness*, Boston, MA: Shambhala.

Neumann, Erich (1959/1974) *Art and the Creative Unconscious: Four Essays*, Princeton: Princeton University Press.

Perera, Sylvia Brinton (1999) *Descent to the Goddess: a Way of Initiation for Women*, Scarborough: Inner City Books.

Rowland, Susan (2002) *Jung: a Feminist Revision*, Hoboken, NJ: Wiley.

Rowland, Susan (2005) *Jung as A Writer*, London: Routledge.

Soanes, C., Waite, M., and Hawker, S. (2001) *Oxford Dictionary Thesaurus and Worldpower Guide*, Oxford: Oxford University Press.

Vogler, C. (rev ed. 1998). *The Writer's Journey: Mythic Structure for Writers*, London: Pan.

Vogler, C. (2007) *The Writer's Journey: Mythic Structure for Writers*, London: Pan.

Chapter 3

The Red Woman and the Blue Woman

The Boundaries of the Mask

Traditional and contemporary narratives have always contained elements of female rebellion against societal expectations; moments when the persona was rejected, thrown off; when agency was asserted or when role reversals were attempted. In this chapter, these motifs are grouped under the umbrella terms 'Red Woman' and 'Blue Woman', covering respectively two types of rebellion: open (the Red Woman) and covert (the Blue Woman). Whereas the Red Woman is willing to explicitly challenge the expected behavioural norms, the Blue Woman pretends to go along with them while also undermining the social order underpinning female oppression. Their most prominent examples of these narrative threads are the tales 'Little Red Riding Hood', Charles Perrault's 'Bluebeard', and Hans Christian Andersen's 'Red Shoes' as well as works of literature such as Nathaniel Hawthorne's *The Scarlet Letter* (1850) and Leo Tolstoy's *Anna Karenina* (1873–1877).

Both these narrative types can be regarded as a 'warning' to the female protagonist not to have ambitions or to be too curious; yet both also offer ways of testing the dimensions of the mask of femininity, as well as ways of outlining – and possibly exploring – the consequences of transgression of the boundaries of socially prescribed behaviour for women. The motifs have proved to be popular and pervasive, have been interpreted and re-interpreted in a number of ways, and have migrated from their initial fairy tale incarnations into a number of narrative forms and genres, including literature, cinema and television. Ultimately, the protagonist of the Red and Blue rebellion narratives fails because the entire social structure is not ready for her to succeed; the support for her agency is not in place, and the cultural financial and legal institutions are against her. Her agency is curtailed by the inflexible system.

Both the narrative structures are distinctly modern, with their more complex incarnations exploring the limits of female emancipation, the conflict between the persona and agency, the role of religion and wealth in keeping the patriarchal order in charge, and the role of modernity and progress in female emancipation. The latter often manifests itself in the image of the train. Importantly, the heroines of Red and Blue threads attempt to derail the

DOI: 10.4324/9781003253044-4

predictability and inevitability of the standard journey from being a daughter to becoming a wife – a path that is boring and dull.

The Original Tale: Little Red Riding Hood

The Red/Blue Woman narrative will mostly be discussed using as a base the original tale by Charles Perrault (1628–1703) and the 1812 rendition of it by the Jacob (1785–1863) and Wilhem (1786–1859) Grimm. Perrault's version was published 1697, part of the collection *Histoires ou Contes du Temps Passé* (*Tales and Stories of the Past*). Perrault's version was stylized as compared to the oral folk original (Dundes, 1989: 3). In many ways, 'Bluebeard' and 'Little Red Riding Hood' are contrasted with the compliant female protagonists in tales like 'Cinderella' which teaches that qualities such as patience and victimhood offer an advantage in life. Like the rest of the tales in the collection, it also has an obligatory 'moral' at the end – in Perrault's rendition it looks like a short poem reiterating and justifying the ending, and summarising the text's didactic intention.

The tale opens with the village girl, 'the prettiest that had ever been seen', embarking on a mission of delivering some cakes and butter to her grandmother. The path lies through the woods where she encounters 'old Father Wolf'. The wolf does not immediately eat her because of the presence of woodcutters nearby, but instead directs her to the longer road to her grandmother's house, resulting in the naïve and unsuspecting girl amusing herself by chasing butterflies and making nosegays (Dundes, 1989: 54–55). Meanwhile, the wolf arrives at the old woman's house, and gobbles her up. The girl arrives later, takes off her cloak and climbs into bed with the wolf who dismisses her suspicions in the famous conversation, and swallows her up. The moral elucidates this tragic finale:

> From this story one learns that children,
> Especially young lasses,
> Pretty, courteous and well-bred,
> Do very wrong to listen to strangers,
> And it is not an unheard thing
> If the Wolf is thereby provided with his dinner.
> I say Wolf, for all wolves
> Are not of the same sort;
> There is one kind with an amenable disposition
> Neither noisy, nor hateful, nor angry,
> But tame, obliging and gentle,
> Following the young maids
> In the streets, even into their homes.
> Alas! Who does not know that these gentle wolves
> Are of all such creatures the most dangerous!
>   (Dundes, 1989: 6)

Perrault's imagery (and the moral) connote rather explicitly the warning about the wild nature of male sexuality and the dangers that await 'young maids' when 'amenable' wolves follow them 'into their homes'. It has also been discussed from the psychoanalytic point of view as a parable of puberty with a focus on the development of sexuality, both female and male, by Geza Roheim (1953), Bruno Bettleheim (1975), Alan Dundes (1988), and others. While psychoanalytic studies tend to focus on the Oedipal relational motifs in the tale, there is a wealth of social commentary associated with the tale's origins as well as its perpetual popularity.

As Jack Zipes notes, Perrault's tale is written from a male point of view; it is, essentially, a tale about good men and bad men. It takes a dim view not only of male predatory nature, but also of women's right to be an individual. Little Red Riding Hood insists on her right to self-expression – after all, she 'amuses herself by gathering nuts, running after the butterflies, and making nosegays out of the wild flowers which she found' (Dundes, 1989: 5). Zipes also points out the obvious elements of victim-blaming in the tale. Little Red Riding Hood is punished for her individualism and blamed for her victimhood for she spoke to 'the devil' and laid the grounds 'for her own seduction and rape' (Dundes, 1989: 123). There is something distinctly individualistic about her:

> We already know that she is the prettiest creature around, spoiled by her mother and grandmother. Thus, the image of this young girl suggests that she contains potential qualities which could convert her into a witch or heretic. Her *natural* inclinations do in fact lead her into trouble. In the woods, which was a known haunting place of werewolves, witches, outlaws, and other social deviates, Little Red Riding Hood talks naturally to the wolf because she is unaware of any danger. She trusts her instincts. If it were not for the *male* woodcutters (for only male can serve as protectors), the wolf would have indulged his appetite on the spot, in his natural abode. Instead, he is forced to make a 'pact' with her.
>
> (Dundes, 1989: 122–123)

Importantly, Zipes links the girl's individualistic attitude to social class. Little Red Riding Hood's attire points at her middle class roots, the middle classes being linked to social mobility paving way for the industrial revolution and a fully-fledged capitalist society. Thus, the tale of Little Red Riding Hood, with the individualistic choices made by the protagonist, already contains the seeds of female emancipation – and points to the shift from the communal to the individual:

> Since clothing was codified and strictly enforced under Louis XIV, it was customary for middle-class women to wear cloth caps, whereas aristocratic ladies wore velvet. Bright colours were preferred, especially red, and the skull cap was generally ornamental. For a village girl, in Perrault's story, to

wear a red *chaperon* signified that she was individualistic and perhaps nonconformist. Perrault probably intended that she bear the sign of the middle class, and by giving her a name he made something special out of her.

(Dundes, 1989: 122)

In this sense, Perrault's adapted version can be regarded as a commentary on class relations as well as attempting to keep the existing gender dynamics – quite a complex dual task. Interesting, some of the subsequent renditions of the Red Woman narrative kept developing the social relations dynamic of the original tale, adding it to the already complicated issue of gender emancipation. The social class perspective is consistently developed in later iterations of the Red Woman narrative. For instance, *Anna Karenina* (and its cinematic renditions) has a running commentary on the speed of the industrial revolution, the rapid development of the middle class, and the gradual disappearance of the old feudal relations (presented by Tolstoy, himself an aristocrat, as a sad state of affairs, as a disintegration of a potent and constructive social order and its replacement with a fast-paced age of the individual). Similarly, in Neil Jordan's *The Company of Wolves* (1984), written by Angela Carter and based on her tales, there are several tales of aristocrats turning out to be werewolves.

Grimm's version of the tale, 'Little Red Cap' ('Rotkäppchen'), is slightly different although the message remains largely the same: individualism is an unsuitable trait for young women as it leads to questionable behaviour of the kind that forces men to become violent; that turns them into beasts. In Grimm's version, the male saviours appear at the end of the tale, in time to save the girl and her grandmother. The wolf still directs the girl off path, and draws her attention to the beauty of nature, to sunrays and flowers. At the end of the tale the girl fills the wolf's body with stones to prevent the wolf from running away. She learns her lesson as she thinks to herself: 'Never again will you stray from the path by yourself and go into the forest when your mother has forbidden it' (Dundes, 1989: 11). In a way, this warning runs through all Red Woman narratives although it is not always spelled out so succinctly.

Zipes considers Grimm's version to be more hostile to female agency than the French one thanks to the metaphorical block to her individuation: the stones with which she fills the wolf actually represent the weight that from now on will be keeping her ambition down. In the course of this self-punishment she 'internalises the restraining norms of sexuality in a political manner' (Dundes, 1989: 125–126). As such, the tale turns Little Red Cap into a 'disobedient, helpless little girl' who deserves to be punished in a variety of ways for straying off the prescribed path (Dundes, 1989: 125).

Interestingly, Grimm's version has a short addition confirming that the girl has, indeed, learned her lesson: one day Little Red Cap returns to her grandmother and encounters another wolf; only this time she does not diverge from the path but runs directly to the grandmother's house, they lock themselves in, and outsmart the wolf who is trying to get into the house from the roof. This segment ends with the wolf falling into a stone trough full of water, and drowning (Dundes, 1989: 11–12). This version is quite interesting because, whereas it does imply that the girl has learned the lesson, it also shows her ability to defend herself and her grandmother. This is certainly a more agentic variant of the basic Red Woman narrative. Yet, changing an outlook on female agency and female individuation is a slow process. As Zipes astutely notes, it took two hundred years for Perrault's tale to emerge out of the witch-hunting tradition, and another two hundred years to 'establish a proper bourgeois image of the obedient Red Riding Hood learning her lessons of discipline' (Dundes, 1989: 127). It may therefore take another two hundred years to unlearn these lessons and to unravel the prohibitive-punitive strand of the Red Woman narrative.

Angela Carter's Reversal of the Outcome of the Red and Blue Rebellion

Both Red and Blue versions of the rebellion against the female persona end up in a failure of agency – the woman is threatened and has to be rescued, or she has to die because she has publicly broken the social norms. In her collection of stories, *The Bloody Chamber* (1979) Angela Carter reverses the outcome of the narratives by asserting the decisiveness of the protagonist. Carter's eclectic post-modernist rethinking of traditional tales and authored texts offers potential ways of exiting the mask and explores repercussions for doing so.

The titular story, 'The Bloody Chamber', is based on the Bluebeard narrative; yet, it also contains references to Tolstoy's novel *Anna Karenina* – a Red Woman story ending with the female co-protagonist's death. For instance, after the wedding, Carter's protagonist is travelling to her home by train, with the train suddenly stopping at night at an unknown station:

> The train slowed, shuddered to a halt. Lights; clank of metal; a voice declaring the name of an unknown, never-to-be visited station; silence of the night; the rhythm of his breathing, that I should sleep with, now, for the rest of my life. And I could not sleep. I stealthily sat up, raised the blind a little and huddled against the cold window that misted over with the warmth of my breathing, gazing out at the dark platform towards those rectangles of domestic lamplight that promised warmth, company, a supper of sausages hissing in a pan on the stove for the station master, his children tucked up in bed asleep in the brick house with the painted shutters ... all the paraphernalia of the everyday world from which I, with my stunning marriage, had exiled myself.
>
> (Carter, 1995: 6)

The train, with its clunking sounds and tonnes of metal is merging metaphorically with the heavy breathing of her husband whose bestial, unstoppable masculinity frightens the young wife. The station, with its echoing, disembodied voices of strangers, is a contrast to the banal familiarity of the heroine's life. The heavy machine is also contrasted with the beauty and fragility of the female persona, which the heroine is wearing in her role as the bride. Much like Anna Karenina (whose experience of train journeys will be discussed later on in the chapter), the Blue wife is peeking into the night from the warmth of her carriage and wondering whether the decision to marry Bluebeard is so catastrophic that she has reached a point of no return. Far from being full of hopeful anticipation of new adventures, the (individuation) journey becomes an exile:

> Into marriage, into exile; I sensed it, I knew it – that, henceforth, I would always be lonely. Yet that was part of the already familiar weight of the fire opal that glimmered like a gypsy's magic ball, so that I could not take my eyes off it when I played the piano. This ring, the bloody bande of rubies, the wardrobe of clothes from Poiret and Worth, his scent of Russian leather–all had conspired to seduce me so utterly that I could not say I felt one single twinge of regret for the world of tartines and maman that now receded from me as if drawn away on a string, like a child's toy, as the train began to throb again as if in delighted anticipation of the distance it would take me.
>
> (Carter, 1995: 6)

The wife is surrounded by giant machines taking her on a journey planned and managed by others. Destined to be led and to be out of control of her body and mind, she compares Bluebeard's castle to an ocean liner where the newcomer's authority is, at best, 'tenuous' (Carter, 1995: 9). Clashing stylistically with the train and the liner, these flagship representatives of modernity and social mobility, is the bed which is 'grand, hereditary, matrimonial', 'with gargoyles carved on its surfaces, vermillion lacquer and gold leaf' (Carter, 1995: 9). Unlike the machines which had taken the protagonist from the parental house to her new home, the bed is Gothic and pompous, ancient and static, signifying the end of the protagonist's journey.

   Yet, the wife does derail her journey, destined to end in her death like the other hapless Bluebeard's wives. On the way to the Bloody Chamber, she feels the rigidity of the female persona disappear, and the agentic, the seat of curiosity, melt away the fear and caution. The wife's act of self-emancipation is contextualized within the outdated medieval interior of the castle and its dark secrets: poorly lit, winding corridors, swords, mysterious hidden rooms, heavy tapestries, thick carpets and torture devices. The protagonist is finally realizing that the ocean liner, which is 'adrift in the middle of the silent ocean', is now under her command. Under her orders, it floats 'like a garland of light'. She is finally, yet dangerously, in charge of her own destiny.

   Yet, she also needs to explain to her husband when he comes back why the key she was supposed to keep safe is now blood-stained. Upon learning about his wife's betrayal, Bluebeard announced that she is to be decapitated with a sword which is described as 'sharp as childbirth', another negative link between establishing a family and sacrifice – forgetting one's personality and devoting oneself to others, abandoning one's journey as a unique, motivated, ambitious individual (Carter, 1995: 38). The wife is being prepared for decapitation – the ultimate form of objectification, of dominance, of possession. Symbolically, she is saved by her mother who, presumably, through the act of becoming a mother did not cease to be a fighter: she disposed of a 'man-eating tiger' when she was eighteen, and now she also shot Bluebeard who is so astonished that he has no time to react:

> The puppet master, open-mouthed, wide-eyed, impotent at the last, saw his dolls break free of their strings, abandoned the rituals he had ordained for them since time began and start to live for themselves; the king, aghast, witnesses the revolt of his pawns.
>
> You never saw such a wild thing as my mother, her hat seized by the winds and blown out to sea so that her hair was her white mane, her black lisle legs exposed to the thighs, her skirts tucked round her waist, one hand on the reins of the rearing horse while the other clasped by father's service revolver and, behind her, the breakers of the savage indifferent sea, like the witnesses of a furious justice. And my husband stood stock-still, as if she had been Medusa, the sword still raised over his head as in those clockwork tableaux of Bluebeard that you see in glass cases at fairs.
>
> (Carter, 1995: 40)

If peeking through the mask is the act of looking, still subterranean, still sabotage, the act of throwing off the mask is a full-on rebellion. It is the mother – not brothers, princes, or strangers – who saves the daughter from the female persona, from the possibility of ending her journey prematurely. Yet, there is something left of the mask still on the protagonist's face – a red mark which cannot be covered, a reminder that her real face was once hidden underneath a persona.

Another story in the collection, 'The Werewolf' offers yet another exploration of female unmasking, this time using 'Little Red Riding Hood' as a canvas. The story is taking place in a deeply superstitious 'northern country', the inhabitants of which tend to see the Devil in everything and stone witches to death (Carter, 1995: 126). A girl is sent to visit her sick grandmother, and is met in the woods by a wolf with red eyes who goes for her throat. She takes out her big knife, cuts off one of his paws, wraps it up in the cloth in which she is carrying the oatcakes, and resumes her journey. Upon reaching the grandmother's house, the girl unwraps the paw which by now has become her grandmother's hand. Knowing now that the old woman is a witch, the girl crosses herself, runs out of the house and summons the superstitious neighbours. They pelt the witch until she dies. The girl stays in the house and prospers.

The female persona is heavily guarded by social norms, any deviation from which is punishable. The persona and its absence are two binary states, branded either good or bad, and treated accordingly. The individuation journey, with its subtleties and complexities, does not fit into this binary. Once again, Carter plays with the pre-industrial Gothic 'darkness of the mind' into which the light of modernity has not reached. The witch, the absence of the mask, is a threat, and is inoculated by the religious child, who, like a good girl, sends in the mob to destroy the deviant. Here Carter is simultaneously subverting the traditional version of the tale and echoing another Red Woman narrative, Hans Christian Andersen's 'The Red Shoes', in which a religious girl ends up losing her feet for overstepping the moral line.

Other stories in the collection explore the wild nature of a maskless woman. The protagonists of 'The Company of Wolves' and 'Wolf Alice' choose to transform into wolves over wearing a female persona. The young girl in 'The Company of Wolves' is on the verge of adulthood, 'an unbroken egg', a 'sealed vessel', and she is fearless because she has her knife (Carter, 1995: 133). At the end of the tale, the girl finds her soulmate, another werewolf (who has just killed her grandmother) and stays with him in the grandmother's house. By rejecting the mask, she regains her own nature.

She is what Estes prefers to call 'the Wild Woman'; a new role model (or 'archetype') who stands against all behaviours that are traditionally seen as feminine and dainty: compliance, dependence on men, fear of venturing out on your own and exclusive focus on sheltered and 'protected' existence. Estes asserts that the Wild Woman is 'robust, chock-full, strong life force, life-giving, territorially aware, inventive, loyal, loving'; she is 'an ally ... leader, model, teacher' who helps women see 'not through two eyes, but through the eyes of intuition, which is many-eyed' (Estes, 1992: 12). What, essentially, Estes is trying to do is shift metaphorical representations traditionally associated with women from frail and beautiful creatures such as butterflies, dragonflies, birds and cats to an animal not traditionally associated with the female persona: the wolf. In fact, even in negative, cunning (absence/negation of persona) allegorical representations women have been associated with snakes (Medusa), birds (harpies), and fish (sirens, mermaids), but never wolves. The wolf, with its associations of aggression and strength, hierarchy and camaraderie, fearlessness and confidence, matches the patriarchal description of male behaviour in a hierarchy. Attaching the wolf metaphor to a woman means rethinking socially-defined femininity and dissolving the female persona.

Estes argues that wolves and women have a lot in common: they are relational, resilient, fierce, strong, brave and adaptable. In other words, they combine the agentic and the communal. They are keen to protect their pack. Yet, both are 'hounded' and 'harassed'; essentially, misunderstood as 'devouring', 'devious' and 'overly aggressive' (Estes, 1992: 2). She contrasts the confidence of the wolf-woman with the female persona in its angel-whore variations: 'tightly girdled, tightly reigned, and tightly muzzled', staggering in high heels or dressing for the church (Estes, 1992: 3). This muzzled woman, the *creatura*, the mask, sometimes falls and reveals a tail and pricked ears because 'a woman's issues of soul cannot be treated by carving her into a more acceptable form as defined by an unconscious culture, nor can she be bent into a more intellectually acceptable shape by those who claim to be the sole bearers of consciousness' (Estes, 1992: 4).

One of the most attractive attributes of the female persona is fragility – belonging to someone else, tolerating (or even enjoying) objectification, being dependent on others, expecting to be saved. The protagonist of 'Wolf-Alice' is raised by a pack of wolves who pass on to her the qualities necessary for survival on her own. Alice is lean and muscular, her nose is sharp, and her hands and knees are callused (Carter, 1995: 140). She is found by nuns, and passed on to an old Duke whose love of mirrors and reflections echoes Duke the Bluebeard's narcissistic rage. Carter reverses time, clones Bluebeard and makes him old and frail haunting his own Gothic castle full of cobwebs, old ball gowns, and even a bloody chamber. Stuck in the ageing monster's castle, neither a wolf nor a human being, Alice explores her liminal nature by looking at her own reflection in the mirror. She is also dealing with the onset of puberty, and trying on the dresses which once belonged to the women who have been long dead now – playing with the remnants of the dusty, dead mask – of someone else's female persona (Carter, 1995: 146). Alice discovers her own shadow, and remembers how natural it was for wolves to play with them (Carter, 1995: 146).

Refreshingly, the protagonist does not progress into becoming fully human, into accepting the female persona, or into taking the persona seriously, because joining a society of humans would inevitably mean compliance. She remains in the liminal zone, living among the shadows. The last scene shows her licking blood and dirt from the wounded Duke's face, like a wolf would, comfortable in her animal skin. Yet, she is also friends with mirrors and shadows, accepting the dark, dangerous, pre-human side of herself, shunning society, rejecting the shame together with the artificiality of the mask. Eventually, her face comes through in the mirror 'as vivid as real life itself' while Alice is licking the Duke back to health (Carter, 1995: 148). Alice's animal traits are reflected in the mirror, a combination of animal-instinctual and the (human) moment of consciousness, of self-recognition.

The act of looking in the mirror is the act of self-discovery, of self-realization, of the acceptance of one's own image. Referring to Angela Carter, David Punter notes that the so-called 'female Gothic' is an unnecessary linguistic doubling because there is an intrinsic link between 'femininity and the Gothic imagination' because the Gothic imagination is peopled by women – as forbidden objects of desire (or as wearers of the female persona, to use the Jungian definition) (Punter, 1998: 120). Being 'locked in front of the mirror' comes with a sense of inescapability where 'vision only comes in the form of the most unthinkable (sexual) transformation of all' (Punter, 1998: 120). Alice acquires power by familiarizing herself with the various aspects of her animal nature, and learns to accept these aspects. Her animal side is not shamed and repressed, but normalized. Alice integrates her shadow and chooses to live with it instead of joining the village community outside the castle walls.

As Estes points out, being the wild woman means 'familiarizing oneself with the arcane, the odd, the "otherness" of the wild [...] Learning to face great power – in others, and subsequently one's own power. Letting the frail and too-sweet child die back even further' (Estes, 1992: 87). Carter's Red and Blue Women reject societal expectations and move into the liminal zone (the zone of the trickster, the zone of the grotesque). They still struggle with fear and shame, but their (self)-image eventually emerges in the mirror as they learn to live without the female persona.

The Red Woman

Carter's rethinking of the Red/Blue Woman narrative is radical. It acknowledges the complexity of the individuation process and weaves this liminal complexity into the rebellion of the female protagonist against the mask prescribed to her. Her solutions still pit the heroine against the social and do not offer eventual integration, but then again, this may be due to the fact that societies she is depicting in her tales are uncompromising – there is no way the protagonist can build a balance between her interests and society's demands.

Many of the cinematic narratives that centre on the Red Woman motif are dealing with the same issue: the protagonist cannot express her shadow, or build any kind of complexity into her relationship with society simply because society is not ready for the unmasked female, let alone for her adventures and moral dilemmas. The Red Woman is also characterized by curiosity, by the desire to look, by the desire to be visible as the author of her actions. Her narrative thread is branded as 'red' because of this self-inflicted visibility.

Michel Pastoreau, who has written extensively on colours as a symbolic system, points out the duplicity of the colour red – it is simultaneously seen as fascinating and dangerous 'as the flames of Satan' (Pastoreau and Simmonet, 2005: 29). In the Old Testament this colour is sometimes associated with sin and all things prohibited, but other times with power and love (Pastoreau and Simmonet, 2005: 33–34). Moreover, the Reformation has brought yet another negative connotation to the colour red: it was the colour of the Papists, and therefore seen as intemperate and insolent (Pastoreau and Simmonet, 2005: 37). For the Protestants, the colour red is the most immoral of all bright colours. This attitude led to a new colour palette: from the sixteenth century onwards, men did not wear red (with the exception of cardinals and certain chivalric orders) (Pastoreau and Simmonet, 2005: 37). Meanwhile, in the Middle Ages the colour blue had been associated with the feminine and red with the masculine (as a sign of power and war). The Reformation turned the colour symbolism around: blue became associated with masculinity and red with femininity (Pastoreau and Simmonet, 2005: 37). The Western culture has since retained these associations which had permeated many cultural domains, including children's toys and gendered clothing.

The 'Red Woman' motif which places the dual connotation of fragility and danger onto the colour red may as well have been the result of the protestant change in attitude towards colour symbolism. The motif, in all its variations, codes the economic position of women into the binary, gendered, Christian value system reflected primarily in colours: the abusive husband's beard is blue whereas the disobedient wife discovers a room full of blood; a little girl loves her new shiny red shoes but this glamorous dress code is disfavoured in the pious Christian town full of people dressed in black; Anna Karenina who carries a red bag is brave enough to leave her boring husband but is eventually crushed by the hypocritical society.

The contradictory nature of the colour red also reflects the conflict the rebellious protagonist experiences on her individuation path as she struggles to be herself while keeping her persona on and trying to behave according to societal expectations. Individuation, according to Jung, is becoming oneself, and it is a 'natural transformation' process (Jung, CW 9/I: para. 255). This is 'rebirth into another being' who is 'the other person in ourselves – that larger and greater personality maturing within us, whom we have already met as the inner friend of the soul' (Jung, CW 9/I: para. 235). The Red Woman sees the mask of femininity as a burden, as something that restrains her when she feels the urge to free 'the other person' in herself. She looks where she is prohibited from looking, she acts when she is required to stand still, and she speaks when she is asked to remain silent. Importantly, she goes against the bourgeois propriety, religious values and everything else that has strict and detailed definitions for the female persona.

The colour red is also associated with the functions of the female body, and with 'pollution' associated with menstrual blood. This association – a taboo in many cultures – leads to the feminine become 'synonymous with a radical evil that is to be suppressed' (Kristeva, 1982: 70). With the Red Woman rejecting to be coded into the binary as either 'the female persona' or 'the abject', she is left on the limen, on the edge of society; she loses her home – metaphorical, social, psychological, and sometimes literal like the protagonists of *Anna Karenina* (in its various incarnations), Victoria Page in *Red Shoes* (1948) or Holly Hunter, the heroine of Jane Campion's *The Piano* (1993).

When a heroine successfully rejects both the persona and the abject labels, and proudly makes the liminal, the grotesque and the carnivalesque her home, paving her own path regardless of what society may think of the 'terrifying' or 'shameful' lack of a female-specific social mask, she becomes the trickster (discussed in the last chapter). BBC's eponymous character Fleabag, Princess Teabeanie in *Disenchantment*, and Rebecca Bunch in *Crazy Ex-Girlfriend* are all convention-breakers foregrounding all the character traits that society sees unacceptable in a woman: they are rude, messy, difficult to embarrass, and independent. Even though they are still dealing with internalized shame, their society does not reject them to the point when they have no place in it. By contrast, the Red Woman still tries to conform to societal standards, still complies with some of the aspects of the female persona; her battle is as internal as it is external. She attempts to disrupt her context, but her society is not ready for her – yet.

Anna Karenina

Leo Tolstoy's *Anna Karenina* (1873–1877) is probably the most famous example of the narrative about a woman who attempts to break free from the impossible pressures of modern personhood in a society with rigid gender norms against the backdrop of political and economic change.

The novel is set in Russia in the last quarter of the nineteenth century, and depicts the country moving from the feudal to the capitalist system. Things are changing, social classes are on the move, and peasants are setting up their own businesses and becoming richer than their masters. The Russian landscape is also changing to suit the needs of the new economic order – railways are built to connect cities and towns across the country to improve transportation and commerce. Yet, in this social and economic turmoil, gender expectations remain inflexible, which Tolstoy – a count whose views on social class and gender roles were rather conservative – is keen to promote by contrasting Anna's attempt to carve out her own path with Kitty's desire for a husband, a family and a house in the idyllic countryside.

The first railway line opened in Russia in 1937, more than a decade later than in Britain. Railways and trains everywhere captured the public imagination as images of power and speed. In his book *Railways and Culture in Britain* (2001), Ian Carter notes that, 20 years after the first railroad was built in Britain, people were disturbed by the economic, ecological, and social implications of the new technology. Cartoonists such as John Leech and George Cruikshank depicted the locomotive as a monstrous creation, with one cartoon calling it 'a dangerous character' and another 'a railway dragon' (Carter, 2001: 64–65). Early railway accidents, too, played their role in the perception of speed as dangerous, and of progress as unrelenting yet traumatic as the motif of death by railway was firmly establishing itself in fiction (Carter, 2001: 76–77).

Carter points out that the train as an iconic machine of modernity (rather like air travel today), despite its associations with order and efficiency, was also associated with fear of a disaster – the fear that modernity could fail at any moment:

> A broken rail or axle, a boiler explosion, a failure in rudimentary signalling systems, a large-scale calamity could – and did – follow. Hence travellers' characteristic response to early railway journeys; excitement at

moving, for the first time in human history, faster than a galloping horse, but mixed with fear for the dreadful consequences which an accident might bring.

(Carter, 2001: 55–56)

Throughout the novel, Tolstoy carefully and skillfully builds up to the motif of death by railway. For instance, at the start of the novel Stiva Oblonsky's kids re-enact a train crash with a box which gets upturned. The daughter, Tanya, shouts in English to her brother: 'I told you not to put passengers on the roof!' (Tolstoy, 1998: 8). The image of the railroad is linked in the novel to symbols associated with the Red Woman, for instance, the red bag.

Anna's red bag features regularly in Tolstoy's descriptions of her states of mind – it becomes a metaphor for a guilty secret, a desire to break with societal norms – in Anna's case, renouncing her socially acceptable family life, leaving her husband and son, and moving in with her lover. The colour of the bag emphasizes the scandalous, rebellious nature of Anna's lifestyle choices: she often flushes in pleasure or embarrassment, like she does when she is trying to process her first encounter with Vronsky while hiding her feelings from her sister-in law, Dolly: she bends 'her flushed face over her tiny bag' and 'blushing to her ears and to the curly black locks on her cheek' (Tolstoy, 1998: 97).

Alongside the bag, the railway is also an umbrella metaphor, representing the unrelenting change brought about by modernity and threatening to destroy the traditional values (including gender roles). After the infamous Moscow ball where she danced with Vronsky, Anna boards the train to St. Petersburg to be reunited with her family, preparing 'with pleasure and great deliberation for her journey' (Tolstoy, 1998: 99). She settles, and unlocks her red bag 'with her deft little hands', takes out a small pillow which she places on her knees and locks the bag again (Tolstoy, 1998: 99). The cosiness of the compartment is contrasted with the snowstorm raging outside the window, the noises of the snow beating against the window, and the moving train. The same bag also harbours an English novel which she tries to read, but, ultimately, does not enjoy it because it requires following 'the reflection of other people's lives' (Tolstoy, 1998: 99). The novel annoys her because she is 'too eager to live herself' (Tolstoy, 1998: 99).

As Gary R. Jahn points out, the railroad, and all it stands for in the eyes of the nobility on the verge of being socially displaced, is present in the novel 'so that it can be attacked' as it represents 'forces harmful to the traditional style of life of the class of which [Levin] "proud to count himself a member"' (Jahn, 1981: 2). Ultimately, Tolstoy punishes his female semi-protagonist (the second being Tolstoy's moral mouthpiece, Levin) for the 'redness' of her existence, for this very eagerness to 'live herself', or, to use Jung's term, to individuate. Struggling to be accepted by society in her new independent state, consumed by anger and jealousy, her mental health eventually deteriorates, and she commits suicide by throwing herself under the wheels of the passing train. The red bag plays a big role in the scene of Anna's death:

> She wanted to fall half-way between the wheels of the front truck, which was drawing level with her, but the little red handbag which she began to take off her arm, delayed her and then it was too late, the middle had passed her. She was obliged to wait for the next truck. A feeling seized her like that she had experienced when preparing to enter the water in bathing, and she crossed herself. The familiar gesture of making the sign of the cross called up a whole series of girlish and childish memories, and suddenly the darkness, that obscured everything for her, broke, and life showed itself to her for an instant with all its bright past joys. But she did not take her eyes off the wheels of the approaching second truck, and at the very moment when the midway point between the wheels drew level, she threw away her red bag, and drawing her head down threw herself forward on her hands under the truck ... [...]
>
> (Tolstoy, 1998: 760)

The bag that she throws away is an umbrella metaphor representing her guilt and the torturous feeling of being trapped, but also the impossibility of an unrestrained freedom for a female in a still fairly traditional society. By this narrative move, Tolstoy simultaneously indicts modernity (with its trains, industrialization, and consumer capitalism) and the woman who dares to step outside the norms of her gender. Modernity and gender become entwined in the image of the train.

Screen adaptations of the novel tend to omit the symbolism of the bag, and instead focus on the symbolism of the train – its weight, its power, its unrelenting force. Adaptations focus on the train as a metonymy and a metaphor, the train being an iron beast represented by its deadly parts – the wheels, the pilot, the chimney, the railcars as well as by the screeching sounds of metal parts moving and pushing against each other, and by the thick smoke coming out of its chimney.

The character of Anna Karenina has been played by some of the most beautiful actresses in the history of cinema: Greta Garbo (1935), Vivien Leigh (1948), Sophie Marceau (1997), and Keira Knightley (2012) to name but a few. Anna is invariably presented as sensual and graceful in her furs, net veils, intricate hats and shoulder-baring dresses, the necklaces emphasizing her delicate neck. Such an exquisite creation – the epitome of the female persona – should be handled with care. Next to this monstrous invention of the Industrial Revolution, the locomotive, the woman looks small and frail; she is too beautiful to be left alone in liminal places like train stations full of crowds, and exposed to the noises and the elements like snow, rain and smoke. A fragile and beautiful creature, she is not supposed to be on move, or torn from her family and children. Jahn notes that 'beyond the interior security of the carriage lies an exterior which is fraught with discomfort and danger' (Jahn, 1981: 6). Yet, Anna willingly faces the harshness of the rain and snow: 'Anna's egress from the train suggests a desire to liberate her suppressed sense of the fullness of life, thus explaining the attractiveness of the seemingly unpleasant exterior conditions' (Jahn, 1981: 8).

Yet, however willing, Anna is unable to handle the elements. Prior to her suicide, Vivien Leigh's Anna is standing on the platform in the pouring rain, looking lost and helpless. As she is standing on the rails looking at the locomotive in front of her, the rain gives way to snow storm, and she closes her eyes as if surrendering herself to the elements. She opens them again to face the approaching machine, her feminine fragility – the pale complexion, the beautiful features, the slim figure – about to be crushed by the demon with the glaring eyes. Meanwhile, Sophie Marceau's Anna is enveloped by a cloud of steam as she dives under the wheels, followed by a synechdoche: a black-and-white shot of a trembling, bloodied eye closing for the last time. The next shot shows her smiling, her image fading in snow and steam. The rather disturbing conclusion from the narrative is that the elements, representing the tough life under new conditions, however exciting the opportunities may seem, can break the woman, physically and spiritually.

Tolstoy, and the adaptations (especially the ones that are faithful to the original like Bernard Rose's 1997 version starring Sophie Marceau and Sean Bean), pitch the alienation of modernity against the female persona, against gender expectations. The glimmering lights of the station, the darkness, the snow storm, the rain, the sense of alienation, of not belonging, that comes with living in industrialized spaces whose layout follows the logic of the capitalist order, are oppressive and are bound to destroy the beautiful Anna, both emotionally and physically, whose journey towards an independent existence ends abruptly and publicly. Tolstoy's criticism of industrialization is also a commentary that women do not have a place in the brutality of the capitalist order. The female persona is too delicate to survive in the city's busy liminal spaces.

The Red Shoes (1948)

Railway death is death by modernity; it is death by its most iconic inventions – the steam engine. Seemingly, modernity has brought freedom to the individual, but the Red Woman is shown struggling to individuate, to live, to become herself against the backdrop of social conventions, still being dependent on men socially, legally, and financially.

In Powell and Pressburger's iconic film, Moira Shearer's character Victoria Page is a ballerina dreaming of a breakthrough. She is hard-working and is prepared to sacrifice much for the sake of art (and success). At one point she manages to join the famous Ballet Lermontov managed by a unpredictable and controlling character, Boris Lermontov (Anton Walbrook). She also has an opportunity to star in the new production, *The Ballet of the Red Shoes*, the success of which leads to more dancing opportunities for Vicky.

The problems begin when Lermontov discovers that she is dating the composer of *Red Shoes*, Julian Craster (Marius Goring). Julian leaves the company, with Vicky deciding to follow him. Yet, Lermontov does not give up and manages to persuade her to return to perform the revival of *The Red Shoes* ballet. Julian follows her in order to bring her back. Torn between the impresario and the lover, between dancing and private life, between career and love, Vicky commits suicide by leaping from a balcony onto the railway tracks.

In many ways, *Red Shoes* is a typical representative of the 'Red Woman' narrative which indicates that excessive ambition in a woman would lead to an imbalance in her life, and may eventually become dangerous. Its background narrative, Hans Christian Andersen's fairy tale 'Red Shoes' (1945) is a warning of the dangers of female ambition, of wanting too much and forgetting the 'duty'. It is a female version of the Icarus story. Karen, the protagonist of the original tale, is poor but has dreams beyond her social station: she wants the same shoes as the little princess who wears 'fine white clothes' and 'red morocco shoes' (....). Her ambition, metaphorically represented as the shiny, red shoes, is contrasted with the religious, devout, repressed, stifling town and its inhabitants: 'Everybody looked at her feet; and when she stepped through the chancel door on the church pavement, it seemed to her as if the old figures on the tombs, those portraits of preachers and preachers' wives, with stiff ruffs, and long black dresses, fixed their eyes on her red shoes' (Andersen, 2012). Her ambition, however, turns sour as her favourite shoes start moving and make her dance against her will. Karen is exhausted, and her feet have to be cut off. This is not the end of the story, however: the red shoes keep returning and dancing in front of her until she breaks down and repents. Eventually, the humbled Karen starts reading the prayer-book 'with a pious mind', which leads to an encounter with 'an angel in white garments', and her soul flows 'on the sunshine to God' (Andersen, 2012). Karen dies of humility, having eventually experienced 'peace' and 'joy'.

The story of humility – the quintessential story of cultivating the passive, inoffensive female persona – is woven throughout the film as well. Vicky flies too high, and her desire for success has a toll on her spirit. Yet, it is also clear that Vicky's breakdown is not her ambition, or an obsession with art, but rather the fact that her success, despite her obvious talent and achievements, is not her own. It depends on the two men: the company's director and the composer. They shape her repertoire and make lifestyle choices for her.

Indeed, Craster's and Vicky's creative outputs are not exactly equal. Whereas Craster has a creative vocation and his output is the music he produces, Vicky is a performance artist who does not have a choice in terms of her creative expression. Instead, she is forced to be a doll, ordered to sit still until she is told to move by the company's director. Lermontov's Pygmalionic habit of 'creating' his objects and giving them the silent treatment if they dare to disobey him, means that any prima ballerina promoted by him has no right for any kind of decision-making, be it personal, creative or professional decisions. As a man, he 'asserts his grasp on the world through action and work' while 'human and vital characteristics are merged in him' (De Beauvoir, 2011: 283). By contrast, the mask of femininity is incompatible with success as it would contradict the wearer's ability to be the 'real woman' because she 'is required to make herself object, to be the Other' (De Beauvoir, 2011: 283).

Craster's creative output is closely guided and tightly controlled, and subject to capricious and even tyrannical outbursts, much like everyone's in the company, but at the very least he is respected for his work. By contrast, Lermontov regularly invades Vicky's personal space by sitting or standing too close, or by cutting her short. He sets out limitations and draws lines which she is not supposed to cross since disobedience will result in her being the Red Woman. These limitations extend into all areas of her life, including her daily routine, her body and attire, and her voice (Lermontov speaks, Vicky listens). Any agentic element in her behaviour becomes a danger to Lermontov's fragile ego.

The female persona expected of Vicky – the exaggerated femininity of a ballerina, the absence of the voice, the impossible grace embodied in the movements written by someone else, the heavy make-up, the long flowing hair – is very tight. In fact, this persona is tighter than the tiny-waisted dresses she wears on-and-off stage, and far less forgiving than the 'standard' persona. Vicky is permanently supposed to be the embodiment of ethereal femininity, the empty vehicle for projections. She has to be the most delicate things - the 'flower', the 'cloud' and the 'bird', as Craster puts it when explaining to her what kind of images his music will transform her into. Observing these limitations, being aware of the multiple boundaries, and trying to keep on the stifling mask is something Vicky can do for a while – but not forever.

Indeed, for some time Vicky is happy to mirror Lermontov in order not to tip him into a narcissistic rage. For instance, she repeats his words or reassures him that she shares his ideas and visions. When they first meet at a party organized by Vicky's aunt, Lady Neston, Vicky orders the same champagne cocktail in order to attract Lermontov's attention. The scene ends with Lermontov telling Vicky that they are going to have 'a little talk' to which she retorts that she does not want to talk to him (after all, he has just called her a 'horror'). Lermontov replies that she should not really worry as he would do all the talking himself.

In a scene set in a hotel in Monte Carlo, he calls Vicky into his luxury office and maps out her future with the company. Vicky is sitting uncomfortably on the edge of her chair in her grey gown as Lermontov moves closer and asks her what she wants in life. When she replies that she wants to dance, which is the response he has orchestrated, he sits down opposite her, leans close to her, grabs the handles of her chair and proceeds to describe all the exciting dancing opportunities he can procure for her. When Vicky attempts to say something back, he immediately stops her with a gesture, and assures her that he will do all the thinking while she will do the dancing.

Similarly, when Vicky lies down after a rehearsal with a towel around her neck, Lermontov sits down next to her, towering over and asserting his dominance and his ownership of her body. His moods when he fails to control his faithful object are reflected in the gloomy atmosphere of the darkened hotel room as he growls and punches the mirror, creating a spider web of cracks where his face used to be. He sees himself as her rightful owner, and would rather see her destroyed than belong to someone else.

Vicky's other option is not particularly creative or liberating either: she could be with Craster which would mean starting a family and, as Lermontov puts it, 'becoming a faithful housewife with a crowd of screaming children'; recreating the other aspect of the female persona – still voiceless and power-less. By transitioning from being a beautiful object to becoming a wife and a mother she would simply swap one myth for another, she would replace one 'mysterious slogan' with a slightly different one (De Beauvoir, 1949/2011: 282). Both Lermontov and Craster think for her, one writing the music and the other dictating the movement and the costumes. Trapped between the husband and the impresario, between the two animus voices but still without a voice of her own, Vicky feels stifled and desperate. In the scene preceding her suicide, she is confronted by Lermontov and Craster, one demanding that she goes on stage and dances her part, and the other that she returns with him to London. Vicky is sandwiched between Lermontov and Craster shouting at each other and demanding that she makes her choice. Julian leaves in disgust, and Lermontov consoles the crying Vicky. Her paleness and fragility are emphasized by the white dress and the flaming red hair.

The Red Woman narrative represents crossing the line, and overcoming limitations set out by society as a critical moment; as the kind of move the protagonist is not likely to survive. Like in *Anna Karenina*, this line is drawn in *The Red Shoes* using the metaphor of the train, the railway representing the unsettling influence of modernity on the individual. Additionally, it emphasizes the 'unsettling' effect of modernity on the female persona as familial and communal aspects of human existence are gradually replaced by individualism and assertion of one's unique identity.

The train as a brutal machine is contrasted with Vicky's slim frame and her ethereal make-up and elaborate costumes. The theme of the train station, of meetings and partings, of conversations in compartments, punctuates the film, and runs parallel to the theme of creative organized chaos of stage life and performances. The company travels extensively in Europe, luxury hotels con-stitute a significant part of the film's mis-en-scène; they represent the attrac-tion of fame and success. For most of the film, Vicky's life is on the (rail) road, unstable, suspended, stuck in the liminal zone. The hotel in which she is staying in Monte Carlo has a large balcony with a beautiful view, but it also opens onto a railway line which runs right underneath it, making Vicky's existence into a paradox, and visually linking all the (red) threads of the travel theme.

Like Anna's, Vicky's life ends on the rails as she realizes that the limitations set upon her agency by the two men in her life run beyond personalities and passions – they are largely determined by society. As an ambitious and creative woman, her personal and professional choices are still limited. As she is led by an assistant towards the stage as it is her turn to appear, she imagines wearing the red ballet shoes with a mind of their own, taking her outside and towards the station where she leaps in front of a coming train. Most of the scene is a synecdoche, as the camera follows Vicky's feet in red shoes, which now determine her destiny, down the white staircase and onto the balcony over the station platform. The destiny of the female artist who cannot escape the constraints of her society is marked by the colour red as the only way she can express her agency is by committing suicide.

For Vicky Page, to dance means to live, but her existence is controlled and heavily framed by the men competing for control over her body and mind. Both Anna and Vicky have men fighting over them, but this does not make them happier, or more accomplished – on the contrary, they become depressed and lose the will to live. Accomplishment is agency, and their agency is obstructed by social, legal, and moral expectations of femininity, self-expression and motherhood. Their attempt to break free of these shackles is tragic and revolutionary.

The Company of Wolves (1984) and Red Riding Hood (2011)

Some of the contemporary attempts to rethink the Red Woman narrative involve the heroine being assertive and surviving the experience of stepping off the prescribed path. Neil Jordan's experimental *The Company of Wolves,* co-written by Angela Carter and based on the story from *The Bloody Chamber*, challenges the traditionally tragic ending for the female protagonist, showing instead her ability to read the context and to successfully deal with danger.

The film features a number of tales told by the grandmother (Angela Lansbury) to the protagonist, Rosaleen (Sarah Patterson), Rosaleen to her mother (Tusse Silberg) and to the werewolf (Micha Bergese). Typical of playful postmodernist structuring, the stories are framed as part of Rosaleen's dream, which is itself inserted into the main frame: a young girl from an affluent family living in the nineteen eighties dreams that she lives in the eighteenth century and has a sister who is killed by wolves. Most of the narrative is taken up by dream sequences in which tales of werewolves are shared between various characters. They include the story of a werewolf husband who returns to haunt his wife; the tale of a young man who becomes a werewolf after drinking the devil's potion; the story of a pregnant girl turning a party of aristocrats into a pack of wolves, the tale of a she-wolf, and, finally, Rosaleen's own involvement with a werewolf – her meeting the huntsman in the forest and later becoming a beast herself.

Later renditions of Red/Blue Woman narratives are often anachronistic, and tend to fluctuate between indeterminate early modern rural and more pronounced modern-industrial imagery, which reflects the liminal position of the original publication by Perrault and its subsequent rendition by the Brothers Grimm. The gender dynamic is mired in complex, convoluted discussions of class relations inherited from the original tales. For instance, *The Company of Wolves* references the social class hint present in Perrault's tale – 'The worst kind of wolf may be not what he seems' – men whose predatory instincts are hidden behind the veneer of gentlemanly behaviour are the most dangerous. The persona, shaped by one's class, does not eliminate the dark forces raging in the unconscious – on the contrary, they may become even more powerful, accumulating energy the more they are suppressed. This combination of class and gender, the merger of the two acute issues of modernity, intensifies in the rebellious protagonist's bid for freedom and her attempts to claim her agency (which include her body, her sexuality, and her individuation).

Carter's shifting of female sexuality (and agency) from the merely passive to the active in the original collection is also reproduced in the film. Splitting off the shadowy animus does not result in any kind of progress on the individuation path but instead feeds the female persona, keeping the character in a permanent state of hypervigilant fragility. She is locked in the vicious cycle of being a potential victim, always looking for the (also split-off) 'good' animus to arrive *ex machina* in order to punish the 'bad' split-off animus. Carter's female protagonists acknowledge and integrate the shadow instead of merely splitting it off, and projecting it on to the (beastly) animus. They carefully collect the information, given to them in abundance by mothers and grandmothers, about the dangers of straying off the path yet do not seem to be put off by it. Although terrified and still learning about predatory human beings, they look in the mirror because their own nature is not much different from that of the 'werewolves' they were taught to avoid.

As Jung puts it, 'the darkness which clings to every personality is the door into the unconscious and the gateway of dreams' from which the shadow and the soul-image (anima/animus) emerge (Jung, CW9/I: para. 222). Rosaleen, like the titular protagonist of 'Wolf Alice', is encountering and recognizing her own shadow in the mirror – contrary to the cautionary tales which imply that female persona owners do not possess the inferior function – that there is nothing to integrate; nothing to see in the mirror. When she sees the wolf boy's reflection in her own bedroom mirror, she does not only see the 'male' shadow' staring at her – she also faces her own inferior function. It is good to see, in the closing story, that she chooses to integrate rather than reject it by putting on the socially accepted mask of fragility and victimhood.

Similarly, Katherine Hardwicke's *Red Riding Hood* replicates this dissolution of the female persona via the act of recognition of the shadow metaphorically represented by werewolves. The storyline opens with a flashback to

Valerie's (Amanda Seyfried) childhood as she is playing in the woods with her friend Peter (Shiloh Fernandez). Now that she is of age, her parents plan to marry her off to Henry (Max Irons), the son of a wealthy blacksmith. Unfortunately, Peter's social standing and his earning potential (he is a woodcutter) prevent him from marrying Valerie.

Meanwhile, the werewolf that plagues the village murders Valerie's sister, Lucie (Alexandria Maillot). A renowned witch hunter, Father Solomon (Gary Oldman) arrives to capture the beast. Meanwhile, during one of the werewolf attacks, Valerie realizes that she can communicate with the wolf, which results in her being accused of being a witch by Father Solomon, and forced to do a 'walk of shame' before the village inhabitants. Father Solomon is bitten by the wolf and has to be killed in order to prevent him from becoming one. In the culmination it is revealed that the wolf is Valerie's own father, Cesaire (Billy Burke); he was cursed and would like to pass this curse on to his daughter. At this moment Peter arrives and fights with the father who bites him. Valerie kills her father, Peter turns into a werewolf because of the bite, and Valerie moves into her grandmother's house in the woods where she is visited by Peter.

Much like Carter's renditions of the Red Woman narrative, Hardwicke's version implies the protagonist's rejection of the female persona despite the dangers coming both from the internal, (unconscious-instinctual) and the external (prohibitive-societal) forces. After all, Father Solomon's prejudice and brutality are the perfect match to the bloodthirstiness of the wolf. The representative of the system, with its punishments for deviants (the iron elephant; the walk of shame), he is the one who draws the (red) lines separating civilization from wilderness. The film's colour palette emphasizes this separation: except for blood and Valerie's crimson coat, the colours are muted and greyish. Father Solomon also falls prey to this wilderness when his hand is bitten off by the beast, and one of his team has to shoot him.

Swyt notes that in Carter's 'The Company of Wolves', the howling outside the grandmother's house as the protagonist is kissing the wolf, celebrates 'the murder of sense and order and celebrates the encroachment of darkness and dissolution' (Swyt, 1996: 322). Swyt's Freudian interpretation of the tale emphasizes the fact that desire escapes the system, upsetting 'the stability of female sexuality as a signifier' (Swyt, 1996: 322). Hardwicke's version essentially follows in the same footsteps, ending with a celebration of the female desire outside of the system based on prescription (who to marry), approval (who to become) and prohibition (do not step off the beaten path). Meanwhile, the replacement of the father (Cesaire) with a young man (Peter) reflect the Oedipal dynamic of attachment to the father and refusal to grow up. Only the symbolic gesture of 'killing' the father can help the young woman move on, accept the reality, and welcome a new partner.

However, a Jungian reading reveals a richer dynamic: both the father and Peter combine the qualities of the animus and the shadow, fusing individuation issues from Themes 1 and 2. Valerie's rebellion against societal rules (not wanting to marry Henry, wanting to make her own choices) are inseparable from her attraction to Peter. Focusing purely on the sexuality aspect of female coming-of-age (the Freudian approach) would mean missing a whole plane of female individuation issues: namely, establishing the boundary between independent thinking and social approval; developing one's individuality, and finding oneself among red lines and social prescriptions.

The Handmaid's Tale (2017–)

Based on two novels by Margaret Atwood, *The Handmaid's Tale* (1985) and *The Testaments* (2019), the series explore a dystopian patriarchal society called Gilead in the aftermath of a US civil war. The heteronormative, patriarchal utopia owns women's reproductive rights. Those capable of bearing children are forced to reproduce as babies become a high-value currency. Women are allowed to perform a limited number of roles in the society's operations: they can be 'Handmaids' who are metonymically reduced to 'wombs' and used to produce children. Those who are infertile are used as house servants and are called 'Marthas'. Handmaids are assigned to families of 'Commanders' whose wives are infertile and who treat Handmaids as incubators to expand their own families.

Physical and ideological control is guaranteed by overseers called the Aunts – older women who explain and maintain rules and rituals, and administer punishment for any kind of independent thinking or behaviour. They are brutal and have the right to mutilate Handmaids who mock the order or break the rules. The worst of them is Aunt Lydia (Ann Dowd) whose devotion to Gilead makes equal her fanaticism and sadism. Women who do not conform to Gilead's heteronormativity by being 'gender traitors' (euphemism for 'gay') or rebels, are labelled 'Unwomen' and sent to the 'Colonies', or labour camps, where they are worked to death.

Women's roles are colour-coded in accordance with their status and duties: Handmaids wear red, Marthas' assigned colour is muted green, and the Aunts' uniform is brown. Commanders' Wives wear tailored teal-coloured dresses emphasizing their femininity and subservience.

The protagonist, Offred (Elizabeth Moss) loses her family when she is captured by Gilead representatives, her child is taken away, and her husband supposedly killed (it later emerges that he managed to escape). Her name, June, is taken away from her and replaced by a new one that indicates her belonging to a particular household. Moss is often typecast in domestic abuse survivor roles, playing paradoxical characters – strong victims capable of rising above the circumstances, and avenging themselves (for instance, detective Robin Griffin in *Top of the Lake* (BBC, 2013–2017), created by Jane Campion and Gerard Lee). Their rage is the rage of the Red Woman – the anger of someone who refuses to be subjugated; who harvests her anger at being helpless in the moment of her rape to come back a stronger person and destroy her abusers. The anger of Moss's characters is the anger resulting from the sense of entrapment within a rigid, patriarchal order. It is agentic anger, born out of the will to act, to escape, and to survive.

However, the angry agency goes beyond the act of survival and vengeance, and into further individuation activities. At best, it remains a sublimation of the terrifying feeling of helplessness. For instance, in Season 1 of *Top of the Lake,* detective Griffin, whose specialism is sexual assault, investigates a statutory rape while the flashbacks from her own rape trauma feed her enthusiasm and lead her in her dark quest – a quest for the truth and also the quest deep into the damaged self. Her 'redness' is reflected in her rebellion, her rejection of bullying informed by patriarchal values as well as the strength with which she breaks through external and internal oppression. With her large eyes and soft features, Griffin is mistaken by men for a victim, only to discover that she is capable of fighting back with superhuman force.

Similarly, Offred is deceptively meek and compliant; yet, she manages to regularly undermine the rules laid out by Gilead. Handmaids are only allowed to have sex with their Commander, and the event is a ceremonialized rape. For instance, she has sex with Nick (Max Minghella), an 'Eye', or a member of the secret police attached to the Waterford household. She also tells the truth about Handmaids to the Mexican ambassador and passes the note to her husband through the ambassador's assistant (S1, E5).

The Handmaids are the ultimate red women, albeit in retrospective – they are subjected to various purification rituals, ranging from physical mutilation to rape ('the ceremony') to communal work (cleaning out the blood of those executed, for instance) as punishment for their 'sinful' past in which they had freedom to choose partners and were financially independent. Their uniform, with its red cape and exaggerated white 'wings', blocking their peripheral vision and worn on top of bonnets, form the symbolic and metaphorical background of the narrative. Handmaids are only allowed to take off the wings in exceptional cases, for instance, during a 'particicution' when a crown of handmaids beats a man, who broke the law, to death.

In fact, this colour combination of 'purity and danger' is linked to the sociocultural perception of the Red Woman as simultaneously desirable and dangerous, as someone whose desire for an agency is to be destroyed so that she could rejoin the inflexible social order. With its sinister and oppressive purpose of limiting the view of the wearer, the wings form part of the female persona. Echoing the cape and bonnet worn by the Red Riding Hood, the cape and wings deliver a warning similar to Perrault's: keep the mask on, or else.

From a traditional Jungian perspective, Handmaids are captives of the anima projection created by the ideology that works in rigid binaries. Gilead is a strict return to the masculine-feminine binary into which the entire society, with its functions and structures, is squeezed. The woman becomes de-individualized; a pure archetype, a pure mask, dressed in symbolic clothes and performing theatrical gestures.

Yet, many Handmaids are also rebels, including Offred, Moira (Samira Wiley) and Ofglen (Alexis Bledel). The Red Woman is the first step towards the female trickster; the Handmaid, dressed in red and constantly reminded of her sinful past, chooses irreverence in an attempt to regain control over her body and mind. The first step towards erasing the very concept of the abject – trickster's main job – is acknowledging the social and systemic origins of the shame and rejecting it because 'abjection is a coexistence with social and symbolic order, on the individual as well as collective level' (Kristeva, 1982: 67). Meanwhile, defilement is 'jettisoned from the symbolic system' (Kristeva, 1982: 65). In the case of Gilead, defilement and abjection, which it associates with the female body and its functions, is redefined in religious terms and coded in the strict colour scheme and brutal rituals in an attempt to contain it. Fertility, sex and childbirth are ritualized in order to contain their unclean, abject nature. Gilead is a hyperbole of a system attempting to control human nature. Offred, the ultimate Red Woman, reabsorbs the shame and turns it against her captors. Yet, she is a rebel and not the trickster yet as she is still self-conscious as well as conscious about her mask. The 'advanced' rebel would be the female trickster who is not aware (or does not accept) labels and is not afraid of bodily functions including sex, pregnancy, childbirth and excrement (she will be explored in Chapter 7).

The Blue Woman and the Bluebeard Narrative

If the Red Woman acts, the Blue Woman's rebellion is more surreptitious – she dares to look. She is seemingly compliant and willing to accept the rules of the game created by her owner or captor. Deep down, however, she is resentful and prepared to sabotage both the man and the social order that makes her his servant, and an insignificant and voiceless addition to someone else's household. Unlike the Red Woman who often perishes, either killed off by the aggressor or ends her own life because of the social pressure, the Blue Woman usually survives thanks to a combination of her shrewdness and various helpers who come to her rescue.

The tale of the secret room which a young woman is prohibited to enter is one of the most enduring motifs recycled in screen narratives. The original tale was written by Charles Perrault and published in 1697. Bluebeard's wife, who is only identified as 'the younger of the two sisters' from a noble family that lived not far from one Bluebeard's 'fine houses'. When her husband goes away 'on an important business matter', he gives her a set of keys which could open all the storerooms and jewel-boxes in the house (Perrault, 2010: 104). One key, however, is forbidden to be used, else 'there is no knowing what I might do, so angry would I be' (Perrault, 2010: 104).

Her friends and neighbours comment on how lucky she is to own so many nice things (cue a detailed description of silver cutlery, luxury furniture and opulent upholstery). In terms of the accomplishments of the female persona, the wife has certainly hit the jackpot. Yet, she is unhappy; all she wants is to know what lies behind the door of the private room downstairs. The room is dark, and at first she cannot see anything, but gradually she starts discerning the horrifying details: pools of clotted blood, in which dead women, tied along the wall with their throats slit, are reflected. Shocked, the wife drops the key to the bloodied floor, and subsequently cannot remove the stains as they keep reappearing.

When Bluebeard returns from his 'business trip' earlier than planned, the wife welcomes him with feigned joy. Naturally, he asks for the key, sees the blood and threatens to slit her throat. Her tears do not touch the husband, for 'so beautiful was she, and in such distress, that she would have moved the very rocks to pity, but Bluebeard's heart was harder than rock' (Perrault, 2010: 108). The tale has a happy *deus ex machina* ending: by stalling, the wife secures enough time for her brothers, a dragoon guard and a musketeer, to arrive and slay Bluebeard. Because he had no heirs, she inherits all his wealth and even marries 'a man of true worth' (Perrault, 2010: 113).

Perrault's tale has two morals, the first being a warning against an excessive curiosity:

> Curiosity's all very well in its way,
> But satisfy it and you risk much remorse,
> Examples of which can be seen every day.
> The feminine sex will deny it, of course,
> But the pleasure you wanted, once taken, is lost,
> And the knowledge you looked for is not worth the cost.
> (Perrault, 2010: 113)

The second moral concerns 'the modern husband's' behaviour: when dissatisfied, he should be 'as quiet as a mouse' as 'it is not easy to decide which is the master of the house' (Perrault, 2010: 114).

Both the morals attached by the original author to the tale are, however, somewhat misleading. Even though they claim to be about female curiosity and male obedience, the tale itself is primarily about trust – and more so about men being able to trust women than mutual trust within a heterosexual couple. The themes of female agency, creativity, intelligence and curiosity are also present, but in a negative rather than a positive light; as a dangerous venture which luckily – this time – ended well for the female protagonist.

Despite this being a fairy tale with characters being sketchy, Bluebeard's wife has several distinctive behavioral traits which are also emphasized and explored in cinematic adaptations and feminist renditions. She is a woman with a backbone who is determined to triumph in difficult circumstances. When she is marked with the colour red – which her owner assumes is the victim's colour – she fights back and gets him killed. She now owns the colour red and is not afraid to display it. Her rebellion against 'the order established by the males', which decides whether she is 'freed from her original taint', to use Simone de Beavoir's analysis of the position of women in society, is also successful in monetary terms as she gets to keep her husband's immense wealth.

De Beauvoir's analysis of the relationship between private property and the dependent position of women in *The Second Sex* (1958) throws light on the emergence of the blue and red woman narratives, and particularly its Bluebeard variation which is directly linked to wealth. De Beauvoir explains that 'woman was dethroned by the advent of private property, and her lot through the centuries has been bound up with private property' (De Beauvoir, 1997: 113). With the emphasis on inheritance came strict expectations of the wife's conduct: 'as long as the property lasts, so long will marital infidelity on the part of the wife be regarded as the crime of high treason' (De Beauvoir, 1997: 115).

Even in narratives in which the female rebellion against being treated as part of the property is accomplished, she often has to be saved from the predatory males by *deus ex machina* men, including brothers or a stranger passing by. From the feminist point of view, therefore, the wife's escape from Bluebeard is not a victory even though she has the husband killed as it still leaves her dependent on male authority (brothers or a metaphorical father figure) for the actual act of survival. De Beavoir's writes:

> The only question is whether the woman after marriage will remain subject to the authority of the father or her older brother – an authority which will extend also to her children – or whether she will become subject to that of her husband. [...] She is only the intermediary of authority, not the one who holds it.
>
> (De Beauvoir, 1997: 103)

The best archetype to use in the analysis of the tale of Bluebeard would the animus, or even the shadow-animus, although classical Jungian views on it would have to be seriously revised.

The tale of Bluebeard lays out an archetypal confrontation of the female persona and the brutal animus, and challenges its acceptance by society. The protagonist accepts the meeting with the animus as potentially fatal as well as confirming the female persona, fixing it to the woman's face. The animus in this case is the terrifying version, the shadow-animus, the demonic and ruthless spirit. One of Jung's disciples, Erich Neumann outlines the 'positives' combining the female persona and the animus, and sees this combination as being one of necessity, even though it causes 'a not inconsiderable danger' for the woman:

> The fact that the varieties of patriarchal marriage have preserved their form for millennia proves that, in a certain way, they offer motional

viable ways of life both for men and women. Although the patriarchal marriage presents a not inconsiderable danger for the woman's development, her chances of realising her inner necessities within it – even if secretly – are great enough. [...]

Patriarchal marriage is a collective solution in which man and woman, the Masculine and the Feminine, unite in a state where each props up the other, so that they achieve a symbiosis that forms the backbone of patriarchal culture.

(Neumann, 1994: 30–31)

Moreover, when in a relationship, the woman must 'surrender' her 'natural psychological bisexuality', to allow her masculine side constellate as the animus (Neumann, 1994: 31). This will lead to the 'division of roles' when the woman 'projects onto the [partner] her own unconscious masculine side in the form of the animus' (Neumann, 1994: 32). The patriarchal marriage also results in further solidification of the female persona as the components of the individual's 'bisexual nature not corresponding to the requisite ideal type are repressed or suppressed' (Neumann, 1994: 33).

Neumann admits, however, that modernity's attraction to the individuation process has led to the decay of some of the traditional collective ideals, including the infamous patriarchal marriage: 'when a great number of persons have developed toward individuation to the point that they can no longer suppress the "equivocalness" of their original human nature in favour of an archetypally based collective ideal, a crisis occurs in the patriarchal marriage and the patriarchal structure of culture' (Neumann, 1994: 33).

Another Jungian, Marie-Louise Von Franz, looks at Bluebeard as an example of the demonic, negative animus who stifles the creativity of those he happens to inhabit. Unfortunately, she also continues Jung's biased line of conflating the social with the psychological, and accusing the woman of harbouring 'dark thoughts' instead of unravelling elements of cultural and institutional oppression that deprive the woman of her voice, or make her sublimate the voice into creative alternatives:

One example [of the murderer animus] is Bluebeard who secretly kills all his wives in a hidden chamber. In this form the animus personifies all these semiconscious, cold, destructive reflections that invade a woman in the small hours, especially when she has failed to realize some obligation of feeling. It is then that she begins to think about the family heritage and matters of that kind – a sort of web of calculating thoughts, filled with malice and intrigue, which get her into a state where she even wishes death to others. [...]

By nursing secret destructive attitudes, a wife can drive her husband, and a mother her children, into illness, accident, or even death.

(Jung, 1963: 202)

Von Franz's analysis of the wife's intentions is an interesting case of victim-blaming, diverting the responsibility for male brutality onto the woman herself. It is also somewhat Freudian in that, instead of discussing external female passivity as a social issue forced upon women, it takes it for granted and argues that woman's hidden violent tendencies are split-off into the figure of the animus and waiting for the right moment to erupt. This is why the emancipation of the woman's voice from the projected and projecting shadow animus is long overdue. It is the kind of revision that post-Jungian theory should start taking seriously right now.

Bluebeard's literal fragmenting of wives is a crude metaphor of preventing the woman's psychological wholeness by abruptly cutting her individuation path. For instance, according to another key Jung's disciple, Jolande Jacobi, the animus is akin to a loud, stubborn voice in a woman's head and it needs to be restrained:

> ... the animus does not so often appear in the form of an erotic fantasy or mood; it is more apt to take the form of a hidden 'sacred' conviction. When such a conviction is preached with a loud, insistent masculine voice or imposed on others by means of brutal emotional scenes, the underlying masculinity in a woman is easily recognized. However, even in a woman who is outwardly very feminine the animus can be an equally hard, inexorable power. One may suddenly find oneself up against something in a woman that is obstinate, cold, and completely inaccessible.
>
> (Neumann, 1994: 198)

Moreover, it is not a single figure, but a whole chorus of men ready to argue and to fight at any moment. These men, Jolande Jacobi argues, are full of 'uncritically accepted opinions, prejudices, principles, which make women argue and bicker. [...] They seem to make up a fairly high percentage of their sex, though there may have been some change since the turn of the century, perhaps as a result of the emancipation of woman' (Jacobi, 1973: 121).

It is interesting that Jacoby links the rise in the power of the animus to female emancipation. Both Jacoby and Von Franz imply in their respective analyses of the animus that women should always be 'supervised' by a man who would be able to control, manage and direct their inner voice should they start expressing any 'uncritical opinions'. Meanwhile, both of them worked under Jung's supervision, were part of his school of thought and expanded his ideas. In a way, Neumann, Von Franz, and Jacobi argue that the female persona is an innate set of traits while the necessary, suppressed, resentment it produces in the form of an 'evil' animus is also an unfortunate and unavoidable part of womanhood. There is no discussion of the social roots of the animus or the formation of the female persona.

Given the tendency of cultural canons to associate the feminine with passive and the masculine with argentic/active, this means the suppression of female individuation, of anyone without an appropriate gender mask. It means vanquishing the agentic in women, of forcing it underground where it dwells like an angry trickster waiting to turn into the shadow, for the right moment to escape. Sometimes it starts peeking from behind the mask, disobeying the master, defying his orders, and doing the opposite of what she told her to do. The nameless Bluebeard's wife challenges the obligatory symbiosis with the projected violent animus. As Sue Thornham points out, Bluebeard is 'a story in which female rebellion, curiosity, and action are central, and the object of investigation is not the enigma of femininity but the secrets of the patriarchy' (Thornham, 2019: 103).

Davies points out that 'the imposition of order identified with Bluebeard is no straightforward matter because in fact it constantly produces its own Other and opposites, so that such order is always fragile and threatened by chaos or rebellion, often embodied in the female protagonist' (Davies, 2001: 233). Davies notes that:

> the 'terrible' husband Bluebeard is not a perverse individual flouting the demands of civilized behaviour, but is in fact upholding those standards. Thus, the real scandal and transgression of the tale lie less in the fact that it involves violence in the family than in that it reveals that violence, necessarily present but usually hidden, which in more recent times especially has become a taboo subject.
>
> (Davies, 2001: 54)

The original Bluebeard story emphasizes the dangers that come with peeking outside the female persona, of lifting off the mask, even a little bit, even temporarily and surreptitiously; of adopting slightly more proactive position, of reclaiming the right to look instead of standing still. Contemporary authors like Angela Carter and Margaret Atwood have explored this crisis of the agentic in their stories 'The Bloody Chamber' and 'Bluebeard's Egg'. Carter shifts the birth of female agency and the feeling of frustration with the stifling mask onto the mother figure who comes to rescue her daughter.

It is the older, more confident woman that destroys the animus-husband – as well as challenging the notion that the female persona is destiny, that the husband nailing it to the wife's face is doing it for the noble reason of maintaining the necessary status quo, and that meeting with the animus constitutes the finale of the heroine's journey. The archetypal symbiosis Neumann mentions also 'works out much less favourably for the Feminine and for women than for the Masculine and for men' (Neumann, 1994: 33).

Margaret Atwood's 'Bluebeard's Egg'

In 'Bluebeard's Egg' Atwood rethinks the issues of trust and agency by reversing the roles of the looking agent and the object, and discovers that the surreptitious agency of quiet observance, or even saboteur-style irreverence and defiance, are still not enough to protect the 'wife' from being hurt. Sally, the story's protagonist, is a neglected wife whose husband Ed has a mysterious past and a mysterious present: he was married twice but cannot explain why the marriages failed; he is also very attractive and often surrounded by women. The story opens with Sally's inner monologue about Ed's perceived stupidity – a sort of reversal of values, an attempt to take off the female persona. Ed is likened to a 'dumb blonde' whose 'monumental stupidity' is endearing despite being a successful medical professional – a cardiologist (Atwood, 1997: 132). Her sentiments are shared by other women: Sally's stylish friend, Marylynn, likens him to a 'cute button', the kind one would like to get bronzed and kept on a mantel-piece (Atwood, 1997: 136).

Yet, Sally's attempt at diminishing Ed's importance in her life aims at establishing some kind of equality between them as well as compensating for Sally's feeling of inferiority: in reality, she 'worries that she is a nothing', with her part-time job ('comfortable enough' and engaging 'only half of her cogs and wheels'), her identity overshadowed by the role of a wife. She is the one organizing meals and makes sure the meals are catered to Ed's preferences (Atwood, 1997: 141). Meanwhile, her friend Marylynn is a self-made woman, independent and the owner of a successful business (Atwood, 1997: 138). When Sally says she is 'nothing', this means she feels nothing outside the established persona, the role of the diligent and quiet wife.

In reality, Ed's 'stupidity' and his lack of awareness of being a magnet for women are part of his pretence. A cardiologist, a 'heart man' as Sally calls him, he x-rays, dissects, and moves on to the next victim. He once took Sally to the hospital to show off the new machine, 'a thousand times better than an electrocardiogram' because it revealed 'the faults, the thickenings, and the cloggings' (Atwood, 1997: 143). As she lay on the examining table, wired to the new machine and feeling vulnerable, she saw her 'insubstantial', exposed heart displayed on the screen while Ed was 'absorbed in his machine', distant and in control (Atwood, 1997: 145).

As part of the homework given by her creative writing instructor, Sally has to flesh out a modern Bluebeard story based on the skeleton premise of a wealthy wizard repeatedly handing an egg to young women for safekeeping and forbidding them from entering a secret room. The first two disobey his orders, enter the room, and drop the spotless egg into a vat of blood which results in them being killed by the prospective husband. The last candidate cleverly places the egg on a shelf before entering the room, reviving her sisters, and controlling the now powerless wizard. An alternative ending included the wizard meeting his comeuppance and burning to death (Atwood, 1997: 156).

Sally is struggling with the task as she is trying to grasp the metaphorical significance of the egg. A fragile and precious object, does the egg represent Ed, someone who needs to be cherished and watched over? Before she has a chance to finish the story, however, she catches Ed and Marylynn together at a party for Ed's colleagues, Ed's 'left arm held close to his side, the back of it pressed against Marylynn. Her shimmering upper thigh, her ass to be exact' (Atwood, 1997: 160). All three pretend that nothing happened.

Yet, Sally is deeply upset and spends the evening thinking about the incident. Her female persona, with its requirement for patience and suffering, does not allow to say anything to Ed: 'she can't afford to be wrong, or to be right either' (Atwood, 1997: 162). Then she realizes that the fragility of the egg metaphor is not applicable to Ed who is perhaps not the precious find, the amazing treasure she thought he was. Perhaps the egg represents her own fragility in the face of a treacherous husband, a serial womaniser whose dark secret she has just uncovered. Finally it becomes clear what happened in Ed's two previous marriages, why he calls the cleaner (just like her predecessor) 'the woman', 'as though they are interchangeable', and why he wanted to see Sally's heart on the screen of the new medical device. Ed regards women as objects, discardable and replaceable, important only in terms of feeding his ego, and interesting as far as they can be pinned to the examination table as he is dissecting hearts and souls and satisfying his need to be in control. Sally now feels that she has no control over her own heart, which is fragile and exposed, 'beating with insubstantial moth-like flutter' (Atwood, 1997: 163). She also has the vision of the egg hatching, it is alive although it is still unclear who will emerge out of it.

Atwood's apt modern rethinking of the Bluebeard narrative highlights all the key themes of the story: the passivity of the feminine persona, the fragility of the woman underneath the mask, and the 'insignificance' and smallness of her budding identity which is hoping to hatch out of gendered expectations. The Blue Woman's rebellion is tentative, still in progress, still evolving, she is afraid of it like Sally is afraid of the egg's aliveness and potential (as well as of being a divorcee, someone previously defined by a relationship with a successful man). The egg and the key are supposed to be clean, spotless, perfect, intact, while simultaneously, oxymoronically symbolizing societal expectations and highlighting societal fears concerning taboo subjects associated with female bodily functions. The story about reclaiming the 'bloody' mystery and destroying the one who dictates the binary attitude to women opens narrative options for a more wholesome image of a female character, the one who can act, who can think outside the binary partnership, and the one who is prepared to individuate.

A range of cinematic adaptations picked up on the budding, tentative emergence of the female agency against the backdrop of objectification and the social demands of the persona. It is worth having a look at some of the more modern versions, including Jane Campion's *The Piano* and Catherine Breillat's *Bluebeard*, as narratives reflecting the changing attitudes towards the entanglement of the social and the economic in the treatment of the female heroine.

The Piano

The Piano is a tale of a female voice. An invariant of *Bluebeard* (which is explicitly referenced in the film), it focuses on the female protagonist's attempt to escape from the circle of victimhood and to regain her agency. Ada McGrath (Holly Hunter) is forcibly married off to a wealthy New Zealand farmer Alastair Stewart (Sam Neill), and has to travel across the world with her daughter Flora (Anna Paquin) and their possessions to settle in her new home. In the opening scene, Ada explains that she has not spoken a word since she was six, which his father (the person who made the decision to marry her off) considers to be a 'dark talent'. Ada explains that she does not consider herself to be silent, and that her voice is expressed through the music she plays on the piano.

Still part of the opening sequence, her music is interrupted by the shadow of a chaperone, a reminder that it is time to leave Scotland and join her new husband. The next scene cuts to her arrival on the shore, a combination of metonymic close-ups and long shots designed to paint a picture of psychological fragmentation: the fingers (a recurrent synecdoche throughout the film), the face, the wet shoes. These fragmentary representations are meant to convey a character who, despite being broken by the circumstances, still manages to pull herself together though defiance and creativity. The mother and daughter are left on the shore with their possessions, the long shot framing the little figures, the heavy instrument and the numerous boxes as small and insignificant against the darkening sky. Ultimately, Ada has to leave the piano on the beach as there is no space for it in Alasdair's house.

Two metaphors are consistently woven into Ada's story throughout the film: self-expression through music and shadow play. The first is also a metonymy, serving as a substitute for Ada's absent voice which is lost in protest against the rigidity of the female persona. The missing voice both emphasizes and rejects the passive aspects of the persona, drawing attention to the brutality of the mask's socially established properties. The silence simultaneously mocks social expectations and reshapes them by transforming the female voice into music. If the woman's task is to be an 'enigma' that has to be (incorrectly) deciphered and projected upon, one might as well stop speaking altogether and become the resentful representation of the voiceless woman. No one wants to hear this voice anyway. If Ada cannot have her individuating voice, she will translate it into a different language, the one that cannot be taken from her so easily.

And yet, this other language – music, self-expression – are frowned upon by various representatives of the shadow-animus in her life; to the extent that Ada has to defend this other voice as well. Her hobby is frowned upon in her home in Scotland, the piano is abandoned on the beach in New Zealand, and, eventually, her new husband chops off her finger in revenge for her infidelity, but also as a way of stifling her voice, of destroying her self-expression.

Shadow-animus is the central archetype of the narrative, delineating Ada's relationships with the successive men in her life: the father, the unknown lover who gave her Flora before abandoning the mother and child, and the new husband. They are represented in the Christmas rendition of the Bluebeard shadow play as the recurrent menacing monster. They are also associated with the visual synecdoche, with her psychological and then literal fragmentation when her finger is severed by Alasdair for her affair with George Baines (Harvey Keitel). The voiceless wife ends up in Bluebeard's bloody chamber and pays for independence and self-expression – both of which are linked with her sexuality and the right to choose her romantic partners instead of being assigned one by her father.

Marie-Louise von Franz notes that, like the other archetypes, the animus is characterized by duality, sometimes appearing as a 'demon of death' (Jung, 1963: 199). Its characteristics are influenced by the person's father, who endows the image with 'the special colouring of unarguable, incontestably "true" convictions – convictions that never include the personal reality of the woman herself as she actually is' (Jung, 1963: 199). The shadow-animus-father inevitably imprints itself on the woman and results in subsequent encounters with a similar figure until the issue is resolved. In Ada's case, the cruel father with his projection of a 'dark talent' becomes the cruel husband who first prohibits any female self-expression, and then brutally punishes his wife for overstepping the line.

The shadow-animus Bluebeard makes his appearance in the pageant shadow play staged by the settlers. The play, which uses animal blood, features Bluebeard's shadow looming over his victim with a raised axe. Later on Stewart will raise his axe to chop off Ada's finger, a horrible and spiteful act which would ruin her ability to play the piano. Full of remorse after the incident, Stewart sets Ada free. Before she settles with Baines and her daughter in Nelson, New Zealand, Ada attempts to drown herself but changes her mind and is eventually pulled to safety. The Blue Woman, full of pain and feeling powerless, musters all her courage to continue living after her traumatic encounter with the beastly animus.

According to Estes, Bluebeard's wife's voice in his rough process of awakening and rebellion does not necessarily have to be refined – far from being musical or beautiful, it can be a howl. Her cry 'travels over a long intrapsychic distance to where her brothers live, to where those aspects of the psyche that are trained to fight, to fight to the death if necessary, live' (Estes, 1992: 57). Ultimately, Ada's shrewdness and psychic awakening are aimed at 'overwhelming the captor', be it 'a destructive religion, husband, family, culture or a woman's negative complexes' (Estes, 1992: 56). In *The Piano*, the protagonist's wildness is expressed through her sexuality, defiant and rebellious, as she repeatedly rejects the normative and accepts (and even emphasizes) the stigmatic, by having a child outside marriage, and later on by cheating on her new husband.

Bluebeard (2009)

Catherine Breillat's 2009 version of the Bluebeard theme is a story of fearlessness and ambition, at times resembling another European narrative celebrating a resilient female persona – *Beauty and the Beast* (originally written by Gabrielle-Suzanne de Villeneuve and published in 1740).

Breillat's film follows two parallel time-frames. Two sisters, presumably in the 1950s, are reading Perrault's tale in an attic (which presumably, they are forbidden to enter). The characters in the book come alive to enact the drama of possessive love, curiosity and ambition. The tale starts in a Catholic convent where two sisters, Anne (Daphne Balwir) and Marie-Catherine (Lola Creton) attend a boarding school. They are summoned to the office of Mother Superior to be told that their father, and sole provider, died while trying to save a child. This means that they would have to leave the convent as the family would be unable to pay for their education. As they are riding in the carriage, they notice Bluebeard's castle, and the younger, Marie-Catherine, expresses an interest in who their wealthy neighbour might be. At home they are met by a dishevelled mother who dyes all their clothes black.

The whole story of the convent and the father is absent from the original tale. Perrault's version has a very brief premise – no more than a few lines – and goes straight into action. By contrast, Breillat spends around 25 minutes (inclusive of the parallel narrative) exploring the young characters. While Anne is angry and believes that her father unreasonably wasted his life by trying to save a child thus leaving his own the family impoverished, Marie-Catherine appears to be kinder and more accepting as she tries to understand his motivation and acknowledges the moral complexity of the incident and its consequences for the family. In the convent scene the younger sister is shown testing the boundaries of authority by being late for the meeting with Mother Superior. She is seemingly full of contradictions: simultaneously curious and careful, brave and delicate, naive and wise. Bluebeard captures her paradoxical character when he says that she is simultaneously innocent and proud.

Yet, Breillat does not add completely new and alien elements to the narrative; she simply expands on what is already in the original tale. One example of this is the focus on wealth. Perrault's text is peppered with references to the houses, furniture, and jewellery Bluebeard owns. The young woman makes the decision to marry him after a party at which his wealth and social standing are put on show. Similarly, Marie-Catherine loves her wedding dress –particularly because it is brand new and made-to-measure. She also wants her sister to envy her new social status. When Bluebeard is away on business, the visitors to the castle are awed by the affluence and prosperity of their friend's new husband.

Breillat uses this theme to emphasize the fact that the young wife is by no means a naïve victim of circumstances. She makes the decision to marry a man with a shady reputation because she grabs an opportunity to climb the social ladder. In this sense, Marie-Catherine is coldly calculating and decisive rather than a victim of circumstances. She uses the shadow-animus to move up in society, linking the tale to the emergence of the middle class.

Estes presents an alternative view on the shadow animus, identifying the site of the projection and separating the inner voice of the woman from the oppressive patriarchal and societal assumptions. Estes moves the woman from the set of civilized assumptions and into the forest of wild instincts and desires, turning her into a wolf, making her a predator rather than a prey. The wolf-woman is initiated into her 'proper instinctive senses' while the predator is 'identified and banished' (Estes, 1992: 56). This is 'the moment in which the captured woman moves from victim status into shrewd-minded, wily-eyed, sharp-eared status instead' (Estes, 1992: 56). Similarly, Marie-Catherine's first encounter with the future husband shows her as decisive and open-minded rather than helpless. She tells Bluebeard that she is not afraid of him even though he has the reputation of a monster. She is prepared to experience things herself instead of relying on rumours and public opinion. She looks unflinchingly at the trembling body of the beheaded goose slaughtered for the feast at the castle. The camera close-up reflects her calculating gaze showing a complete lack of fear in her cynical hunt for wealth. Like Carter's wolf girls, Breillat's young heroine is also somewhat a monster, and is determined to acknowledge and integrate this part of herself.

Estes points out that Bluebeard narrative powerfully breach 'the injunction against "looking"' (Estes, 1992: 61). In this sense, Breillat emphasizes the investigative streak of Bluebeard's wife as it is this streak - the desire for looking, searching and researching – that transcends the female persona that is based on passive observance and non-intervention. Bluebeard's wife is certainly keen to intervene. Not only does she want to explore her husband's possibly difficult character and take risks associated with it, but she also disobeys him and opens the forbidden room. For this, a traditional society assumes, she must pay with her life.

Breillat's version of Bluebeard's wife transgresses the bounds of the female persona in a number of ways: by not being afraid of self-proclaimed monsters, by expressing her curiosity, and by causing the death of her husband by skilful stalling. She prefers to find out things for herself. Being a detective is not part of the female persona, and Marie-Catherine is a detective investigating a dark secret that her husband harbours.

Conclusion

The warning narratives detail the consequences and penalties for transgressing the boundaries of the female persona and present these transgressions as horrible death in the hands of a shadow-animus. Interestingly, they also link the budding, rebellious female agency to the concepts of bourgeois individualism and the rise of modernity. 'Individualistic and nonconformist', as Dundes puts it, the Red and Blue heroines resist the constrictive bounds of society in which their agency and sexuality are regarded as non-existent, and their status as victims is reiterated in warnings about predation and other dangers, physical and psychological (Dundes, 1989: 122). While the Red heroines often die as a consequence of their choices, the Blue ones survive by integrating the shadow animus, realizing their (class) ambitions and revising their victim status. They prepare the way for the less fearful, more openly transgressive heroine unafraid of open conflict, of looking ridiculous, or of getting herself into dangerous situations.

References

Atwood, Margaret (2000) *Bluebeard's Egg and Other Stories*, London: Vintage.

Beauvour, Simonede (1949/2011) *The Second Sex*, London: Vintage Books.

Carter, Angela (1995) *The Bloody Chamber and Other Stories*, London: Vintage.

Carter, Ian (2001) *Railways and Culture in Britain: the Epitome of Modernity*, Manchester: Manchester University Press.

Davies, Mererid Puw (2001) *The Tale of Bluebeard in German Literature: from the Eighteenth Century to the Present*, Oxford: Oxford University Press.

Dundes, Alan (1989) *Little Red Riding Hood: a Casebook*, Wisconsin: University of Wisconsin Press.

Estes, Clarissa Pincola (1992) *Women Who Run With the Wolves: Myths and Stories of the Wild Woman Archetype*, London: Rider.

Jacobi, Jolande (1942/1973) *The Psychology of C. G. Jung* (8th Edition), Ralph Manheim (trans.), New Haven and London: Yale University Press.

Jahn, Gary R. (1981) 'The Image of the Railroad in Anna Karenina', *Slavic and East European Journal*, 25 (2) (Summer), pp. 1–10.

Jung C.G. (n.d.) *The Collected Works*, Herbert Read, Michael Fordham and Gerhardt Adler, (eds.) R.F.C. Hull (trans.), London: Routledge. (Except where a different publication was used, all references are to this hardback edition.)

Jung, Carl Gustav and von Franz, M.-L. (eds.) (1964/1978) *Man and His Symbols*, London: Picador.

Kristeva, Julia (1982) *Powers of Horror: an Essay on Abjection*, New York: Columbia University Press.

Neumann, Erich (1994) *'The Fear of the Feminine' and Other Essays on Feminine Psychology*, Princeton, NJ: Princeton University Press.

Pastoreau, Michel and Simonnet, Dominique (2005) *Petit Livres des Couleurs*, Paris: Editions Points.

Perrault, Charles (2010) *The Complete Fairy Tales*, Oxford: Oxford University Press.

Punter, David (1998) *Gothic Pathologies: the Text, the Body and the Law*, London: Macmillan Press Ltd.

Swyt, Wendy (1996) '"Wolfings": Angela Carter's Becoming-Narrative', *Studies in Short Fiction*, 33 (3).

Thornham, Sue (2019) 'Beyond Bluebeard: Feminist Nostalgia and Top of the Lake (2013)', *Feminist Media Studies*, 19 (1), pp. 102–117.

Tolstoy, Leo (1998) *Anna Karenina*, Oxford: Oxford World's Classics.

Von Franz, Marie-Louise (1964) 'The Process of Individuation', in Carl Gustav Jung and Marie-Louise von Franz (eds.) *Man and His Symbols*, London: Picador, pp. 159–254.

Zipes, Jack (1989) '"Little Red Riding Hood" as Male Creation and Projection', in Alan Dundes (ed.) *Little Red Riding Hood: a Casebook*, Wisconsin: University of Wisconsin Press.

Chapter 4

Bildungsroman

Rejection of the Mask

It is refreshing to see the emergence of a female bildungsroman in both cinema and television: this is the sign that the industry has been finally paying attention to female individuation and identity. Moreover, the young female individuand emerging out of childhood and learning to negotiate with the world encounters a whole range of archetypal themes and motifs where she had previously been limited to the issues belonging to Theme 2 (parents and lovers/husbands). She is no longer simply passed on from her childhood home to her new family where her journey ends. By contrast, the new female bildungsroman contains elements of Theme 1 (the trickster and the shadow) and Theme 3 (the child, the hero and the self). Sometimes several themes are combined, like they do in Disney's *Brave* (2012) in which the protagonist, a young princess called Merida, is struggling with her own shadow as well trying to maintain a relationship with her problematic mother. Meanwhile, another Disney character, Elsa from *Frozen*, is trying to find the self through handling her shadow, expressed in her ability to turn objects she touches into ice.

The involvement of the themes of social integration and inspiration/motivation also mean that the protagonist is not regarded to be someone endlessly caring and accepting (stereotyped behaviours woven into the female persona) but possesses a degree of conflict, both within herself and externally, with society. These new narratives explore the complexities and conflicts that come with growing up, with individuating, with adjusting one's emerging interests and values to those of one's surroundings. Human identity generates conflict as it goes through the process of social contextualization, and it is this conflict that female characters have often been denied. Yet, bildungsroman it also touches on other archetypal themes and figures – particularly the hero's journey (as a potential), and the entanglement of parental past (mother/father) and romantic present (anima/animus) which dominate Theme 2.

Bildungsroman and The Child Archetype

As a genre, Bildungsroman – the story of growing up, either in its literary of cinematic form, has traditionally focused on the male protagonist, with

DOI: 10.4324/9781003253044-5

female characters often used as props in the male drama. The *Dictionary of Critical Theory* defines Bildungsroman as:

> A sub-genre of novel focusing on the personal development of the pro-tagonist, usually from childhood through to adulthood. The prototype is J. W. Goethe's Wilhelm Meisters Lehrjarhre (Willhelm Meister's Appren-ticeship, 1795–6), but the form was widely adopted in Europe throughout the 19th century. [...] the development is not merely personal, inasmuch as it generally takes the form of both a move away from rural origins towards the modern city and an upward movement from one social class to another. In this regard, the personal history can be read as an allegory of a particular trajectory within a national history.
>
> (Buchanan, 2010)

Bildungsroman normally follows a young man's trials and tribulations as he matures, learns about his powers and limitations, learns to understand society and to obey its laws, and, eventually, becomes integrated into it. Issues of social status and class inevitably underlie this genre because, ultimately, the protagonist has ambitions and wants to achieve a position of visibility in society. Charles Dickens's *Great Expectations* is a classic example of this narrative: a poor boy called Pip falls in love with a privileged young woman Estella, inherits some money and becomes a gentleman; then loses his wealth, and eventually learns to leave within his means while building a more realistic relationship with Estella.

Film and television favour this genre because it offers opportunities to explore an unblemished world of a young person, with their hopes, dreams and first (often cruel) disappointments. Bildungsroman works in a number of genres and formats. For instance, it can explore the emergence of a young superhero: *The Adventures of Young Indiana Jones* 1994–99, created and directed by George Lucas; the *Spiderman* franchise; the *Harry Potter* franchise, and more recently, Netflix's *Stranger Things* (2016–), created by the Duffer brothers. It can also take darker undertones and explore social realities and inequalities, such as John Singleton's social drama *Boyz n the Hood* (1991), Richard Linklater's *Boyhood* (2014), and Shane Meadows' *This is England* (2006).

Coming of age is an interesting, exciting yet dangerous part of the indivi-duation process when a young person learns about the world and plans their future. It is mainly focused on the theme of self-actualization and centres around the archetype of the child – the present prodigy, the future hero. Although 'at first sight it may seem like a retrospective configuration', in the psychology of the individual the child motif signifies 'anticipation of future developments' (Jung, CW 9/I: para. 278).

Jung is keen to emphasize that the child motif has nothing to do with rea-lity as such, actual or psychological; it has nothing to do with the Freudian personal complexes, but is rather a generic metaphorical imprint for the feelings of trying to find (or restore) one's unique self. Having its imprint in the collective unconscious, the image is 'not a copy of the empirical child but a *symbol* clearly recognizable as such: it is a wonder child, a divine child, begotten, born, and brought up in quite extraordinary circumstances... [...]. Its deeds are as miraculous or monstrous as its nature or physical constitution' (Jung CW9/I: para. 273 cf). The motif has its stock elements, which include abandonment or neglect, supernatural qualities or prodigious abilities, having two sets of parents (human and divine), vulnerability and uniqueness (Jung, CW 9/I: paras. 281–282).

Bildungsroman shares with the child archetype the themes of awe and wonder in anticipation of future adventures. The child works out how to use their agency, at first uncontrollable, and to make its power and direction compatible with society. Alternatively, the child is so special and powerful, their skills so magical, that they are above society's rules and expectations. As a genre, Bildungsroman has traditionally been male-dominated while young female characters, with a few exceptions discussed later in the chapter, were not expected to display miraculous skills, have supernatural abilities, to have ambitions, to overcome difficulties, or to display a fascinating combination of weaknesses and strengths. Bildungsroman implies emergence, as well as recognition, management and acceptance, of one's voice and agency, reflected in the metaphorical struggles of the child figure. The maturation narrative of being unusual, a prodigy, or a weirdo, or having dubious or potentially dangerous abilities (such as turning things you touch into ice), does not fit in with societal expectations for a woman whose worth is contained in her ability (and willingness) to be a hearth-keeper – someone available, someone exuding warmth, someone looking after the physical and emotional needs of others.

Rather echoing the psychoanalytic concept of the Electra complex which suggests that the girl's maturation process is channelled via identification with the (passive) mother and linked to the realization of one's 'lack', the existing examples of literary and cinematic female bildungsroman, with a few exceptions such as George Eliot's *The Mill on the Floss* (1860), have focused either on the refusal to grow up (*Alice's Adventures in Wonderland* (1865), *Through the Looking Glass* (1871), *Pippi Longstocking* (1945)) or on the monstrous feminine inversely reflecting the horrors of being female in the world built for men. The latter was already expressing itself in various nineteenth-century Gothic texts such as Charlotte Bronte's *Jane Eyre* (1847).

In the second half of the twentieth century, cinematic representations of 'becoming a woman' in particular have centred on the horrors of the lack – on female reproductive system and its functions – leaving the female child's futurity with limited choices as to self-expression, creativity or psychological development. This kind of Bildungsroman has been firmly rooted in surrealism and horror, which distorted the young women's development or infused it with dark tones. William Friedkin's *Exorcist* and Brian de Palma's *Carrie* (and the more recent Kimberly Peirce's adaptation (2013)) represent growing up as a terrifying liminal experience during which the protagonist loses control of her body and mind.

Questions of identity, psychological changes and normal biological processes become the sites of shame and horror as the young female protagonist finds herself out of control of her life and destiny, lacking in agency that has not been afforded to her by ideological structures underpinning her society. Commenting on Brian de Palma's *Carrie*, David Greven notes that the director emphasizes his characters' 'position in patriarchy, affirms and identifies with their desire to transgress against its structures, especially in matters of sexuality…' (Greven, 2011: 92). Similarly, *The Exorcist,* as a failed coming-of-age narrative, depicts a violent and bloody rejection of reality that goes beyond transgressive. Focalization is usurped by the representatives of the Symbolic, and the female monster is eventually forced to concede with societal rules for women. The exorcism is performed by the Symbolic to tame the demonic feminine principle.

The horror elements in the female Bildungsroman reflect both the projected fear of castration, and its rejection by the carrier of the projection. The young female initiating into the Lacanian Symbolic gradually realizes that not only she is going to deemed 'not whole', 'an empty signifier' with nowhere to go, but also judged on her ability to wear the mask of femininity. Quite correctly (rather than excessively), the horror versions of the female Bindungsroman depict the rage of the teenage girl violently rejecting the mask, and destroying (or attempting to destroy) the order in which their destiny is to be a fixed signifier, forever waiting to be filled with meaning.

From the post-Jungian perspective, whenever the heroine is presented as the monstrous mother or anima – the negative side of the archetype – she is essentially locked in Theme 2. As a secondary or tertiary character she is an obstacle on the male protagonist's path. When she moves to Theme 3 and becomes the 'dark child' – usually the protagonist – her agency is still judged negatively, her developmental trajectory curtailed, and her abilities condemned by society. She is ostracized and expected to be cured into conformity. To an extent, this is in line with male versions of the dark child, including the bloody doll of the *Chucky* franchise (1988–), the teenage killer from *We Need to Talk about Kevin* (2011) or Tim Burton's *Vincent* (1994) and *Edward Scissorhands* (1990). Yet, the female versions of the horrible child also seem to be more intense, and created more in response to society's perception of the female futurity, as a sort of anticipation of the exclusive mother/wife role from which a girl cannot escape no matter how hard she tries.

Luckily, in recent years the female Bildungsroman has been detaching itself from the horror genre and taking a variety of forms, including animation, fantasy and realism; feature length films, mini-series and even lengthy fantasy drama. The heroines of the new Bildungsroman still have the rage and still fight against what Lacan calls 'being excluded by the nature of things' – but they also confidently survive their social context, challenge their assigned social status, and protest their prescribed roles. They utilize the archetypal powers of the child image to carve out their own path. They have their own – imperfect and often meandering – journey, they make mistakes, they get hurt and they hurt in return. In other words, the female initiand is finally able to mature beyond the Electra complex, and to challenge the very structures that insisted that following in the footsteps of the passive mother is simply 'the nature of things'.

Essentially, bildungsroman is about the boundary between the personal and the social in the individuation process; it is about becoming yourself while also learning to wear a social mask – and fine-tuning the persona to the newly-found identity. The cultural expectations of the female persona, meanwhile, presuppose that an authentic identity in a woman is unnecessary – or, at least, should remain invisible. The challenge for the female bildungsroman then would be to restore the balance between the personal and the social in female individuation; to create narratives in which the female child would learn to find this balance without altogether sacrificing the search for the authentic self.

The protagonists in this latest ensemble of female Bindungsroman narratives have a range of options beyond the second archetypal theme (family creation). For instance, both in *Ladybird* and *The Queen's Gambit* the ending is open, leaving the young women with no conclusive partner choice, thus refocusing the narrative on self-actualization, creativity and personal achievement rather than romantic or sexual choices. Although present, these choices (along with the second theme of the anima/animus) do not dominate the narrative and merely constitute a portion of the journey. The protagonists confidently enter the Lacanian Symbolic while rejecting its requirements for women: to compensate the supposed lack with a baby. Yet, they survive and thrive, and the audience is left guessing as to their plans to have a family at all.

Finally, the focus of female Bildungsroman is not on the abject, and not on motherhood as the final destination either. It is not about having a child. Rather, it is about being the child - a special child, planning one's future, dreaming, despairing, and making mistakes. Importantly, it is also about being the future hero who has 'somewhere to go' instead of being 'already there' (to use Campbell's expression).

Disney's Female Bildungsroman

The new generation of Disney's female leading characters – Merida in *Brave* (Disney/Pixar, 2012), Elsa in *Frozen* (2013–) Moana (*Moana*, 2016), the protagonists of *Raya and the Last Dragon* (2021), *Cruella* (2021), *Encanto* (2021) and *Turning Red* (2022) – is markedly different from the traditional Disney princess with her fixed maturation and individuation path which inevitably leads to finding a 'perfect' partner (e.g., Cinderella or Snow White). The new heroine goes on adventures, gets into trouble, doubts herself, and, importantly, has a dark side which she explores and with which she attempts to reconcile. While she gets help on the way, it does not come in the form of a handsome prince.

In fact, neither of the narratives end in finding a partner, or are even focused on looking for one. While the protagonists do learn to compromise with their surroundings and acknowledge the importance of others, it does not at all mean not exploring the various options open to them as individuands (and as individuals). All the narratives discussed further in this chapter employ different archetypes to accompany the girls on their respective individuation routes – a welcome diversion from the single-track story of waiting to be saved/collected by a prince on a white horse.

Brave *(2012)*

Brave is one of the fresher, more unusual narrative canvasses that emerged in film and television over the past decade. Its coming-of-age thread has themes of growing out of parental influence and finding one's unique voice; a combination of Themes 2 (particularly the Mother archetypal theme) and 3 (the Child and the Hero). The combination of the Mother, the Child and the Hero create a thread which effectively questions the necessity for a teenage girl to learn to wear a social mask (in narratives with a male protagonist the theme of adjustment is usually dealt using elements of Theme 1 – the Shadow and the Trickster).

Merida (voiced by Kelly Macdonald) is a flame-haired, wild girl, living in make-believe Medieval Scotland. She excels at archery, loves adventure and enjoys horse riding and rock-climbing. The story opens with her enjoying her carefree childhood, misbehaving and breaking gender norms unaware of her mother's plans to have her married off to an heir of one of the neighbouring clans. Her mother Elinor (Emma Thompson) is a true persona-wearing lady: the keeper of the peace, the wisdom of the house, and the preserver of 'proper' feminine behaviour. Merida is none of these, but Elinor is keen to teach her the ways of the mask: singing, dancing, poetry-reciting, sewing, and calming a hall full of drunken men.

While pseudo-Medieval male characters are allowed to live without the mask and behave the way they want, the character of Merida is constrained by her mother to Theme 2 which means that she will be passed on from the parental home to the home of her husband. Thus, she will lose out on the adventures associated with other themes: going on a journey, struggling with one's internal darkness, discovering one's inner voice, becoming a rebel or experiencing the liminal turmoil while her life is on hold. Persona-building functions are about prohibition, restraint and shame – they are about introducing the word 'no' into the world of an otherwise carefree child. They are meant to limit the individual's narcissistic impulses and to direct the developing personality towards communal goals. Usually represented by the Trickster and the Shadow, the impulses need to be tamed lest they overwhelm the individual – and destroy the social order.

In the course of her education into the female persona, Merida is constantly told that 'a princess should not raise her voice' or 'place her weapons on the table' (or even not to have weapons at all). She should be 'compassionate, patient, cautious, clean, and, above all, a princess strives for perfection'. The mask of perfection is supposed to cover Merida's boisterous, curious personality until it becomes so heavy and thick that it suffocates this personality completely.

On the day when the clan heirs compete for her hand, Merida is made to put on an uncomfortably tight corset and a headdress which restrain her beautiful red hair. Both quite explicitly represent the female persona and would make it difficult for her to do anything adventurous. The dress, constructed to encourage passivity and to induce 'a modest consciousness of [her] authentic condition', it is here to arrest Merida's development as an individual (De Beauvoir, 2011: 205). Luckily, her personality (and the will to individuate on her own terms) prevail, and the princess tears off the restrictive corset and the headdress, grabs her bow and arrow and announces that she is going to shoot for her own hand. She then proceeds to hit every target better than any of the heirs. The female persona is a construct so rigid that it is not even allowed an imprint of the shadow/trickster stage, the natural moment of personal struggles, and proceeds straight into Theme 2 (parental issues and marriage). By rejecting the persona publicly, Merida refuses to be 'docile to threaten men's work', and to limit herself 'to enriching and softening of their too sharp edges' (De Beauvoir, 2010: 204).

What Merida deserves is to go through the same developmental stages as a male character would in a bildungsroman: to meet with the shadow, or to deal with a trickster. In other words, she should be allowed to grapple with her own inner darkness, to learn to tame one's antisocial traits, to assert her personality, and learn to negotiate with the system. She should be able to build the social mask naturally instead of being issued with one that is supposed to fit the entire womanhood.

In *Brave*, Merida is given this opportunity when she runs into the woods and encounters a witch who makes her an enchanted cake, which would later turn Elinor into a bear. By feeding it to the mother, Merida expresses her shadow side. Without learning about this side of herself, she cannot graduate from the child to the hero; or, indeed, to formulate a persona that goes beyond the one-fits-all template of the mask of femininity. The shadow needs to be acknowledged and then integrated, its power harvested lest it becomes repressed, pushed into the unconscious, and later turns into something uncontrollable (Jacobi, 1973: 110). An encounter with the shadow does not just affect the persona – it also 'runs parallel to the development of the ego' (Jacobi, 1973: 110). In fact, this difficult encounter helps the individual develop an understanding of the precarious balance between one's conscious personality (the ego) and social requirements (persona). By giving her mother the poisoned cake, Merida makes this process happen, unaware of the challenges ahead and the damage this act can inflict on her family.

Once Merida's adventure starts, the character of Elinor becomes dissolved in the numinosity of the mother archetype, and reborn as a spectrum of mothers: the bear (wild, brutal, clumsy, terrified, or the fearless mother bear ready to fight to protect her cubs), the old witch in the forest who is linked to the mother archetype via her hobby of carving bear figures out of wood, and the internalized oppressive mother that needs to be destroyed, cut off, or, at the very least, challenged and reformulated via a compromise with reality.

In her numinous incarnations, Elinor embodies the dual nature of the mother archetype which can appear to the protagonist as a helpful woman or a wicked witch, and can symbolize now 'wisdom and spiritual exaltation' and 'helpful instinct and impulse that ... cherishes and sustains', and now 'anything secret, hidden, dark; the abyss, the world of the dead, anything that devours, seduces and poisons' (Jung, CW9 I: para. 158). The mother is ambivalent as she is both 'the loving and the terrible mother' (Jung, CW9/I: para. 158).

Both the mother and the shadow are important milestones on Merida's individuation path. Both are necessary for her maturation and development as a hero. The fact that Elinor is perceived by the princess as a destructive force, acts as a motivating impulse on her individuation path. Coupled with the shadow, the negative mother serves a good purpose. The Jungian analyst and writer Clarissa Pincola Estes notes in *Women Who Run with The Wolves* (1992), that the 'too-good mother' offers no advancement for the female psyche. Estes points out that in traditional narratives the death of the good mother and a subsequent trip into the woods (albeit a forced one because the girl is sent there by her envious, evil stepmother and/or stepsisters), is, in fact, a positive event in the life of the female protagonist. As an example, she uses the Russian fairy tale about the young woman Vasilissa whose mother dies at the beginning of the narrative, and who ends up visiting Baba Yaga (in Slavic folklore, Baba Yaga is the goddess of death living in a hovel which stands on chicken legs) (Estes, 1992: 81–82).

One of the trials on the female questor's path, the old woman symbolizes the power of the wild as well as tests her guest's survival ability. A frequent feature of Eastern European fairy tales, an old goddess whose power is unmitigated by patriarchal structures, actually points out at the necessity and ability of the individual to be resourceful and resilient. A heroine, thus, should be 'able to stand the face of the fearsome Wild Goddess without wavering' (Estes, 1992: 81–82). The goddess of death challenging the protagonist on her journey is therefore necessary for the individuation process to advance. What a female looking at the prospect of individuation and determining her position in society really needs is some form of rejection, a lack of acceptance, a weakness in the bond between mother and child:

> In the natural process of our maturing, the too-good mother must become thinner and thinner, must dwindle away until we are left to care for ourselves in a new way. While we always retain a core of her warmth

this natural psychic transition leaves us on our own in a world that is not motherly to us. [...]

Vasalisa's [sic] initiation begins with learning to let die what must die. This means to let die the values within the psyche which no longer sustain her. Especially to be examined are those long-held tenets which make life too safe, which overprotect, which make women walk with a scurry instead of a stride.

(Estes, 1992: 81–82)

In *Brave* the role of the goddess of death is performed by the bear-carving witch (Julie Walters) who lives in a small hut in the woods. Alongside the bear/oppressive matriarch, she is one of the several negative incarnations of the mother archetype whose qualities prompt the protagonist into the survival mode and motivate her to find answers to her own identity questions. An understanding and accepting mother would not necessarily lead Merida, the female initiand, far from the parental home, improve her as a human being, or assist her in her journey of self-discovery.

Merida's reaction to the 'bad mother' challenge goes beyond the motif of the poor girl/evil stepmother pairing which traditionally ends with the poor girl being saved by a prince – Cinderella and Snow White in the Western canon, numerous hapless female protagonists in other folklore canons, such as Nastenka in the Russian traditional tale 'Morozko'. As a rule, early Disney films did not attempt to change the original power balance of traditional fairy tales. Neither Snow White nor Cinderella is given an opportunity to individuate, or to make decisions as to their destiny. Instead, both are victims of evil matriarchs, and both are waiting for a prince to save them from their misfortune. Both are poor, used as servants, and dream of improving their social status by marrying a handsome aristocrat. Both are slim, their feminine figure emphasized by pretty dresses. Both have a similar combination of character traits: they are modest, patient, optimistic, naive, graceful, kind, gentle, caring and maternal, bashful, elegant, hard-working, empathic, and fragile looking. They are also willing to forever tolerate abuse and – referring to Freud's assumptions about 'female masochism' – almost seem to enjoy their misfortunes. In other words, they have wonderful female personas consisting of a rather contradictory combination of fragility, resolve and willingness to be ruled and directed.

Interestingly enough, both are presented as resourceful, skilful and capable, but neither of these abilities and qualities help them climb up the social ladder. In both cases, their feminine qualities are rewarded with a heightened social status and wealth. Neither have a real agency, vision of the future beyond marriage, or aspirations outside of being modest and kind. Their status is lowered by women, and raised by men. The other women in the tale are hostile and lack feminine qualities, and their roughness (e.g., large feet which cannot accommodate pretty shoes) is juxtaposed with the delicateness of the heroine.

In Disney's history of hapless heroines whose stories ended with finding a prince, Merida is different, and she paved the way for other proactive female protagonists such as Moana. Instead of being the victim, meek and submissive, she stands up for herself, even if this means unleashing her own shadow with all the unintended consequences. In fact, Merida's shadow is the very element that advances her individuation and breaks through the power of tradition (and the power of the mother). At the start of the film Merida is watching her father, the clan guests and her little brothers 'get away with murder' – behave in ways that are risky and messy; get into fights and enjoy horseplay, compete, be rough, and eat and drink too much. Meanwhile, she is told to watch her behaviour and to be 'clean' whereby her persona is maintained by suppressing the shadow. By releasing the shadow and rejecting the persona, Merida makes mistakes and hurts people around her – but this is the only way to break free from the chains of tradition and to escape the prison that is the female persona.

Moana

Disney seems to be stuck with the royalty trope, but at least they try to change the protagonist's destiny. Much like Merida, Moana and the princesses from the Frozen franchise, Elsa and Anna, are allowed to exercise their agency and find their own path instead of relying on tradition or waiting for a man to guide or save them.

Moana's path is that of heroism and adventure, and the principal archetype leading her is the trickster represented by the Polynesian trickster and culture hero Maui. She is a chief's daughter who travels across the sea to retrieve the heart of the goddess Te Fiti. The heart was originally stolen by Maui who was then attacked by Te Ka, the demon of earth and fire. They clash and the heart sinks to the bottom of the sea. Moana's task is revive her home island by finding the heart, replacing it and bringing the goddess back to life.

Much like in *Brave*, the use of Theme 1 in the female bildungsroman is remarkable as the archetypes inhabiting this theme are usually the ones breaking or challenging the social order. For instance, the shadow may make the protagonist explore her anger (like it does in *Brave*) and become destructive. The shadow also encourages the character to openly break social codes and even turn into a monster or sabotage the entire social order. Both options often happen in male-led narratives such as Stevenson's *The Strange Case of Dr. Jekyll and Mr. Hyde* and its many cinematic renditions, and *Fight Club* in which Tyler Durden (Brad Pitt) talks the unnamed protagonist (Edward Norton) into undermining the capitalist system. The presence of the shadow or trickster element signals the acknowledgement of the gap between one's identity and persona, between the ego and the mask. It also demonstrates the presence of the conflict between the individual and the social in human beings; a conflict that is always present, that will never be resolved and that is often explored in creative works. Male protagonists like Walter White (Brian Cranston) in TV series *Breaking Bad* (2008–2013) can take as many as five seasons to be converted by their shadow into a sociopath.

Yet, this gap has not been properly explored for female characters. Traditional narratives automatically assume that the woman has no issues with wearing the female persona, and would not rebel against it. Openly evil female characters (like witches or stepmothers) are often shown as already belonging to the 'dark side' rather than grappling with a complex moral dilemma. Female protagonists who disobey and rebel against the mask – like the Red or Blue Woman discussed in the previous chapter – are told by society that venturing outside the prescribed boundaries is too dangerous for a female, and may result in being ostracized or murdered.

Both the trickster and the shadow have been traditionally avoided in depiction of female characters, probably because they challenge the persona too much. A woman merging with the trickster or displaying trickster qualities (further discussed in Chapter 6) is breaking a whole range of taboos and blatantly ignoring the prescribed social mask. In both traditional and cinematic narratives, tricksters are often shameless and lewd characters who like to have sex and are not particularly picky about who they have it with (like Jim Carrey's *Ace Ventura in Ace Ventura: Pet Detective* (Tom Shadyac, 1994) and *Ace Ventura: When Nature Calls* (Steve Oedekerk, 1995)), are dishonest and unscrupulous to the point of being criminals (Randall Patrick McMurphy (Jack Nicholson) in *One Flew Over the Cuckoo's Nest* (Milos Forman, 1975)), are creative in a messy way (Mozart (Tom Hulce) in *Amadeus* (Milos Forman, 1984)), and break boundaries accidentally or deliberately, embarrassing everyone around (Beetlejuice (Michael Keaton) in Tim Burton's *Beetlejuice* (1988)). Trickster and shadow characters behave as if social norms do not exist – a direct contradiction with the very principle of the female persona, which is all about supporting the social order. Challenging and changing the order of things, or exploring the dark side, has traditionally been the domain of male characters while female ones were expected to stick to admiring or supporting them (Melissa (Courney Cox) in *Ace Ventura: Pet Detective*), or, alternatively, to be disgusted by their darkness. Walter's wife Skyler (Anna Gunn) alternately does both throughout the five seasons of *Breaking Bad*.

In *Moana*, the darkness is relegated to the volcanic demon Te Ka, and is not particularly explored as part of Moana's identity. It is later revealed that the demon is Te Fiti's shadow, which disappears when Moana restores her heart. The shadow is caused directly by the trickster's irresponsible actions. The assault on Te Fiti and the birth of the shadow constitute the side-lined Theme 2 of the narrative. Meanwhile, Moana is on the quest to save the earth Goddess from her own dark side and meets Maui who helps her discover her inner strength in this dangerous task.

In many ways, Maui is a typical trickster: unreliable, boastful, blundering, irresponsible, messily creative, unaware of any boundaries and limitations, stupidly confident, a thief and a shapeshifter. The trickster archetype is about the stubborn ability to display and sustain agency against all odds; against the backdrop of a restrictive social order. Moana's 'call to adventure' can be traced back to Maui's actions as a thief when he steals Te Fiti's heart. Her suffering leads to the island's demise and makes Moana to believe that she is the one who can restore peace and prosperity.

In the original Polynesian tales, Maui has all the hallmarks of a typical trickster. He can turn into insects and birds. He steals fish from his brothers and claims that it is his catch. He repeatedly visits the underworld for various reasons. He is reckless and does not recognize his physical limitations: he disrespects death, engulfs the sun, and separates the sky and earth, creating an inhabitable world. Importantly, his immense creativity, energy and ambition result in various innovations for mankind: a number of legends recall the discovery of fire by Maui which only happens thanks to his resilience and determination. He also invents the kite and learns to control the winds (Westervelt, n.d.). Maui combines antisocial behaviour and bravery in his quest to bring inventions to the people.

Moana does not have to start embodying the trickster's duality in order to be inspired by his power. She takes from Maui all that she needs in order to explore and express her agency: she crosses the boundary she is told would be difficult to cross (goes beyond the island's reef), and borrows some of the trickster's recklessness, wit, optimism and creativity. Armed with these new qualities, Moana becomes determined and creative, which helps her confront the burning demon Te Ka. Maui fights alongside her, a separate yet acknowledged and integrated psychological entity whose powers can be harvested for personal and communal advancement.

Many tricksters are also culture heroes, assembling cultural elements and passing on knowledge to the people. This seems paradoxical given the antisocial nature of the trickster. Yet, it makes sense as the trickster guards the culture's ability to renew itself, helping the community survive in the changing world. Thanks to Maui, Moana becomes adaptable and learns to find the way out in difficult situations. Importantly, the trickster figure is allowed to be a significant part of the female bildungsroman, unencumbered by the usual cultural demands that a female protagonist remains passive, prudent, or risk-averse.

The Frozen Franchise

Much like *Brave* (less so Moana which follows a pretty standard tale of a hero saving an oppressed female goddess), *Frozen* rethinks the destiny of the female protagonist by integrating a shadow into her personality and then learning to manage it. Inspired by Hans Christian Andersen's tale, 'The Snow Queen' (1844), *Frozen* is story of Princess Elsa, the future queen of the kingdom Arendelle. Elsa has the magical ability to create snow and ice and to freeze objects and people. Elsa is very aware of the danger her skill poses to others as she remembers inadvertently hurting her little sister during a horse-play. Elsa's 'cursed powers' present both beauty and danger. In order to limit their effect, and to protect herself and people around her, she has to wear gloves. Another misfortune follows: Elsa and her sister Anna lose their parents to a sea storm and learn to live on their own – a motif that often accompanies the child archetype. Tied to a child figure in narratives, the abandonment motif prompts the young protagonist's individuation process.

Frozen differs significantly from the original 'Snow Queen' story. The Queen in Anderson's tale does not have a name, only a title; she is a prop in the individuation of the male character while his female companion acts as a secondary protagonist. The story itself centres around the friendship of two children, Kay and Gerda, whose bond is suddenly broken when a tiny splint from Snow Queen's magic mirror finds its way into Kay's eye and freezes his heart. The mirror makes Kay become snappy and lose the ability to see beauty in the world. Primed by the Snow Queen to become cold and une-motional, he is then kidnapped by her. Gerda is determined to save her friend, and after many adventures she arrives at the Queen's palace and defrosts Kay's heart.

Archetypally, the tale is focused on the rather Oedipal version of Theme 2 – dependence on and separation from the parents and learning to be with a partner. It also showcases the female co-protagonist who is brave enough to confront and conquer the mother while the focus of her efforts remains pas-sive in a palace far away, waiting to be rescued. The Queen herself possesses the requisite ambivalence of the mother archetype: she is an empty vessel for projections, a sketch, and is simultaneously caring and cruel, attractive and destructive. She looks after Kay and wraps fur around him to keep him warm as they are travelling in her sledge, but she also unleashes snowstorms and has no heart.

The Queen is as beautiful as she is frightening, and Kay is fascinated by her perfection as he is watching her emerge out of a snowflake through the window: 'The flake of snow grew larger and larger, and at last it was like a young lady, dressed in the finest gauze, made of a million little flakes like stars. She was so beautiful and delicate, but she was of ice, of dazzling, sparkling ice; yet she lived; her eyes gazed fixedly, like two stars, but there was neither quiet nor repose in them' (Andersen, 2012).

As the mother figure and potential partner fight over Kay's destiny (and his heart), their power is presented as a categorical set of opposites: the Queen's magic is injurious and narcissistic, cold and dangerous, while Gerda's empa-thy and unequivocal love saves the day. The Snow Queen resides in a 'resplendent' remote palace with a hundred halls, 'all lighted by the powerful Aurora Borealis' (Anderson, 2012). It is all mathematical perfection and pre-cision, with no joy, warmth or emotional connection. The Queen is sitting in the Mirror of Understanding, which looks like a frozen lake (Anderson, 2012). Made to play with pieces of ice, Kay is dying from cold in the palace until he is saved by Gerda's warm embrace and 'burning' tears (Anderson, 2012). Between the two extremes personified by female characters, and despite Gerda's bravery and resilience, the balance is still on the side of the female persona with its implications of sacrifice, victimhood, unequivocal empathy and tolerance. The shadow belongs entirely to the Snow Queen.

Frozen's treatment of Theme 2 is unusual for a female-led narrative in that it does not constitute the central problem for the protagonist – i.e., she is not an anima, a mother, is not looking for a prince and is not being passed on from one house to the next one. Instead, Theme 2 merely becomes the background to Themes 1 and 3 and allows them to blossom – the child-hero growing up, finding her voice and dealing with the shadow within. Elsa and Anna's parents die at sea, establishing one of the multiple versions of the 'abandonment' motif, which is a precursor for the child's strength and independence. Whereas some analyses of *Frozen* have used the post-Freudian paradigm to examine Elsa's coldness towards men, it would actually be more useful to focus on her individuation as well as her ambition and creativity rather than romantic and sexual interests. The primary cluster of issues she encounters in her individuation process belongs to the shadow rather than the animus/anima. This shift of focus from Theme 2 (parents and lovers) onto Theme 1 (the shadow) is also what makes Disney's version different from the original tale. Although *Frozen II* further develops Theme 2 in the form of 'parental curse' (King Agnarr and Queen Iduna's tribes used to be at war; Anna's magical abilities have to do with this split), the main focus is still on the protagonist's motivation, self-discovery, and the shadow.

The shadow in *Frozen* is linked to Elsa's search for identity, or even for the (Jungian) self. The original Snow Queen is the shadowy-negative mother and nothing else, which makes her rival look angelic. In *Frozen*, Elsa is given the Snow Queen's powers while Anna gets Gerda's inner strength, passion, and survival skills. Neither set of qualities is praised or demonized. The gilt about possessing the power – and possessing the shadow – is replaced with the call to explore and celebrate it while, refreshingly, empathy and love are not foregrounded as essentially female properties and integral elements of the female persona. Neither Elsa nor Anna follows in the footsteps of Disney's traditional patient and virtuous princesses. As a result, the narrative encourages the protagonist (and those watching the film) to build the persona naturally, by integrating the shadow rather than negating it or burying it under a rigid mask.

Traditionally, a female character is not allowed to be antisocial or narcissistic – to display any kind of struggle with the shadow; or even elements of the shadow. In female characters, the shadow is usually split into the figure of a witch or a stepmother, it is not integrated; it occupies the entire character. Women can either be entirely good (and wearing the female persona) or entirely bad (and ignoring societal rules). A female character is either solely the shadow, or she is perfect. By contrast, the male shadow is allowed to be explored as part of the protagonist's maturation process, its acknowledgement and acceptance integral to the individuation loop.

Elsa is terrified of her own powers because she knows that without the female persona, she will be regarded as evil – much like generations of evil queens in traditional narratives (many of whom have been replicated by Disney). Her first public display of power happens when she becomes angry with Anna at the coronation after-party, and creates a wall of ice, shocking her guests and prompting accusations of 'sorcery'. Elsa's fear of her own emotions are informed by cultural cues such as the misogynistic approach to the female shadow. One either hides it, or one is the witch. Her intuition is right – she is branded an evil sorceress by the Duke of Weselton immediately after she loses her temper, and is later on ordered to be killed by him. Essentially, the moment she lets the persona slip, she needs to be destroyed.

She is so terrified of her own abilities that she runs away. Alone in her ice castle, she sings 'Let It Go' which essentially explores the conflict between the shadow and the female persona: on the one hand, it is hard to control one's affective state, such as rage, which feels like trying to 'control storm' and 'control the curse'. On the other, genuine, 'unladylike', powerful expressions of affect in women are seen as disturbing by society and are erased from social protocols. As Elsa puts it in the song, maintaining the female persona can be summarised as a prohibition to feel. Dundes et al. argue that Elsa is powerful because 'her conflicts are no tempest in a teapot, as befits a woman' (Dundes et al., 2018: 11).

Yet, individuation is not about maintaining a mask without understanding its principles or accepting at least some of them. Individuation involves developing a functional mask and learning to relate in meaningful ways. According to Jung, the urge to individuate is the urge to self-reflect (Jung, CW11: para. 401). Individuation is conscious listening to the inner voice (Jung, CW 17: para. 308). Yet, rejecting the persona to sustain the inner voice does not in itself comprise an individuation process – this is individualism. The 'communal' individuation component is supported in the narrative by Anna who (much like Gerda in the original tale) drags the protagonist out of the pit of self-isolation and teaches her to relate to others. In the culmination scene Anna sacrifices herself to save her sister from Hans, and turns into a frozen statue. Elsa's tears offer the solution to the persona/identity dichotomy. They become the connecting, empathic, human element, the missing bridge between the individual and the social in human beings.

Frozen II (2019) goes even further in expanding the female individuation process and in offering the female protagonist an identity that is in conflict with social norms; the same right male protagonists have been afforded for centuries – discovering one's voice, going on an adventure, searching for the self, and learning to maintain the balance between the persona and one's interests. In the second instalment of the franchise, Elsa hears the mysterious voice repeatedly calling her – the very metaphor of Jung's inner voice calling one to go on a journey of self-discovery.

Having incorporated the shadow and learned to master her powerful ice-making abilities, Elsa is summoned to solve the mystery of her ancestors and to manage the spirits of the Enchanted Forest. The voice of her mother Iduna calling her to an adventure can also be interpreted as the voice of the self, the uniting feature of the psyche. At the end of the story, she saves Arendelle from flooding and becomes the protector of the Enchanted Forest, leaving Anna to govern the kingdom. Anna has been afforded a proper individuation process leading her from a strict persona to rebellion, and, eventually, to uniting her own interests and abilities with communal and societal require-ments, and using them for the common good. This can be seen as a victory in terms of representation of female protagonists who are usually expected to unequivocally display communal behaviour without any agentic elements involved. They are not allowed to follow a trajectory that allows them to explore the tenuous relationship between the individual and society.

The *Frozen* franchise plays with decades of Disney's narrative traditions when Anna falls in love with prince Hans and decides to marry him after they sing a song together ('Love is an Open Door'). This had been the standard individua-tion ending for generations of Disney princesses whose journey ended abruptly because love (and marital union with a man) was presented as the pinnacle of female achievement. Her sister explains to her that she cannot marry a man she has just met. With her other love interest, Kristoff, Anna seemingly has a power balance. He is not at all taken aback by her display of decisiveness and bravery. At the end of *Frozen,* Anna also gifts him a new sleigh (read: a car), the kind of gift that is traditionally given by men to women.

Yet, even though many of the narrative stereotypes are self-referentially dismantled in *Frozen*, some of the visual representational conventions still remain. As Rudloff notes, the sister's dresses are still conventionally tight and emphasize slender figures, tiny waists and slim wrists. With their large eyes, the princesses resemble the childlike characters of Japanese manga. Their features are exaggerated in order to convey this childlikeness (Rudloff, 2016).

Meanwhile, male characters, particularly Kristoff, are visually styled as stereotypical men: tall and broad-shouldered in contrast to the slenderness of Anna's build. Predictably, the visual inevitably feeds into the textual as, despite her bravery, Anna still ends up being a 'damsel in distress', locked by Hans in a room and waiting to be saved by a prince (Rudloff, 2016). As such, *Frozen* is both a site of disruption and maintenance of gender stereotypes (Rudloff, 2016).

Industry insiders' stereotypical views on gender representation do not help to improve diversity of narratives on screen. For instance, *Frozen*'s head of animation, Lino DiSalvo, once mentioned that female characters are notor-iously difficult to animate because, apparently, they need to remain pretty in the process of expressing their emotions (Mesure and Lewin, 2013).

Some of the character features attributed to Anna specifically may be said to counter the standard prettiness of her face: she is clumsy, messy and outspoken, often tripping and falling instead of daintily watching her step, and often embarrassing herself when she is supposed to wear a solid persona (such as when she is standing next to her sister during the coronation ceremony). Yet, there is still a dichotomy between the narrative and the visual representation of female characters in *Frozen*: they both end up – playfully (Anna) or violently (Elsa) resisting the female persona yet replicating the standard look of femininity: tight dresses, full make-up and pretty hair. More likely, this conflict is at the heart of the ageing entertainment giants who emancipate their heroines gradually, by making them individuate via 'difficult' archetypes such as the shadow and the trickster while still keeping them slim, pretty, and childlike.

Encanto *(2021)*

The protagonist of *Encanto,* Mirabel Madrigal (voiced by Stephanie Beatritz), is born into a family of prodigies. Her grandparents, parents and siblings all possess a superhero quality, such as the ability to make weather, to shapeshift, to communicate with animals, or to lift very heavy objects. Their abilities are revealed to them on a special day, and the joyful news are shared with the entire community. On Miranda's 'gift-revealing' day, however, nothing happens. It turns out she is the odd one out in her family, an ordinary person untouched by magic. This leads to her being treated as deficient, and sometimes shut out of family celebrations.

The matriarch of the house, grandmother Alma Madrigal (voiced by María Cecilia Botero) is particularly concerned about Miranda's lack of magical abilities as this constitutes a public relations issue – after all, the family is regarded by the community as special and therefore much respected and admired. This respect and admiration put a lot of pressure on the matriarch, and her wards who constantly have to prove their worth to others. After a while, some of the repressed and neglected issues begin to emerge – metaphorized as physical cracks in the Casa Madrigal. One of these repressed issues is Uncle Bruno (voiced by John Leguizamo) who has to hide in the basement because his gift (of prophesy) is too alarming, and therefore inconvenient for the family. Another is the fact that some of the family members are by now tired of being constantly perfect: Mirabel's strongwoman sister Louisa complain about the pressure being too much, and the fear of failure. This leads to a disaster and subsequent re-assessment of priorities by Alma Madrigal who realizes that her special children and grandchildren are human beings rather than superheroes on permanent display.

The child archetype is associated with tales of being special, possessing magical qualities and having unusual parents and a miraculous birth (Jung, CW9/I: para. 281) while also being depicted as fragile and exposed, as being in danger (Jung, CW9/I: para. 282). This set of motifs adds to the futurity aspect of the archetype – the emergence of the personality out of primordial darkness, the potential for self-fulfilment and the 'insuperable obstacles' one has to overcome when maturing out of the collective unconscious. The child is 'smaller than small yet bigger than big' – an oxymoron and a metaphor for the dialectic between childhood omnipotence and environmental limitations and expectations. This dialectic comes out of the omnipotence of the primary relationship (unity with the mother) which does not yet contain 'intrapsychic tension between the ego and the self' (Neumann, 2002: 17). The magical gifts originating in the child archetype and keeping the hero protagonist motivated later on, too, have roots in the lost unity with the self. Mirabel is a child who disappoints her relatives by failing to live up to their expectations because she is human, and her gifts are real rather than magical. Or, in a way, her gifts *are* magical as they restore and revive her family and its fortunes as she exposes the familial shadow.

Mirabel's story mostly cuts across Themes 1, 2, and 3 focusing on individual contributions feeding into the communal canvas. In many traditional narratives, the protagonist has to leave their community in order to find themselves (the theme of 'going out to seek one's fortune'). Yet, Mirabel finds herself, her destiny, and her individuation path while still linked to her family, she is its integral part regardless of the fact that she has no special gift to offer. Rather, her gifts are introspection and self-reflection which the rest of her family do not possess as they pursue perfection at the expense of psychic (and familial) balance.

The tension in the narrative culminates in the scene of the destruction of the Casa Madrigal and Mirabel's subsequent guilt for pushing things too far, for trying to expose the invisible cracks in the house and the psychological cracks of its inhabitants. Mirabel makes up with Alma and makes the Casa Mirabel even stronger than it was before. Her individuation is closely linked with the life of her community but not dictated by it.

It is also refreshing to see Mirabel depicted as plain-looking instead of being a pretty, slim princess, unlike her mother or some of her sisters. Appearance is one of the female persona's strongest elements, or, at least, the one that is immediately noticeable. It forms the outer layer of the mask. Appearance is often seen as a valid substitution for agentic qualities. Mirabel wears large round glasses and has an unruly curly bob. Her clothes are not tight fitting or fancy but colourful: an embroidered blouse tucked into a long skirt. She is rather clumsy and lacks the elegance of her mother and sister Isabela, with their feminine gifts of cooking, healing, and pretty homemaking.

Mirabel's double lack – the persona with its many requirements including appearance and behaviour and the special gift – is rare among female Disney protagonists. Even the more progressive characters such as Elsa, Mulan (*Mulan*, 2020) and Raya (*Raya and the Last Dragon*, 2021) are pretty or have special powers, or both. Mirabel's weightlifter sister Luisa has superhuman strength even though her female persona is missing. Mirabel has neither but she does not need them to individuate. Being special in any way is not a pre-requisite for looking for one's destiny and finding one's path in life. She has agentic qualities and she is an irritant of the established order which is a good enough starting point for the individuation process.

Turning Red (2022)

Turning Red (directed by Domee Shi) is a Pixar/Disney coming-of-age animated comedy drama whose protagonist, 13-year old Mei-Mei Lee (voiced by Rosalie Chiang), is struggling to deal with the physical changes that come with puberty while also dealing with an overbearing and strict family circle. Like *Brave* and *Encanto, Turning Red* explores a difficult mother-daughter dynamic whose brutality is metaphorically reflected in the figure of a bear. The protagonists of both movies are transformed by the mother-shadow archetypal constellation as they learn to relate to society as well as to draw the boundary between themselves as new individuals and parental expectations.

Mei-Mei's mother, Ming Lee (Sandra Oh) is keen on keeping her daughter 'perfect' in everything, which means controlling and directing her every move. Mei-Mei tries to be a good daughter. In the opening sequence the protagonist's life is presented as devoid of internal or external conflicts: she is a top student with loyal friends and doting parents. After school she helps her mother at the Temple of the Red Panda dedicated to her ancestor Sun Lee who, apparently, had the ability to transform herself into a giant red panda. Mei-Mei is assertive and confident; she does not care if she is popular at school. She is also a superfan of the boyband called *4-Town* whose upcoming concert in Toronto she dreams of attending. She appears to already know her path and is careful to balance her personal interests with the community expectations.

Cracks in this perfect picture begin to emerge when Mei-Mei gets her first period. She is shocked to discover that she possesses an ability to shapeshift into a red panda every time she feels emotional. She also learns that this transformation runs in several generations of her family, but her mother and other female relatives managed to control their pandas by locking them into amulets, for which they had to undergo a magical ceremony. A similar ceremony to lock up her shadow-trickster panda is planned for Mei-Mei by her family at the temple.

Female puberty, traditionally represented as a curse and relegated to the horror genre, in *Turning Red* becomes the metaphor of the bear into which the protagonist transforms every time she feels emotional. This is a significant representational advancement as the previously abject and taboo subject – puberty, associated with the female shadow – is finally given a prominent narrative space but not as something terrifying and disgusting. Mei-Mei's physical and psychological changes do not turn her into a witch, a, uncontrollable monster or a homicidal maniac – all poster images of the 'implacable enemy of the symbolic order' associated with sex, irrationality and closeness to nature and threatening to 'unsettle boundaries between the rational and irrational, symbolic and imaginary' (Creed, 2007: 76). The abject feminine disrupts the law that 'sets down the rules of proper sexual conduct' (Creed, 2007: 61). Grotesque othering and shame are the principal ways of keeping the female agency in check. Or, to use Jungian terminology, shaming is a way of establishing and managing the individual's shadow.

The expectation to put on the female persona the moment 'the monster' appears to protect both the young woman and the society in which she lives, is central to young women's socialization. Female emotion is denounced as irrational, and therefore split off from everyday existence. Horror versions of the cinematic bildungsroman such as *Carrie* (1976) show the girl's family as the conduit of societal shame aimed at subduing the budding personality and stemming her journey. The shadow is presented as demonic, as bloody, as something that cannot co-exist with the ego; as something that has to be cast off.

Yet, even before the 'red moment' Mei-Mei had been her own person and therefore ready for an upcoming pressure to denounce her shadow. When the red panda makes its appearance, Mei-Mei is shocked but has a good enough support network to withstand the fear and shame. Likewise, when she is embarrassed by her mother in public, when, for instance, Ming offers Mei-Mei a sanitary pad in front of all her classmates, she does not collapse into a heap of shame leading to her becoming murderous and slaughtering everyone in her vicinity. This does not happen because she can rely on her environment for support.

Her naïve, teenage infatuation with *4-Town* and dreams of pretty boys are shared and normalized by her immediate circle even though they are rejected by her parents as something silly and nonsensical. Rejected by the mother, Mei-Mei's teenage obsessions and temper tantrums are nevertheless accepted by the friends and the father, and Mei-Mei sees it being liked and admired. As Mary Dougherty notes, the inferior function 'must be made conscious in order to produce a tension of opposites, without which no forward movement is possible' (Hauke and Hockley, 2011: 232). She decides to keep the panda – the shadow – instead of ritualistic banishing and imprisoning it in a pendant, like her mother and other female relatives did. The protagonist's defiance and refusal to accept either the Red Woman or the lifeless persona destiny, culminates in a fight with the mother, who gets so angry that she turns into an enormous, menacing red panda.

Importantly, Mei-Mei's ability to look in the mirror and integrate the shadow is linked to society's willingness to see the female shadow as an important part of the agentic female, instead of locking it behind the carefully coiffed female persona (both Ming and grandmother Wu (Wai Ching Ho are elegant and polished)). By navigating the mother-shadow conflict, protagonist chooses and defends her own path, however silly and naïve it may look at present. Ultimately, Mei-Mei appropriates the stigma by inoculating it, and integrating it into her path.

The Awkward Theme 2: Animas, Animuses, and Parents

Disney stories featuring young female protagonists have been currently avoiding the soul-image altogether in their versions of the female bildungsroman; perhaps because they do not want to revert to the old narrative stereotypes of patriarchal marriage which had dominated their stories for decades.

Yet, the role of romantic partners in the individuation process have been explored in a range of other contemporary moving image narratives, including *Ladybird* (Greta Gerwig, 2017), *Sex Education* (Netflix, 2019–), *The Queen's Gambit* (Netflix, 2020), and TV adaptations of Sally Rooney's novels, *Normal People* (BBC/Hulu, 2020) and *Conversations with Friends* (BBC/Hulu. 2022). Protagonists and branch characters like Lady Bird/Christine McPherson (Saoirse Ronan), Beth Harmon (Anna Taylor-Joy) in *The Queen's Gambit,* Frances (Alison Oliver) in *Conversations with Friends*, Marianne (Daisy Edgar-Jones) in *Normal People*, and *Sex Education*'s Maeve (Emma Mackey), Lily (Tanya Reynolds), Ola (Patricia Ellison) and Aimee (Aimee Lou Wood) all learn about themselves through the process of falling in love (or in lust) with others. However, their romantic and sexual entanglements do no result in marriages, children, or the end of their journey. The journey for the self continues, complete with painful and happy experiences, difficult and satisfying choices, and actual or anticipated accomplishments.

The two sets of elements in Theme 2 – parents and partners – are sometimes difficult to tell apart in coming-of-age narratives because of the developmental continuity of young characters who gradually learn to disentangle their projections and childhood imprints from real people. This Theme mostly concerns the 'leaving home' part of the maturation process although it does not presuppose that finding a partner is the end of a journey should be treated as the goal in itself. Unfortunately, this theme has dominated the trajectory of female characters for millennia, echoing the assumption that the woman as a personality is not important, or even does not exist, outside of the family.

Jung's own descriptions of the animus are, at best, conservative and, at worst, sexist. His disciples, even the female ones like Jolande Jacobi and Marie-Louise von Franz, do not fare any better. Apart from a seldom acknowledgement that culture views women as inferior, it is clear from their views that 'masculine', animus-controlled women should regain their feminine nature by acknowledging and resisting the unconscious power of the soul-image.

The animus is the 'contrasexual', male soul-image residing in a woman's psyche. He often appears as multiple images, and can become projected onto celebrities or politicians (Jacobi, 1973: 116–121). The chorus of animus-voices can be quite loud, and women have to handle these creatures carefully lest they become unruly and overwhelm the owner (Jacobi, 1973: 121).

The inner masculine in women, Jung asserts, brings on inspiration and creativity (Jung, CW7: para. 336). Yet, he can also be oppressive and lead the owner down the path of masculinization: 'A woman possessed by the animus is always in danger of losing her femininity, *her adapted feminine persona* (my emphasis), just as a man in like circumstances runs the risk of effeminacy' (Jung, CW7: para. 337). He continues to discuss the anima, the animus and their owners in stereotyped binaries, confusing the adapted female persona with a 'natural' propensity for communal behaviour with which the too-intense animus can interfere: 'The conscious attitude of woman in general is far more exclusively personal than that of man. Her world is made up of fathers and mothers, brothers and sisters, husbands and children. [...] The man's world is the nation, the state, business concerns, etc' (Jung, CW7: para. 338).

In a somewhat less biased discussion of the animus, Jolande Jacobi does mention that its conception is closely tied with societal treatment of women: '... in consequence of the patriarchally-orientated development of our Western culture, the woman too tends to think that masculine as such is more valuable than the feminine, and this attitude does much to increase the power of the animus' (Jacobi, 1973: 117). The oppressive effect of this culture on men is also tangible as it results in discouraging them from showing any 'effeminate' traits (Jacobi, 1973: 117). This often results in men projecting their 'unconscious', unrealized, unrecognized femininity on to women instead (Jacobi, 1973: 117).

Another issue that arises from the above definitions and descriptions it that the soul-image is envisaged as primarily heterosexual, implying that women have inner animuses and not animas while men invariably have animas. Contemporary dramas are finally dealing with inherent heterosexuality of the 'romantic interest' motif by introducing more bisexual, lesbian and gay characters into their narratives. For instance, in series 2 of *Sex Education*, Ola starts dating the protagonist, Otis Milburn (Asa Butterfield), but eventually realizes that she has feelings for Lily (Tanya Reynolds). Both unsuccessfully date men before realising that this is not working for them (Ola, for instance, discovers that she is pansexual). The expected 'contrasexual' image waiting to be romantically unleashed onto a love interest in the real world is simply not there; instead there is a same-sex image.

Luckily, the new bunch of heroines do not intend to stop developing as individuals by marrying a total stranger (as Elsa would call it), by marrying young, or even by marrying at all. Beth Harmon in *The Queen's Gambit* is a child prodigy who learns to play chess while in an orphanage. The narrative follows her through the years as she deals with her tranquilizer addiction, mood swings, repressed parental issues, romantic obsessions and her overwhelming passion for chess. Boys and men (and one woman) are not a goal in itself, but stepping stones on her path towards a greater understanding of herself. Throughout the series, the audience witnesses Beth grow up and nurture her talent as well as have relationships, which does not hinder her competitiveness or her progress in the world of chess.

Beth's major romantic involvements – the elusive Townes (Jacob Fortune-Lloyd), the awkward, geeky Harry Beltik (Harry Melling), and the arrogant genius Benny Watts (Thomas Brodie-Sangster) all happen to be chess players. They are all very different people: the only trait they share is a good ability to play chess. As she is going through matches at different competition levels, Beth experiences a series of physical and psychological transformations, gradually becoming confident and building her unique social mask instead of relying on stereotypes. She has no intention of hiding her femininity, which expresses itself in extravagant clothes. In fact, a lot of emphasis is placed on her appearance, with costume design by Gabrielle Binder almost being a separate character in the narrative.

Yet, Beth does not exactly dress for the boys – she dresses for herself. Her white dresses and chequered coats are not meant to construe, or even to support, a female persona. They are meant to emphasize the fact that the female persona is irrelevant, that gender is irrelevant, when it comes to ambition, motivation, and talent. Beth beats her male opponents without hesitation or regret, and without an intention to appear 'attractive' by pretending to be fragile, weak or submissive. The men with whom she falls in love and has sex can be regarded as an imprint of her chess-playing animus, the inspirator, the vague and mysterious muse residing inside and driving her in her quest for success. Townes, Beltik and Benny can even be seen as incarnations of this elusive animus, if we are to accept the Jungian premise that there is more than one animus, or that he has the propensity to multiply into different voices which offer 'opinions' and 'principles' (Jacobi, 1973: 121).

Beth's world certainly does not consist of 'mothers and fathers, brothers and children' while her chorus of disparate animuses helps her achieve her dream of beating the world champion Vasily Borgov (Marcin Dorocincki) – a combination of the arch-enemy, level boss, and ultra-animus, the ultimate negative inspiration. *The Queen's Gambit* ends with Beth's triumph, also celebrated by the 'animuses' who all gathered together in Benny's flat in New York to watch her play in Moscow and to help her with the game. Beth is not made to pick any of them; moreover – she is not even expected to fully mature and to move on from her 'imaginary' inner male to a real one via the process of accepting the real person. After all, male characters had been allowed to objectify their muses, and use them for inspiration, for a long time.

Likewise, the protagonist of *Lady Bird,* Christine, goes through a series of romantic involvements before moving to New York to study at NYU. With her red hair and quirky nickname, Christine is both troubled and driven, determined to escape poverty and to attend a prestigious college. Her exploration of her identity (complete with her made-up name), being ashamed of her family's low social status, her insistence on an independent point of view (which causes her to be suspended from the Catholic school), and her relationship with boys, is full of social, economic, and maturational issues, but it never becomes a search for 'the one'. Instead, it is a search for the self. The young men on her way – Danny (Lucas Hedges) and Kyle (Timothee Chalamet) are integrated into her bildungsroman narrative, but they do not overwhelm it. Neither does she build a female persona aimed specifically at men. Instead, she remains focused on the goal of getting the kind of education that would make her succeed in the tough and ultra-competitive environment that is neoliberal capitalism; to succeed on her own, without relying on the mask of femininity.

The protagonist of *Conversations with Friends* (based on a novel by Sally Rooney), Frances Flynn, falls in love with a handsome married man, Nick Convay (Joe Alwyn) but has no end goal in mind. In fact, Nick becomes an individuation and initiation device while Frances is figuring out what to do with herself as she is finishing the university and mapping out her life. The narrative is slow and meandering, shot voyeuristically, as if the viewer becomes privy to someone's everyday existence – or, rather, a fragment of someone's individuation process. Frances' relationship with the female persona is notable: she is very much herself, an introvert, wears little make-up, plain clothes, has unremarkable hair, and has no intention of copying anyone else's style, manners, or trying to be more attractive than she is. Her outer plainness and inner complexity present a dilemma for her friends and the people she dates (including her ex-girlfriend Bonny (Sasha Lane)). She uses Nick just as much as he uses her; he is not the centre of her existence but rather an inspiration and a temporary guide on a long and difficult journey. Nick is a rather typical animus – mysterious, handsome, and seductive – but he does not get to dominate Frances' journey; she remains firmly the centre of the narrative, as evidenced by frequent framing her in close-ups and mid-range shots, sitting pensively in rooms, cafes, and train carriages. Her journey is internal as well as external and physical, between parents, friends, and lovers in real life as well versions of them living in her head. It is slow and detailed, documented in on-screen chats, emails, and printed and recited poems. It is a journey of growing up, and a journey with animus as a guide minus the female persona even though its shadow is still there in the form of societal expectations and constant self-doubt.

Conclusion

Rejection of the female persona in narratives dominated by female characters, particularly the ones focusing on young protagonists deciding what to do with life and how to succeed without relying on an (actual or metaphorical) prince, is a sign of slow and gradual progress in the entertainment industry. Regardless of the genre (animation or live action; film or TV series; schematic or detailed; comedy or drama), the observable tendency is to move away from the rigidity of the female persona to a character possessing a moral complexity and internal tension, manifested by a shadow or a trickster; a character who is in conflict with the world; who is learning to exist independently in an unwelcoming environment, to develop resilience and to survive against all odds. This new protagonist is allowed to be harsh and difficult as she learns about the world and herself. Young female protagonists are finally getting their own individuation paths which do not end in a marriage, children, or being someone else's disembodied inspiration.

References

Andersen, Hans Christian (2012) *Hans Christian Andersen's Fairy Tales*, Acheron Press.

Bassil-Morozow, H. (2018) *Jungian Theory for Storytellers: A Toolkit*, London: Routledge.

Buchanan, Ian (2010) *Oxford Dictionary of Critical Theory*, Oxford: Oxford University Press.

Creed, Barbara (2007) *The Monstrous-Feminine: Film, Feminism, Psychoanalysis.* London: Routledge.

Dundes, Alan (1989) *Little Red Riding Hood: a Casebook*, Wisconsin: University of Wisconsin Press.

Dundes, L., Streiff, M., and Streiff, Z. (2018) 'Storm Power, an Icy Tower and Elsa's Bower: The Winds of Change in Disney's Frozen', *Social Sciences* 7 (6), p. 86; doi:10.3390/socsci7060086.

Estes, Clarissa Pincola (1992) *Women Who Run With the Wolves: Myths and Stories of the Wild Woman Archetype*, London: Rider.

Greven, David (2011) *Representations of Femininity in American Genre Cinema: the Woman's Film, Film Noir, and Modern Horror*, New York: Palgrave Macmillan.

Hauke, C. & Hockley, L. (2011) *Jung & Film II: The Return, Further Post-Jungian Takes on the Moving Image.* London & New York: Routledge.

Jacobi, Jolande (1942/1973) *The Psychology of C. G. Jung* (8th Edition), trans. Ralph Manheim, New Haven and London: Yale University Press.

Jung C.G. (n.d.) *The Collected Works*, Herbert Read, Michael Fordham and Gerhardt Adler, (eds.) R.F.C. Hull (trans.), London: Routledge. (Except where a different publication was used, all references are to this hardback edition.)

Mesure, S. and Lewin, A. (2013) 'The difficult princesses: Animating Female Characters is Harder, Says Disney Boss, Because of their "Range of Emotions"', *The Independent*, 14 October.

Neumann, Erich (2002) *The Child: Structure and Dynamics of the Nascent Personality*, London: Karnac.

Rudloff, Maja (2016) '(Post)feminist paradoxes: The sensibilities of gender representation in Disney's Frozen', *Outskirts (Online)*, 35, pp. 1–20.

Westervelt, W. D. (n.d.) *Legends of Maui, a Demi God of Polynesia, and of His Mother Hina*, Amazon (print on demand).

Chapter 5

The Mother

This chapter examines recent representation of motherhood on television as a shift from the mask to self-reflection and self-awareness, and from passive acceptance of the abject label to rejection of shame and acknowledgement of awkward and difficult identity struggles. Firstly, it looks at a range of recent TV comedies. Shows such as *One Day at a Time* (2017–2020)*, Better Things* (Netflix, 2016–), and *Motherland* (BBC, 2016–) as well as other comedies with parenthood as side narratives (for instance, *Crazy Ex-Girlfriend* or *Killing Eve*) challenge traditional visions of motherhood and parenthood, exploring the pent-up shame under the mask, and liberating and redefining the roles of the mother, wife, and parent. The chapter also looks at a range of television shows and films in which the 'negative' mother acts as an inspiration and a developmental milestone for the female protagonist, including *Disenchantment* (2018–) and Disney's *Encanto* (2022).

The mother archetype, belonging to Theme 2, is fairly tricky to improve in terms of representation because of its generally static nature. It too, however, can be made progressive if narratives move away from rigid representations of motherhood as well from the construction of the agentic mother as being abject/terrifying (a culturally-coded image) and to the more dynamic versions of this figure. Thus, genre plays an important role in varying representations of the mother figure. For instance, she stops being a bland character when portrayed along the horror/comedy split. As a protagonist, the horror mother tends to suffer from guilt and resents her loss of identity; as a background character she may be the mother of a serial killer or a psychopath, or form a kind of metaphorical background – an alien mother laying eggs that produce people-eating monsters.

The Mother and the Monster

Traditional moving image representations of motherhood depict the role of the mother as something that comes naturally to a woman; as something every girl dreams of becoming. Erich Neumann writes that 'the feminine's fulfilment, granted by nature, lies in the primal relationship and pregnancy'

DOI: 10.4324/9781003253044-6

(Neumann, 1994: 23). The mother is a body, a vessel, a medium via which new life is generated. A more progressive representation of motherhood would treat it as an aspect of a person's life rather than a sole purpose; it would also remove the objectification and *particularly abjectification* of the maternal, or the birthing parental, and inscribe the experience of having a child into the overall narrative of a person's life.

Predictably, the mother in moving image narratives has traditionally been studied from the Freudian and Lacanian angles. She is the physical mother, the Oedipal mother, the one whose body is a mystery, and a source of secrets. Its functions – pregnancy, childbirth, and all the associated transformations are abject, simultaneously disgusting and appealing. Physically leaving this gestational vessel and reconciling with it could be equally difficult, and may never happen for some children. The horror genre has explored this ambivalence towards the material body and its perceptions in society. As Barbara Creed points out in *The Monstrous Feminine: Film, Feminism, Psychoanalysis* (1993), horror represents reconciliation with the maternal body (Creed, 1993: 14). Horror also relates to the construction of the border between the clean and the unclean as 'the maternal … is constructed as unclean specifically in relation to menstruation and childbirth' (Creed, 1993: 41).

The menstruating and gestating body are terrifying precisely because the ability to produce new life is magical, powerful, and is not entirely controllable by science and medicine despite decades of research. Reproduction, whether 'natural' or 'artificial' is still unpredictable, still largely out of human control. Yet, both literary and moving image narratives reflect obsessiveness with which society, via religion or science, wants to master and manage these processes. Narratives such as *The Handmaid's Tale* (both the book and the show) depict the fear and brutality of the patriarchal order controlling the female reproductive function upon which depends the survival of an entire species. This function needs to be reined in, masked, squeezed into a narrow set of definitions, subdued, and reorganized according to pseudo-rational rules. Its 'owners' will be treated metonymically, as mere carriers of the function defined by it rather than agents or individuals.

If the function cannot be controlled, it will be feared. Creed argues that the archaic mother so popular in horror narratives 'does not depend for its definition on the masculine' (Creed, 1993: 27). Importantly, horror genres label the woman abject when she has been 'unclean' and imperfect, when she has made 'a spectacle of herself' (Creed, 1993: 42); in other words, when she has lost her persona, her 'clean' and 'proper' mask. Losing the mask pushes the feminine into the realm of abjection, she becomes disgusting, rejected – and terrifying like the invisible alien mother in Ridley Scott's *Alien* (1979), Nola Carveth (Samantha Eggar) in David Cronenberg's *The Brood* (1979), or like the uncontrollable, raging teenagers, Reagan (Linda Blair) in *The Exorcist* (directed by William Friedkin, 1973) and Carrie White (Sissy Spacek) in Brian de Palma's *Carrie* (1976). More recent horror narratives focusing on bad mothers unravel the trail of secrets, neglect, and abuse (*Hereditary*, 2018) or troubled, exhausted mothers suffering from depression and struggling with parental responsibility (*We Need to Talk about Kevin* (2011); *The Babadook* (2014)).

Depth psychology, including the Freudian and Jungian branches, has traditionally stereotyped the mother as an empty vessel doing all the biological, physical, and emotional labour in a one-sided relationship with the baby (who, narcissistically, uses her as literal and metaphorical food). As Irigaray points out in 'The Culture of Difference', Freudian thought follows the patriarchal cultural perception of motherhood as the ultimate sacrifice, and the situation is exacerbated by the obsession with the mother-son relationship – the crux of the Oedipus complex (Irigaray, 2007: 40). Thus, parenthood is both gendered and fetishized in depth psychology theories while the mother-daughter and father-daughter relationships remain neglected at the expense of the 'castration threat' drama:

> One of the distinctive features of the female body is its toleration of the other's growth within itself without incurring illness or death for either one of the living organisms. Unfortunately, culture practically inverted the meaning of this economy of respect for the other. It has blindly venerated the mother-son relationship to the point of religious fetishism, but has given no interpretation to the model of tolerance of the other within and with a self that this relationship manifests. A woman's body in fact gives equal opportunities of life to the boys and to the girls conceived in it through the coming together of male and female chromosomes.
>
> (Irigaray, 2007: 39)

What Irigaray pinpoints in this paragraph is the cultural imperative that showcases the mother in an idealistic light, as a tolerant, caring individual; as a vessel rather than a person. Yet, Irigaray also highlights, the relationship between the mother and the foetus, and subsequently mother and child, is a two-way communication. It involves mutual respect and growth rather than blind sacrifice of a stereotyped mother. The carrying parent is not just a vessel hijacked by an alien body, the two being inseparable and undifferentiated up to the point of the father's arrival into the child's world. The father is presumed to intrude into the organic, perfect, gestational relationship and to make a civilized being out of the small narcissistic human by introducing (him) to the concepts of duty, law and order. In the cultural imagination there is a split which presents the baby now as the alien and intruder, now as a helpless creature completely dependent on the mother.

In her interview with Helene Rouch, Irigaray also emphasizes that the separation of the mother and baby exists before the introduction of prohibition by the social. The separation, the difference is already there – in the form of the placenta which mediates it. While psychanalysis 'justifies the imaginary fusion between a child and its mother' and presents their separation as 'loss of paradise, traumatizing expulsion and exclusion', in (biological) reality this relationship is not as parasitic because

> there has to be a recognition of the other, of the non-self, by the mother, and therefore an initial reaction from her, in order for placental factors to be produced. The difference between the "self" and the other, so to speak, is continuously negotiated.
>
> (Irigaray, 2007: 35)

The mother is a social role, and one of the several aspects of the mask of femininity. Recent examples of 'motherhood horror' genre have been focusing on the parent's perspective rather than the oedipal-patriarchal version of it. On the surface of it, this is a gain for feminism. Yet, upon closer look, films such as *The Babadook* and *We Need to Talk about Kevin* are about women trying to deal with the mask, and one of the facets of the female persona – the perfect motherhood. Thus, the films are still dealing with the burden of objectification albeit this time it is self-objectification reflecting society's expectations of female parents.

Post-industrial societies, with their focus on individualism and nuclear family and the severing of communal ties, place the burden of responsibility for the child's physical and emotional development on the mother who, as a result, may become exhausted or depressed. For the sake of the child's future as an emotionally stable, independent, professionally and personally success-ful individual, the mother is expected to give up her ambitions, her personal time, or even her sanity. Such a radical sacrifice would – supposedly – result in a perfect child, amazing mother-child bond, and lay the foundations for a highly empathic, secure, successful individual. The good mother is thus the perfect mother who does not make mistakes, who sacrifices herself to the child to the point of losing her identity and her personality. Eliane Glaser remarks in *The Guardian* that motherhood is 'one of our modern, enlightened society's awkward little secrets'. Despite decades of feminism, mothers are still underpaid, isolated, underpaid and 'perpetually guilty' (Glaser, *The Guardian*, 18 May 2021). While support is minimal (the availability of affordable childcare, for instance varies greatly between Western countries), strangers are often quick to judge a mother or to assume that she is not taking good care of the child. Glaser adds that she feels lonely and judged by stran-gers; she also notes that combining work and childrearing has been chaotic and made her feel like a failure (Glaser, *The Guardian*, 18 May 2021).

As Amanda Konkle notes in her analysis of *The Babadook*,

> Mothering, women are told, should be done 'by the book,' but mothering by the book, especially if that book is an attachment parenting tome can be a horrifying enterprise. Ideologies of intensive parenting underscore

the breakdown of the distinction between child and mother, producing an abject horror that traverses national boundaries ...

(Konkle, 2019: 1)

This kind of approach creates 'horror from a woman's perspective' – a realization that society stereotypes motherhood and dictates the rules while leaving the parent to fend for themselves – the worst of both worlds. The film is 'the critique of the horrors of intensive mothering ideologies' (Konkle, 2019: 1).

The book Konkle refers to is *The Baby Book* by Dr. Bill Sears – the advocate of 'attachment parenting', a school which presupposes anticipating the child's needs before the child explicitly expresses them. Sears' view of the mother's autonomy are bleak: a good mother feels incomplete without her child as if a piece of her is missing (Sears, 2001: 8, quoted in Konkle, 2019: 1). This extreme view brings to mind Lysa Arryn (Kate Dickie) in *Game of Thrones* who greets her guests while breastfeeding her obviously grown son, Robyn (Lino Facioli).

Whereas postnatal depression and psychosis affect a significant number of women, they are rarely realistically represented on screen. A survey by the parents' charity NCT has found that

half (50%) of mothers experienced mental health problems at some time during pregnancy or within the first year of their child's birth. These can include postnatal depression, anxiety, obsessive compulsive disorder (OCD), post-traumatic stress disorder (PTSD) and postpartum psychosis.

(NCT, 2017)

The mask of perfect motherhood is artificial and superficial. Traditionally in narratives the mother keeps running in the background as a figure of support for the protagonist or other characters. Full of warmth and acceptance, 'good' mother characters fill a space on the protagonist's path and do not contain much complexity. The horror genre has developed a heightened, metaphoric, euphemistic representation of a new mother struggling with her feelings about the child, showing depression being projected outwardly on to a make-believe figure or the child themselves. Horror mothers expose the split between representational fantasy and the reality of contemporary motherhood.

The Archetypal Mother

The mother's guilt is compounded by the burden of responsibility for an individual's future. Traditional Jungian view of the mother's role does not make her burden any lighter. For instance, Erich Neumann supports the fusion of social expectations and archetypal characteristics that bring together the human mother and her archetypal counterpart: the good mother supplies 'the feeling of security and shelteredness' whereas the bad mother can cause a disruption in the development of the baby's consciousness. The good mother is thus 'the mother of growth and nourishment' connected to the experiences of 'satiety, warmth, awakeness, consciousness and light' (Neumann, 2002: 112).

The real human being who gives birth, therefore, carries an enormous responsibility for the child's success as a future individual – not just as part of the dual 'primal relationship' ('an expression of total relatedness') but also later when child's ego-consciousness starts to develop. Moreover, for all the 'goodness' the good mother dispenses she should not expect anything in return, for motherhood is de-individualizing, turning one into a generic, archetypal selfless carer:

> [Acts of mothering have] nothing to do with blood kinship, for the true mother is more or less replaceable by a figure playing an analogously affective role. In other words, it is not the personal individual, but the generically maternal that is the indispensable foundation of the child's life. The mother of the primal relationship is the 'good Great Mother'. She is the being who contains, nourishes, protects and warms the child, and who is affectively bound to it. She is the foundation not only of its physical but also of psychic existence. She gives security and makes life in this world possible. In this sense she is anonymous and transpersonal, in other words, archetypal, as the one part of a specifically human constellation which operates between her and the child. Her unconsciously directed behaviour, which enables her to coincide with the mother archetype, is vitally necessary to the normal development of the child.
>
> (Neumann, 2002: 21)

The good mother also manages transitions between sleep and the state of being awake, leading the baby into the world of consciousness:

> The good mother of the primal relationship is also the guardian of consciousness and its development; she is Sophia, whereas the 'bad mother' is always hostile to the development of consciousness because she intensifies the tendency to remain in, or return to, the darkness of the unconscious.
>
> (Neumann, 2002: 113)

Yet, at the same time, the bad mother can also positively affect the child's development as 'fear of the terrible mother usually tends to strengthen consciousness and often plays a positive role in the development of consciousness in the first half of life' (Neumann, 2002: 113).

And yet, the transposition of the dual archetypal mother onto real women makes the expectations of motherhood impossibly high. Neumann does not really delve into this in *The Child: Structure and Dynamics of a Nascent Personality* as the book is focused on the baby rather than the mother, but

Analytical Psychology in general has a lot to say about the dangers of over-identification with an archetype. After all, the perfection assigned to a goddess or a mythical figure – the archetypal image – is impossible to achieve for a human being. Archetype is an idea (for instance of motherhood), and archetypal image is its concrete realization (e.g., Virgin Mary), but no real person can embody an archetype without losing a grip on reality. Trying to embody an archetype is a dangerous path as it does not take into consideration all the complex, detailed context with which human beings are surrounded in society: community, relatives, family roles, jobs, friends – and now also social media. Trying to achieve the perfection of an archetypal image also means trying to identify with the collective psyche. The alternative to this is becoming aware of societal projections, of mediatized representations of the collective psyche, and resisting the pressure to become one of them. The perfect mother only exists in the collective unconscious, in the collective psyche, both inside, and outside – in societal expectations and media representations.

Jung points out that 'succumbing to the fascinating influence of the archetypes', particularly if one does not realize that this is happening, as identification with an image coming from the collective psyche may lead to over-inflation and even psychosis when archetypes 'escape from conscious control altogether and become completely independent, thus producing the phenomena of possession' (Jung, CW9/I: para. 82). Yet, the perfect mother is nothing, it is a template, she is an empty vessel devoid of personality, of needs. As Simone de Beauvoir writes in *The Second Sex*, the mother is a 'little simmering consciousness lost in a fragile and contingent body' (De Beauvoir, 1949/2011: 570). She

> ... expects no compensation in exchange for her gifts, she justifies them with her own freedom. This generosity deserves the praise that men forever bestow on her; but mystification begins when the religion of Motherhood proclaims that all mothers are exemplary. For maternal devotion can be experienced in perfect authenticity; but in fact, this is rarely the case. Ordinarily, maternity is a strange compromise of narcissism, altruism, dream, sincerity, bad faith, devotion and cynicism.
>
> (De Beauvoir, 1949/2011: 570)

The perfect mother is thus viewed as no longer an individual. No wonder that 'possession by motherhood', and reduction of the person to the 'little simmering consciousness', is the stuff of cinematic nightmares.

What is required, therefore, is a revision of the role of the mother – in real life as well as in narratives. Donald Winnicott's concept of the 'good-enough' parent is a healthier example of motherhood and parenthood than identification with the mother archetype. He states that 'It is part of the normal process that the mother recovers her self-interest...' (Winnicott, 2006: 22). Only if the mother is good enough (as opposed to perfect), 'does the infant start a process of development that is personal and real'. (Winnicott, 2006:

23) The good-enough mother, from Winnicott's view, should astutely sense how to take away the infant's omnipotence without overwhelming it with a feeling of helplessness and despair. Meanwhile, using the mother as a transitional object, the child should be allowed to retain an illusion of control – for the time being: 'The mother's eventual task is gradually to disillusion the infant, but she has no hope of success unless at first she has been able to give sufficient opportunity for illusion' (Winnicott, 2005: 11).

Women are socialized to be patient, and to take care of others, at the expense of their own comfort and mental health. Bad mothers, rebellious mothers, different mothers who do not conform to this stereotype are relegated to the horror genre, just like angry teenage girls who refuse to be the victim (*Carrie*, 1976) or do not conform to the 'nice type' (*The Exorcist*, 1973).

Yes, things have been changing lately. A range of comedy-dramas, including *One Day at a Time, Better Things* and *Motherland* raise the issue of parental guilt and explore societal expectations of motherhood and parenthood. These shows display good enough rather than idealized mothers – mothers who can get impatient and angry, embarrassing and messy; mothers who draw boundaries when they need to and when they should not, acting selfishly instead of being physically and emotionally available to the child.

Recent Stories of the Imperfect Mother

The imperfect mother is not necessarily bad; it's that she fails in some aspects of her parental duties. She is often juggling family life and a career, either neglecting one or attempting to have both, and feeling that she is not really succeeding in either. The characters of *Motherland* variously fail to achieve perfection either as mothers or as professional women (and men). Pamela Adlon's protagonist in *Better Things*, Sam, is a single mother and a moderately successful actress who tries to juggle auditions and childrearing. In the recent version of *One Day at a Time,* Penelope (Justina Machado) is also a single mother who does her best to keep the three generations of her family alive and well while also working full-time as a nurse.

All three sitcoms, despite their cultural differences, move motherhood into the trickster zone, discussing its real pitfalls instead of presenting it as a polished, smooth, beautiful experience. All three sets of characters maintain their personhood despite the connotations of sacrifice attached by society to motherhood. They also navigate the dangerous waters of inter-generational wars by acting as a fragile bridge between grandmothers and grandchildren. The grandmothers, representatives of the baby boomer generation, are confident, conservative and either attention seekers or emotionally unavailable. In other words, they do not offer much support to the overworked daughters – on the contrary, embodiments of maternal ambivalence, they often offer criticism and negativity, and they can also be socially embarrassing.

All three narratives use the inter-generational connection to explore the evolution of the feminine persona, in its mother guise. *Motherland* follows the lives of a group of friends and acquaintances (several mothers and one father) living in London. Most of the narrative action happens in cafes, during school events or at the school gates. The main character, Julia (Anna Maxwell Martin) is bumbling and permanently angry. Her life is hectic and she is completely unsupported by her mother and husband who share a lot in common: both are neglectful, selfish, pursuing their own interests and hobbies, and unwilling to spend time with the family.

Other mothers (and fathers) in the show are equally dysfunctional: they are all struggling with the multi-faceted persona; a combination of social class and motherhood. All of the characters, even those who at first sight appear to be confident, popular and successful, are panicked and lost underneath the mask. Amanda, with her slim figure, expensive clothes and perfect hair and make-up, is an overconfident bully and the leader of the 'alpha mums' – a secretive group into which Julie is not invited. Yet, over the seasons, it is revealed that she herself is the product of a narcissistic, superficial mother (brilliantly played by Joanna Lumley) who loves being the centre of attention and putting her daughter down. Amanda's husband, Johnny (Terry Mynott) leaves her and later finds a very attractive replacement who he is planning to marry. Like her mother, Amanda is nothing but the mask, always in denial, and attempting to make up for the lack of real personality and confidence with good looks, superficial leadership and a range of attention-seeking stunts.

Julia's own unemotional mother, Marion (Ellie Haddington), likes to spend her time lunching with friends instead of providing (free) childcare. Borderline neglectful, she admits that she never came to her daughters' school sports competitions, is perpetually embarrassed of Julia and avoids her whenever she can. Julia keeps being rejected by her mother in a number of ways: instead of helping Julia, Marion is going to stay with her other daughter who has just had a baby. Julia keeps chasing her mother's approval and demanding her attention whenever she bumps into her, both deliberately and accidentally. For instance, she meets Marion at the school sports day, only for Marion to admit that she is not here for her family – she is here on official duties as she is a member of the school board (S2, E12).

In an interview with *Vogue*, Sharon Horgan, one of the writers on the show, explains her decision to make Marion cold as introducing a form of rebellion against social pressure on women to provide free care. The creators wanted a character who would say 'I am not doing it anymore' (Schama, 2018).

Marion's rebellion is against the part of the female persona that codes the feminine as endlessly caring and devoid of selfish thoughts. Yet, eventually the mother and daughter are forced to confront their feelings about each other when Marion suffers a heart attack at the end of Series 2, and has to move in with Amanda in Series 3. However, physical proximity does not improve their relationship, proving that the issues they are experiencing are deep. Julia, who had spent chasing Marion for most of Series 1 and 2, is now terrified that her mother would have to stay with them forever: in fact, when she gets a phone call from Marion's doctor telling her that Marion won't be able to live on her own, Julia runs into the bathroom and starts screaming out of anger and frustration.

Similarly, in *One Day at a Time*, the eccentric grandmother Lydia (Rita Moreno), although not exactly neglectful, is self-centred and attention-seeking to the point that she just has to outshine her daughter, be it in cooking skills or physical attractiveness. In her seventies, Lydia likes to wear bright, tight-fitting clothes and is absolutely confident in her appearance. She owns the mask and controls it, enjoying its effect on her admirers – including Penelope's boss, Dr. Berkowitz (Stephen Tobolowsky). She also despairs that the younger generation have lost respect for the female persona – for instance, she tries to make her granddaughter Elena (Isabella Gomez) wear (rather gaudy) make-up, with very limited success.

Penelope (Justina Machado) cannot always rely on Lydia's support: Lydia is quick to criticize her when things do not go the way she wants. Even though she does eventually realize that she was wrong, Penelope spends much of the learning curve on her own, simultaneously trying to solve the issue and deal with her mother's lack of support. For instance, when Penelope's problematic ex-husband, Victor (James Martinez) returns, lies that he no longer has a drinking problem and wants to restart their relationship (S1, E12), Lydia chooses to believe Victor rather than her own daughter. However, when Penelope finds an empty alcohol bottle, Lydia switches sides.

At the same time, Lydia can serve as an example of resilience – a Cuban immigrant who has had a lot of hardship, she is full of *joie de vivre*, even after a stroke. She celebrates every moment of her life, wears bright clothes and make-up, and loves dancing and going out. In fact, she has integrated her feminine persona into her personality; it has become part of her survival and a sign of resilience. Perhaps when she expects her daughter and granddaughter to be the same, she does not only mean for them to be superficially feminine; she wants them to be in control of their own destiny; to keep celebrating life even in tough times.

Like Julia and Penelope, Sam, Pamela Adlon's character in *Better Things*, lives next door to her mother Phyllis (Celia Imrie) and has to deal with her shenanigans every day. Sam acts as a parent to both her mother and her three daughters, Max (Mikey Madison), Frankie (Hannah Alligood) and Duke (Olivia Edward) while also working as a moderately successful actress. Like Lydia, Phyllis is selfish, eccentric, and a hoarder, refusing to part with any of her belongings. Like Lydia, Phyllis also regularly embarrasses her daughter – for instance, when she nonchalantly recalls a racist story when Sam brings home a film director and potential love interest, Mel (Lenny Kravitz) (S1, E3), or when she decides to do some gardening, naked.

All three daughters – two of them single and one with an unsupportive partner (Julia) deal with the emotional absence of their own mothers while trying to be good mothers to their own children. While Marion, Lydia and Phyllis are more of a burden than support to Julia, Penelope and Sam, the three daughters have more self-awareness than their mothers, and accept the fact that they are imperfect as parents – and that they do not need to be perfect. Instead of being in denial, they embrace imperfections – their own, their mothers', and their children's. All three daughters accept that the female persona has holes in it, that it is an impossible construct that needs to be examined and negated while their mothers simply quietly sabotage it (they lack the necessary self-reflection to openly reject societal expectations).

Meanwhile, the younger generation is very aware of the dangers and oppressiveness of the mask. Sam and Penelope make an effort to understand their Gen Z children, with their activism and identity politics despite the fact that their own mothers were not good examples of love and acceptance. The middle generation also learns from their daughters that the female persona is obsolete, and needs to be challenged. Penelope's daughter Elena (Isabella Gomez) is an LGBTQ+ activist, attending various protests and marches. When Elena comes out as gay (S1, E8), Penelope has to process her own feelings and to accept her daughter's identity. Later on Elena starts dating Syd (Sheridan Pierce), who is non-binary, and both Penelope and, surprisingly, the very conservative Lydia, are very supportive of their relationship. Penelope, who only decides to defend her rights (for instance, her right for equal pay in S1 E2) after tolerating the injustice, soul-searching, and getting angry, is a less confident person than her daughter.

Julia, Penelope, and Sam have to rethink the female persona – their lives are too busy for it. They also have no time for the abject, or for shame. They celebrate difference and contrast between all three generations, and exist in the liminal zone – between their mothers and their daughters; having a job and a career while also trying to mediate family relations. They act as a bridge between people, perpetually stuck 'betwixt and between' family and work; between identities and generations. They are the ones holding things together – on their own, without (male) partners, and without much social support. They are the new liminal mothers.

'Solving' the Mother: the Protagonist's View

Liminal or ambivalent mothers like the ones described in the previous section serve as an effective dramatic device which provides a colourful context for the protagonist's pain and subsequent victories, internal as well as external. The 'wounding' parents is a potent motif as it lays the narrative ground for the child's future with its misfortunes and fortunes.

Compared to Theme 1, which is home to the shadow and the trickster, Theme 2 may seem relatively tame and narrow. However, it still produces significant conflicts; sometimes so powerful that they become the leading motif in the protagonist's journey. It is also worth reminding that in traditional narratives, the bad mother as an element of the protagonist's path, is often destroyed or humiliated as the protagonist is released from her spell.

So, the mother can be killed off or integrated. Recent Disney creations have been moving away from the destructive option. For instance, Mirabel's conflict with Alma in *Encanto* is crucial in finding a direction of personal development and in discovering what makes Mirabel special. While Alma is in denial, Mirabel has wisdom and insight – which at first do not look like special gifts – to scrutinize her family's success and to point out its failures and secrets. In the end the grandmother accepts that Casa Mirabel is not as stable and perfect as she wanted it to be, and the family is united again. Overcoming Alma's inflexibility and forging her own path are important elements of Mirabel's individuation. Similarly, Merida in *Brave* overthrows her mother's plans in a bid to acquire her own agency and to decide her own destiny. The mother – metaphorically presented as a bear – is the aggressive force, which Merida has to overcome, and accept, before becoming free to make her own decisions.

A number of recent film and TV narratives, including Disney's *Disenchantment* and *Cruella,* and BBC's *Fleabag*, depict the mother-daughter (or stepmother-stepdaughter) conflict as unresolved, and unresolvable. The mother does not die, physically or metaphorically, and continues to haunt the daughter, adding dynamics to her individuation process. The protagonists' relationship with the mother figure is destructive, obsessive, and, ultimately, not leading to any form of acceptance or even a compromise which the daughter expects and demands. In this sense, returning, obsessively, to the mother, and expecting love and care, only results in re-traumatizing and further fragmentation.

The protagonists of 'failed mother' narratives feel the darkness within, and act out the trauma. Paradoxically, they repeat and deepen the trauma in an attempt to heal themselves. The mother, Neumann emphasizes, is a key element of the primal relationship. She plays a significant role in the child's future individuation because the primal relationship is a 'foundation of all subsequent dependencies, relatedness and relationships. [...] ... the dependency of the small and infantile on the large containing vessel stands at the beginning of all existence' (Neumann, 2002: 17). Importantly, 'a decisive step in the development of the child within the primal relationship is the formation of a *positive-integral ego,* an ego that is able to assimilate and integrate even negative or unpleasant qualities of the outer and inner worlds, such as deprivations, pain, etc' (Neumann, 2002: 58). The mother acts as a compensatory self which communicates to the child that negative factors and events are not permanent and things will eventually improve (Neumann, 2002: 58). When the mother fails in her physical role as a guarantor of emotional security for the child, she also fails in her archetypal role as the builder of the child's future life narrative.

This unresolved, and unresolvable, primal conflict plays out throughout the chaotic, fast-changing narrative of *Disenchantment*. Its protagonist, Princess Teabeanie, is trying to find the answer to the 'mother issue' which is forming a solid narrative block regularly repeated, with some modifications, throughout the seasons, propping and directing Bean's individuation journey. The mother, Queen Dagmar (Sharon Horgan), also undergoes a number of transformations, all part of her dangerous and unpredictable character. For instance, in Season 1 she only exists as a statue and is admired by the Bean and King Zog (John DiMaggio) who are trying to find a way of reversing the spell that turned her into stone. The statue of an elegant, suffering and self-sacrificing mother is a personification of the female persona. However, when Dagmar is revived, it quickly becomes clear that she is not the idealized mother and good wife she was regarded as but a hell-dealing witch who is scheming to marry her daughter to the devil himself.

Throughout the series, Bean is hunted by Dagmar who wants to screw a metal crown to her head. The motif is also increasingly surrealistic as it is unclear in later seasons if the mother who has the habit of following Bean and popping up at various right and wrong moments, is 'real' or just a dream figure. Dagmar's visits are accompanied by the intradiegetic eerie melody which plays every time Beans opens a music box, her mother's gift. The music punctuates Bean's individuation and follows her into dreams and adventures. Bean does not want the crown or status just as she rejects any other aspects of the persona, and particularly its female version. She wants to be her messy self, not a figure split into tortured perfection and demonic cruelty.

Ultimately, the mother motif is related to the shadow and culminates at the end of Season 4 in Bean fighting with her own double who she slays, enraging the mother. Christopher Hauke writes that confronting the shadow means facing the abject and notes that Jung suggests that there may be a space in Hell for the aspects of the psyche associated with the shadow (Hauke and Hockley, 2011: 109). Bean's numerous adventures often land her in Hell, and at some point even betrothed to the Devil. Bean's individuation path is fragmented but it does lead her to a better understanding of herself. Her erratic agency takes her on a journey from being an aimless alcoholic to an individual who is trying to figure out what to do with the shadow-mother. Yet, reconciliation with Queen Dagmar may never happen. Despite the narrative expectation of reconciliation, the daughter is not owed a closure and peace with the female parent – just like the female parent is not expected to be perfect. Imperfection, often stemming from Theme 2, is one of the biggest drivers of the individuation process.

Conclusion

It is refreshing to see the new generation of narratives focusing on the complexity of the mother figure, exploring both her role in the female protagonist's life and her own struggles with motherhood, simultaneously comedic and terrifying. Liminal, imperfect, 'bad'; tricky and tricksterish, ignorant of or ignoring the demands placed onto them by society, their imperfection and lack of commitment often cause intergenerational problems. Yet, these rifts and issues are no longer confined to the horror genre – an imperfect mother is a fact of everyday life. One can certainly see the funny side to her.

References

Beauvour, Simonede (1949/2011) *The Second Sex*, London: Vintage Books.

Creed, Barbara (1993) *The Monstrous-Feminine: Film, Feminism, Psychoanalysis.* London: Routledge.

Glaser, Eliane (2021) 'Parent trap: why the cult of the perfect mother has to end', *The Guardian*, 18 May.

Hauke, Christopher and Hockley, Luke (2011) *Jung and Film II: the Return*, Hove: Routledge.

Irigaray, Luce (2007) *Je, Tu, Nous*, New York and London: Routledge.

Jung C.G. (n.d.) *The Collected Works*, Herbert Read, Michael Fordham and Gerhardt Adler, (eds.) R.F.C. Hull (trans.), London: Routledge. (Except where a different publication was used, all references are to this hardback edition.)

Konkle, Amanda (2019) 'Mothering by the Book: Horror and Maternal Ambivalence in The Babadook (2014)', *Feminist Encounter: A Journal of Critical Studies in Culture and Politics*, 3 (1–2), p. 4.

Neumann, Erich (1993) *'The Fear of the Feminine' and Other Essays on Feminine Psychology*, Princeton, NJ: Princeton University Press.

Neumann, Erich (2002) *The Child: Structure and Dynamics of the Nascent Personality*, London: Karnac.

Schama, Chloe (2018) 'In Sharon Horgan's Motherland, All Moms Are Bad Moms', *Vogue*, May 14.

Winnicott, Donald (1971/2012) *Playing and Reality*, London: Routledge.

Winnicott, Donald (2006) *The Family and Individual Development*, London: Routledge.

Blogs and Websites

NCT (2017) 'Nearly Half of New Mothers with Mental Health Problems don't get Diagnosed or Treated', https://www.nct.org.uk/about-us/media/news/nearly-half-new-mothers-mental-health-problems-dont-get-diagnosed-or-treated (accessed: 13 June 2022).

Chapter 6

The Hero/ine

Technically, in Jungian narrative analysis fighter characters are covered by the archetype of the hero. Thematically, the hero is one of the three archetypes of motivation (the other two being the child and the self), responsible for constructing an individual's personal narrative and for determining the direction of their development. In traditional narratives female protagonists and characters are largely shut out of this archetype, and out of the inspiration/motivation archetypal cluster in general (which constitutes Theme 3). The hero archetype, in all its incarnations (including the fighter and the detective) becomes progressive when it moves from the notion of traditional masculinity as the default gender option for the protagonist.

The most directly agentic of archetypes, the hero is also the one that has been used to break the stalemate in female representation, mainly because it is fairly easily to transpose its structures and components, including archetypal situations, onto female characters whereas other archetypes (for example, the trickster, the shadow or the anima) may require more intensive and intricate efforts of disentangling the character from the social mask. Actually, many of the on-screen female fighters and questors retain some controversial aspects of the female persona – attractive looks and seductive behaviour showing how mechanistic and superficial the process of simply converting a male agentic character onto the female one can be.

This section will cover two variations of the hero(ine): the seeker (detectives, cops and other characters obsessively looking for truth in predominantly crime genres) and the action character (populating mostly fantasy, sci-fi, martial art and other heavily 'defamiliarized' genres although sometimes she also can be found in more realistic narratives).

Truth Seeker: Investigators and Vigilante Cops

The 'Seeker' category contains a range of roles from which female characters have traditionally been either excluded or only admitted on certain conditions. This character category calls for intellectual self-expression, motivation, resilience and curiosity, and includes detectives and adventurers. Although

DOI: 10.4324/9781003253044-7

female detectives and vigilante cops have been present in narratives for more than a century and, as Deborah Jermyn rightly notes, its presence in TV procedurals has become so commonplace that it is no longer worthy of note (Jermyn, 2017: 260), this persona-defying role is still as acutely relevant to feminist debates as ever. The female detective's creativity, innovation and energy are shown as contributing to the creation and restoration of the order – in other words, she is granted world-building, creationist, function in contrast to traditional representations of anima-like characters whose only task is to be a recipient for others' projections.

Susan Rowland notes that the arrival of the detective protagonist, one of the most popular characters of modernity, coincided with the birth of psychoanalysis: 'Both the detective and the psychoanalyst have to search for clues to a truth that is hidden from view. In both cases the truth sought for is of unknown extent. Both cultural forms additionally structure their quests in terms of seeking an ultimately narrative understanding of knowledge' (Rowland, 2015: 5). Both are about the process, the story of discovery rather than a solution to the mystery (Rowland, 2015: 5).

The seeker has been traditionally associated with masculine rationality even though since the inception of the genre detective protagonists such as Sherlock Holmes have had liminal, deviant, trickster qualities alongside their famous deductive reasoning and impressive analytical skills (Rowland, 2015: 7). Even though the genre's aim is to restore the order in the world which has been rattled by liminal activity, the detective, driven by curiosity and the desire to disrupt the status quo, or to show it that it is flawed, is as much the trickster as the criminal being chased. Both rattle their cages, and often detectives are shown to be mavericks, or 'wounded healers', and opposed to the dull and typically useless policemen.

Importantly, the process in a contemporary detective story has been as much about the seeker as it is about the mystery (Rowland, 2015: 7). Apart from focus on the process, the detective genre, as Kristen Whissel reminds us, operates through defamiliarization, and organizes the narrative around scopic and epistemological pleasures (Whissel, 2022: 49). In the moving image versions of the genre – famously, the films of Alfred Hitchcock – these 'pleasures' were exclusively the prerogative of the male detective (John 'Scottie' Ferguson in *Vertigo* or L.B. 'Jeff' Jeffries in 'Rear Window') while the woman was the one defamiliarized, othered and studied; she was the subject caught up in the process. Multimodal rendition of the hunting for truth brings objectification and scopic activity to the fore, turning the woman into the mystery and the driver of the detective's individuation process.

What happens when the detective is a woman? When she is the one being the seeker of truth, engaging in scopic activities, turning stones, and employing the gaze to reveal the workings of the warped *status quo*? What shape would her process, her individuation, take in a genre associated with 'masculine rationality' and passive-aggressive violence? The fact that the female character is not the cause of trauma (like the Freudian mother) or simply its carrier but the person who does much of the looking for and unlocking of secrets, is a cause for celebration. She is allowed to partake in the transformative process, and to initiate change.

From Nordic Noir (*The Killing, The Bridge*) to BBC's recent crop of procedurals, the female detective or police officer is becoming an archetype in itself, normalizing the woman *with* the gaze, the woman seeker, the hero operating in the shadows. The female detective, the owner of the gaze, is as obsessive and trauma-driven as her male counterpart. Male maverick detectives are often not listened to, their unique vision regarded as bizarre and fantastical while in the case of female detective the situation is worse as her innovative solutions and obsessive drive are conflated with 'hysteria' and hormones. While male characters display 'determination', female ones are seen as 'unhealthy obsessives' if they possess the same qualities. When unemotional and focused Sarah Lund (Sophie Grabol) in *The Killing* spends a lot of time at work, she is accused of being a failed mother. Either way, there is no winning for the female seeker.

As a character, the female detective also involves the reversal of roles, and of archetypes. She is able to look as opposed to exclusively being looked at. From being locked up in Theme 2 – the voiceless anima, the enigmatic woman whose mystery is to be cracked, an inadvertent and passive participator in the scopic regime, or a victim to be saved, the female heroine moves into the agentic Theme 3 which deals with curiosity and motivation. Here she acquires her own problems to solve and traumas to heal. She also has her own path, often running alongside the mystery she is solving.

The woman looking, and searching for the truth within society and within herself, is breaking one of the main aspects of the female persona – the prohibition to question the *status quo*, and to pursue a goal beyond standing still and looking pretty. The female detective (re-)claims scopic and epistemic equality through a whole range of archetypes from Themes 1 and 3, namely, the hero (for drive and agency), the self (for guidance), the child (for inspiration), the shadow (for self-analysis which turns into a drive) and the trickster (for asserting individuality and stirring up the stale and ineffectual *status quo*). These claims, however, are often met with resistance and disdain at the sight of someone who has broken the bonds of both the female persona and – through the trickster/shadow traits – challenged the rules existing for all members of society.

'Lady detective' is a modernist phenomenon which entered the public imagination in the second half of the nineteenth century. As Therie Hearney-Seabrook notes in her article about Catherine Louisa Pirkis's Loveday Brooke stories (1893), the female sleuth was a subversive phenomenon set against the dominance of male looking and speaking. If the detective is someone intrusive, someone proactive, how does the female detective maintain her pace and her dignity in the face of being judged and relegated to her small box? Pirkis argues:

Female vision and visibility were, indeed, culturally problematic but the female voice was regarded with just as much suspicion and dismay, both for its possible content and for the very fact of its delivery at all. The muse inspired because her vocal submission furthered male performativity. What then of the female detective who performs successfully through her own combined abilities of surveillance and speech? The detective must deploy her voice to ask questions generally, interrogate suspects, report findings, summarize evidence, and interpret others' statements and actions in the context of the juridico-legal discourses that define her own public agency.

(Hearney-Seabrook, 2007: 76)

More than a century and many more female sleuths later, scopic and epistemic agency played through the archetypes is still the source of amazement (and amusement): the female detective is the woman who engages in behaviour not matching her gender, who dares to protect and to penetrate instead of waiting to be protected (and penetrated). Mulvey explores the drive to epistemic equality through the myth of Pandora's box. In the myth, Pandora opens the box containing all the evils of the world out of curiosity. Her drive to discover and to investigate 'is directed at a culture in which woman has not, traditionally, been the possessor of knowledge and which has, traditionally, tended to consider femininity as an enigma' (Testaferri and Pietrapaolo, 1995: 4). Pandora's compulsive desire to look and to explore instead of passively mirroring the male gaze is a serious threat to male dominance, and thus is presented as 'the end of the world'. This mythological character, Mulvey argues, represents feminist defiance of objectified passivity expected of women in male-dominated cultures:

> While curiosity is a compulsive desire to see and to know, to investigate which is secret and to reveal the contents of a concealed space, fetishism is born out of a refusal to see, a refusal to know, and a refusal to accept the difference that the female body symbolizes. Out of this series of turnings away, of covering over, not the eyes but understanding, of looking fixedly at any object that holds the gaze, female sexuality is bound to remain a mystery, condemned to return as a symbol of anxiety while overvalued and idealized in imaginary. Hollywood cinema has built its appeal and promoted its fascination by emphasizing the erotic nature of the female star concentrated in a highly stylised and artificial presentation of femininity. [...] The myth of Pandora and the box are similarly imbricated with the structure of fetishism. But Pandora opens the box containing everything that fetishism disavows. The box is, in this sense, a fetish that fails.
>
> (Testaferri and Pietrapaolo, 1995: 18)

Curiosity, Mulvey notes, sets up a 'configuration of space through its association with investigation' (Testaferri and Pietrapaolo, 1995: 9). The box lures

Pandora, and prompts her to act and to discover, thus breaking down the 'regime of fetishism' (Testaferri and Pietrapaolo, 1995: 18). Transgressing the rules of the regime, exposing it to unsafe objects, forcing it to look at the horror of castration without the distance, is seen by the patriarchy not just as a mere act of defiance as it creates an association between the feminine and fear of evil (Testaferri and Pietrapaolo, 1995: 18).

The woman insisting on her right to look is driven by 'epistemophilia'. In this sense, the female detective is the descendant of the Blue Woman, having shaken off the shame, fear and sense of powerlessness:

> Although Eve's story highlights the knowledge theme, the epistemophilia, as it were, inherent in the drive of curiosity, the myth associates female curiosity with forbidden fruit rather than with forbidden space. The motif of space and curiosity can be found again symptomatically in the fairy story *Bluebeard*. The story is about his last wife, a young girl who is given the free run of his vast palace with the exception of one room which her husband forbids her to enter. Its little key begins to excite her curiosity until she ignores the luxury all around her and thinks of nothing else. Then, one day, when she thinks her husband is away, she opens the door and finds the bodies of all his former wives still bleeding magically from terrible wounds and tortures.
>
> (Testaferri and Pietrapaolo, 1995: 9)

The archetypes lead the detective in her double journey for justice and self-determination. The trickster/shadow combination is a visible presence in moving image narratives featuring female detectives. They tend to be the opposite of team players, their difficult character traits causing tension at work and at home. Yet, their lack of perfection which equals the refusal to live with the female persona, also leads them to discoveries others miss. Their trauma and darkness, the shadowy side coupled with the tricksterish (or foolish) impulse to disregard danger to themselves and to others, make them difficult colleagues and lead to all kinds of trouble while also helping them resist open sexism, survive physical and emotional violence and ignore more subtle demands to put on the 'proper face', the nice persona.

For instance, Sarah Lund, *The Fall*'s Stella Gibson (Gillian Anderson, BBC, 2013–2016), *Happy Valley*'s Catherine Cawood (Sarah Lancashire, BBC, 2014–2016), *Top of the Lake*'s Robin Griffin, and *Vigil*'s Amy Silva, played by Suranne Jones (BBC 2021) are all regarded as stuck-up, difficult women. All break rules regularly, enraging their bosses and colleagues; all are relentless and unpredictable in their pursuit of truth, divergent thinking, and messy creativity fuelling the narratives' defamiliarization machine which uproots reality and questions the mundane.

Rudeness and epistemophilia, expressed via the shadow and the trickster, seem to go well together. Yet, a public and blunt subversion of the female persona attracts violence towards the female sleuth. Robin Griffin is regularly insulted and physically assaulted by men. Silva is repeatedly locked in small spaces on the submarine by different men in order to prevent her from doing her job. Gibson is treated with disdain and suspicion by her colleagues as well as physically attacked by the perpetrator, Paul Spector (Jamie Dornan) at the end of Season 3 of *The Fall*. Sergeant Cawood, called 'an old woman' by her nemesis, a serial rapist and murderer Tommy Lee Royce (James Norton), is often on the receiving end of misogynistic abuse both in and outside of her job as a police officer.

The female detective's tricksterish epistemophilia, the unstoppable, impulsive desire to look for the hidden, to seek knowledge, is what restores order by defamiliarizing broken normality and revealing the cracks in it. The impulse to look is the antithesis of the female persona with its implications for standing still and being available for projections. Another challenge to the persona is manifested in the detective's refusal to make conscious efforts to look feminine, as illustrated by Sarah Lund's sweater-jeans-parka combo and Catherine Cawood's unremarkable everyday attire.

This, however, is not the case in all narratives featuring a female police officer or detective. The original crime drama *Charlie's Angels* (1976–1981) features oversexualized and much-copied outfits and hair styles worn by its three protagonists, Sabrina Duncan (Kate Jackson), Jill Munroe (Farrah Fawcett), and Kelly Garrett (Jacklyn Smith). Their boss, the invisible Charlie (John Forsythe) behaves as if she owns them. Some of its subsequent remakes, like the 2000 film *Charlie's Angels* with Lucy Liu, Drew Barrymore and Cameron Diaz, feature a plenty of tight and pretty outfits, high heels and perfect hair, at the expense of the 'seeker' function of the protagonists. They are the ones who are looked at, not the agentic ones who are looking.

In a more recent example, Stella Gibson has a wardrobe of expensive and stylish blouses and is not afraid to flaunt her sexuality. Stella's attention to her appearance has inspired articles recalling, assessing and rating her clothes. For instance, Hannah Marriott writes in *The Guardian* that Gillian Anderson's 'steely cop' has become a fashion icon who emerges out of a sleeping bag at the police station in 'magically wrickle-free' pastel blouses. On Gibson, even the colour pink is 'reclaimed' as tough (Marriott, 2019).

The show's creators, indeed, juxtaposed the colours and textures traditionally associated with the female persona – its luxurious, sensual version – pink, pastels and silk – with Stella's mental toughness, unflappable demeanour, resilience and persistence. Yet, Deborah Jermyn argues writing about *Prime Suspect USA* and *The Fall,* the focus on appearance is clearly voyeuristic as demonstrated by all the constant media obsession with the protagonists' sartorial choices (Jermyn, 2017: 265). A well-dressed detective, Jermyn insists, is a 'superficial but glossily packaged' nod to post-feminist gains, a thinly veiled 'regressive move' (Jermyn, 2017: 266).

The tension between female agency and the appearance aspect of the female persona cuts across a whole range of archetypes and roles female characters embody (as discussed in other chapters) although in the detective it is perhaps the most noticeable because it distracts the audience from the intensity of the character's epistemophilic engagement. Whether attention to appearance is regressive, in fictional characters or in real life, is debatable, but, judging by the amount of media attention blouses, sweaters and hats worn by the protagonists get – this is a powerful addition to the multimodal picture of the sleuth/detective/vigilante cop which draws the focus away from the character's agentic functions.

Happy Valley (BBC, 2014–)

Luckily, not all of the police/detective characters have the love of clothes as an added multimodal value, one of them, famously, being Sergeant Catherine Cawood from BBC's procedural drama *Happy Valley*.

Sergeant Cawood (Sarah Lancashire) is the heart and soul of her community, helping people in need and in trouble within and outwith her professional duties. When she is not catching rapists and drug lords out in the streets of a small Yorkshire town, she helps her family, friends and vulnerable individuals. Cawood is a typical 'wounded hero' with a painful backstory and a temper which often gets her in trouble: her teenage daughter committed suicide shortly after giving birth to a son, conceived by rape in a violent relationship with a man who would go on to become a serial killer. Catherine adopted the child, Ryan (Rhys Connah) who is proving to be hard work and often gets in trouble at school. Cawood's sister (Siobhan Finneran) helps bring up Ryan.

Cawood is someone who deeply cares about truth and obsessively looks for cues, both on-and-off duty. Her intense epistemophilia is not about (Freudian) pleasure but about (Jungian) impulse to get to the core of things. In this, she is inseparable from her community, her individuation process woven into it: while Catherine struggles with her shadow (temper, stubbornness, anger issues, depression), her town is plagued with drug addiction, poverty, violence and misogyny. Cawood individuates against this lacklustre, tough backdrop, dealing both with her personal issues and solving the crimes in her community.

She does this without any nod to the female persona although she admits to parenthood being an important part of her identity. In the fifth episode of the first season Catherine explains to her ex-husband, Richard (David Riddell), that she simply cannot celebrate her own birthday when her daughter, Becky, is dead. In fact, Cawood's unstoppable motivation, her impulsive epistemophilia, are driven in the first two seasons by the desire to avenge Becky's death and to punish her daughter's abuser, Tommy Lee Royce.

Yet, her identity is not locked up in motherhood. Catherine harbours a whole bouquet of archetypes: she is a fighter, has a noticeable shadow, has a tricksterish habit of breaking rules and looking where she is not supposed to look, and is compared to God (the self) by a colleague. These archetypes interweave, forming an intricate set of personal problems leading to a ful-filling individuation path and infusing Cawood's character with vigour, com-plexity and intensity. Her trickster and her shadow are frequently entangled, with Cawood becoming insubordinate or losing her temper with both collea-gues and superiors, and criminals. However, this insubordination also leads to moments of inspiration and discovery like it does in Season 1 when Catherine breaks into the house in which she had spotted the recently-released Tommy Lee Royce, and discovers evidence of kidnapping and rape.

Cawood's shadow is what is driving her success and her epistemophilia since obsessiveness is one of this archetype's chief qualities (Jung, CW 9/2: para. 15). She is certainly angry, most of the time managing to keep it under control and occasionally exploding like she does in the last episode of Season 1 when she finds Tommy Lee Royce in the boat with Ryan, about to set ablaze both himself and the boy, and starts kicking him and spraying him from a fire extinguisher until her colleagues drag her off. This trickster-shadow impulse helps her defamiliarize her surroundings. And to notice things which her 'normal' and rule-bound colleagues and superior cannot see.

Like any trickster, Catherine is both ordinary and extraordinary, human and divine (Jung, CW9/1: paras. 465–472). Her total absence of the 'appear-ance' aspect of the female persona is reflected in her clothes. When not dres-sed in her police attire, she can be seen wearing a fleece, a pair of jeans, a woolly scarf, and a shaggy-looking parka. In this oxymoronic, tricksterish combination or the ordinary and the extraordinary, she is compared to God by her younger colleague and protégée, Ann Gallagher (Charlie Murphy). Ann had been kidnapped by Tommy in Season 1 and, inspired by Catherine, becomes a police officer in Series 2. Ann is drunk and emotional when she does the comparison and cannot explain what she means by it. It does make sense, however: Catherine is the flawed, suffering, limited-omniscient, post-modern trickster-God struggling with her own shadow yet still doing her best to help others. Stanley Diamond notes that God as a trickster is ambivalent, his actions often incomprehensible while Paul Radin calls trickster-God 'creator and destroyer, giver and negator' (Radin, 1972: xvii). Chaotic yet controlling, the one who notices and sees more than everyone else, Sergeant Cawood manages to rise after every blow and to keep moving after dis-appointments and disasters. Importantly, she owns the act of looking despite numerous dangers to her physical and emotional wellbeing. Blundering and imperfect but refusing to live in fear and shame, she is led by the self, and, to the best of her abilities, also shows the way to others.

The female detective, the seeker of truth, is the ultimate reversal of the Bluebeard narrative as the act of looking is owned by the protagonist. Looking may be impulsive, or intense, and may get the owner in trouble, but it is nevertheless an important step in defying and rejecting the female persona. The act, and process, of looking activate a whole range of archetypal roles, from boundary-negotiating the shadow and the trickster, to the archetypes of inspiration such as the hero and the self, taking the protagonist beyond the typical anima/mother passivity.

The Action Heroine/Fighter

From the Dora Milaje warriors of Wakanda (*Black Panther*, 2018) to Rey's and Bo-Katan Kryze's (Katee Sackhoff) exploits on the wastelands of various planets in the *Star Wars* universe, female fighters have been increasingly prominent in action and non-realist genres such as fantasy, sci-fi, horror and dystopia. Vampire and zombie slayers, utopian and post-apocalyptic survivors, telekinetic superheroes, extreme treasure hunters, martial arts champions, space marines, cyberpunk rebels, jailbird mercenaries, medieval and wannabe knights, and secret service agents, both as protagonists and as secondary characters, have been populating imagined worlds for several decades now.

Action heroines have a tendency to capture the cultural imagination (although some, perhaps, for the wrong reasons): Lara Croft, famously portrayed by Angelina Jolie (*Lara Croft: Tomb Raider*, 2001; developed from the video games series *Tomb Raider* (Eidos Interactive/Square Enix)); Beatrix Kiddo (Uma Thurman) from Quentin Tarantino's *Kill Bill* (2003–4), Trinity from Wachowski's *The Matrix Series* (1999; 2003), Imperator Furiosa (Charlize Theron) in *Mad Max: Fury Road* (2015) and many others. Even Tim Burton made a film with a defiant female protagonist going on a quest of self-discovery (*Alice in Wonderland,* 2010). Many of these characters came to screen from video games, comic books and novels. They also come from a variety of genres, from high fantasy to martial arts and procedurals. Animation heroines, such as Merida in *Brave* and the more proactive Disney heroines also deserve close attention.

Television abides in examples of women in 'traditional' individuation quests: *Xena: Warrior Princess* (1995–2000); *Buffy the Vampire Slayer* (1997–2003), *La Femme Nikita* (1997) and *Nikita* (2010–2013), Nordic Noir series *Forbrydelsen* (*The Killing,* 2007–2012) and *The Bridge* (2011-), and the international 'high fantasy' blockbuster *Game of Thrones* (2011–). A host of Marvel and DC heroines appeared too, poised for action albeit scantily-clad – in other words, seemingly breaking the rules by going on a quest while still wearing one of the most prominent aspects of the female persona – projective/introjective sexuality. They include Gal Gadot's Wonder Woman (*Wonder Woman,* 2017, directed by Patty Jenkins); Scarlett Johansson's Natasha Romanoff/Black Widow (the *Avengers* franchise (2012–2019); *Black Widow,* 2021, directed by Cate Shortland); and Margot Robbie's Harley Quinn (*Suicide Squad*, directed by Richard Ayer, 2016; *Birds of Prey,* directed by Cathy Yan, 2020 and *The Suicide Squad* (James Gunn, 2021)). The progress is evident: for instance, Natasha Romanoff and Wonder Woman have an entire movie to themselves instead of being part of a team or a semi-protagonist (like Charlize Theron's Imperator Furiosa in George Miller's *Mad Max: Fury Road*, 2015). Notably, more female directors have been engaged in the making of superhero films thus addressing the concerns outlined in the Annenberg report.

Yet, some aspects of the female persona are more difficult to shift. From Sigourney Weaver's (and Ridley Scott's) Ellen Ripley in *The Alien*, the action heroine has undergone a range of transformations, becoming more masculinized in her behaviour and appearance in the 1980s (Sara Connor in *The Terminator* (1984)), then regaining the erotic appeal while also retaining the hard-won masculine qualities (Lara Croft from the *Tomb Raider* films, 2001 and 2003 respectively; Buffy Summers in *Buffy the Vampire Slayer* (1997–2003)) (Buikema and Van Der Tuin, 2009: 179). The sexualization of the action heroine in the 1990s and early 2000s was in line with the 'girl power' movement and third-wave feminism with its optimistic view on the possibility of women 'having it all'. Anneke Smelek comments on the voyeuristic camera in *Lara Croft: Tomb Raider* (2001) which lingers on Lara's (Angelina Jolie) various body parts, moulding her sex appeal with athleticism, resilience, and bravery (Smelek, 2009: 178–179). Bennett notes the move towards a utilitarian trend towards the end of the decade, with characters such as Jessica Jones, played by Krysten Ritter in Marvel's *Jessica Jones* (Netflix, 2015–2019) eschewing sex appeal completely, both in their appearance and their behaviour (Bennett, 2021: 6). This could be an attempt, 'on the part of the makers of the given show, to vaunt its (supposed) progressive, feminist credentials' (Bennett, 2021: 6).

Yet, despite the tendency to tone down the consumable femininity, many action heroines are still made to look traditionally attractive. Taylor and Glitsos note that while female-led superhero films such as *Wonder Woman* (2017) and *Captain Marvel* (2019) are a sign that female representation is improving in the film industry in particular, their bodies are also stylized and situated in the past (Taylor and Glitsos, 2021: 9–12). For instance, they note that in *Black Widow* (2021) Natasha Romanoff's character (Scarlett Johansson) is heavily sexualized, as per the Cold War mythology of the Soviet *femme fatale*, simultaneously dangerous and seductive: the character is essentialized, and embodies 'a politics which encourages women to weaponize psycho-sexual manipulation' (Taylor and Glitsos, 2021: 11).

This is certainly true of *Wonder Woman*'s Diana Prince (Gal Gadot), a demi-god, whose costumes, particularly her battle suit and the blue gown she wears to the gala at the German High Command, are objectifying and revealing, some to the point of being fetishist, and meant to emphasize her femininity. Although Diana as a character seems to be very straightforward and therefore incapable of deliberately utilizing 'psycho-sexual manipulation', her creators certainly are aware of the power of sex appeal. One reviewer, however, points out that displaying muscular thighs is in itself a subversive, persona-destroying act; particularly because the muscle symbolizes action rather than nurture (Williams, 2017). Basically, Diana fights male violence with 'better violence', which it itself is a 'feminist act' (Williams, 2017).

Quite apart from the visual aspect of the female persona, which has proven to be inextinguishable, the role of the fighter afforded to a female character is in itself a big win. At the very least, female characters moved on from accepted passivity and victimhood to agentic behaviour. The essentialist thinking which underlines traditional narrative construction equates the presence of a penis with proactive behaviour (either positive or negative), and its absence with the waiting position, which also includes victimhood. 'Killer' is the kind of 'vocation' or 'profession' that features very rarely still in films and dramas led by female protagonists, and if you take stock of secondary female characters, the returns are not going to be any more impressive.

In her book *Men, Women and Chainsaws: Gender in the Modern Horror Film* (1992) Carol Clover asks the question why there are not 'more and better female killers' in the horror genre narratives. The killer, she rightly notes, is 'stubbornly male' while the victim is female, which 'would seem to suggest that representation itself is at issue' (Clover, 1992: 47). The problem, Clover concludes, is that the killer asserts his masculinity (often compromised or doubted by society, family or women) by thrusting his phallic objects (knives, drills) into women. A woman has no masculinity to assert, or a phallic object to thrust (Clover, 1992: 47). What kind of killer or a sadist would this deficiency (or lack, as Lacan would call it) would make her? Besides, she is a 'mother' and a nurturer; and killing is an activity incompatible with 'mothering'. So, even on the cruelty front women have been left out. As Zoe Williams notes in her review of *Wonder Woman*, 'women are repeatedly erased from the history of classical music, art and medicine. It takes a radical mind to pick up that being erased from the history of evil is not great either' (Williams, 2017).

Clover stresses that the horror genre was already carefully subverting the 'traditional disposition of sex roles on screen' over a decade before *Thelma and Louise* (1991) introduced female protagonists who refused to be victims of their habitus in general and of men managing this habitus in particular. This film, Clover writes, 'has been a turning point on this score' (Clover, 1992: 235). Clover draws the reader's attention to the fact that the 'rape and revenge' motif had been a prominent feature of horror narratives such as *Carrie* (1976) and *I Spit on Your Grave* (1978) since the middle of the nineteen seventies. The narrative element, Clover laments, has now been absorbed by the mainstream cinema (Clover, 1992: 235–236).

Refreshingly (controversial as it may sound), the new generation of action heroines also take on male enemies and rivals. For instance, Mulan in Disney's 2020 film adaptation protects the emperor by killing the leader of the enemy army, Bori Khan. In season four of *Stranger Things* Eleven/Jane manages to push Henry Creel/One (Jamie Campbell Bower) into the Upside Down where he turns into the evil spirit Vecna. Meanwhile, in Disney's *Obi-Wan Kenobi* (2022), the protagonist is hunted by the strong-willed Jedi-hunter, Revan Sevander (Moses Ingram) who even kills her superior, the Grand Inquisitor (Rupert Friend) because he was in the way of her ambition.

The Heroine's Individuation Process

Jungian analysis shows a new dimension to the action heroine. The female fighter, aligning with the hero archetype and the hero's set of archetypal events, situations, and encounters, is neither passive nor afraid of difficult, even brutal, decisions on her archetypal path. The archetype of the hero is chronologically linked with the child and the self, moving from a challenging yet magical and inspiring childhood to an unattainable perfection, assisted by various other archetypes and going through a range of archetypal situations. Neumann writes that the self is inseparable from the psyche in the early stages of human development (uniting the two archetypes), and the desire to regain this harmony is a chief goal of the individuation process (Neumann, 2002: 91). In this sense, the journey happens in the present while the past, particularly childhood, provides motivation and inspiration and the future is build and shaped as she deals with the challenges metaphorized in archetypal images and situations.

The heroine having a past, a present and a future is an important point even though it sounds banal. There was a tendency for traditional and victim-type heroines to be locked in one temporal mode, or to be frozen in time, for instance, only thinking of the past in the case of rape-revenge narratives or planning a future family while trying to ensnare a husband. By contrast, action heroine incorporates elements of her struggles into her personality. She is building this personality as she is living her journey and learning from the battles and the encounters.

The initial impetus for her to go on the journey comes from the child while the self is clearly the most vocal and influential force on it, but other archetypes also play a role in the formation of the heroine's identity. For instance, Beatrix Kiddo from the *Kill Bill* films is driven by the (negative) animus as she goes on a killing spree of her former boss and their associates. The teenage warrior Arya Stark (Maisie Williams) in *Game of Thrones* is inspired by the father or, rather, the father/animus combination which also merge into the self as she is trained and guided by various men (Syrio Forel, Yoren, the Hound, Jaqen H'ghar) on her physical/spiritual journey to become a fighter and to find her own way in life. Her path is unique and the guidance she receives is almost exclusively provided by men, interchangeable incarnations of her animus, culminating in the figure of the Faceless Man/Jaqen (Tom Wlaschiha) whose ability to change appearance is a direct reference to the plasticity of the animus.

Quite often the archetypal constellation of the child, the father, the animus and the shadow often present in action heroine narratives shows the female character as focused on her external and internal enemies and foregoing – at least, at present, within the current narrative frame – the desire to have a family. There is no space for the female persona in this combination of archetypes. Even when romantic encounters happen, and are given narrative space (as they do in *Wonder Woman* and its sequel, *Wonder Woman 1984*), they do not tend to result in a 'happily ever after' sequence. Wonder Woman's lover Steve (Chris Pine) dies in the first film, and comes back as a spirit in the second, all the while acting as an inspiration for Diana's adventures, enhancing her focus on combat rather than hindering it or distracting her from her duties.

Rey in the *Star Wars* films *The Force Awakens* (2015), the *Last Jedi* (2017), and *The Rise of Skywalker* (2019) is very much focused on her journey as a soldier and a Jedi. She wears gender-neutral clothes, has a tragic and murky background typical of child prodigy destined to be a hero, and most of her encounters are either related to training or fighting. Her only romantic (and controversial) moment involves kissing Kylo Ren/Ben Solo (Adam Driver) at the end of the *Rise of Skywalker*, but this brief unity is cut short as Ben proceeds to die immediately afterwards. Meanwhile, Disney's *Mulan* (2020) does not specify what happens to Mulan's potential relationship with her love interest, Chen Honghui (Yoson An) as she is promoted to the rank of the imperial officer and intends to continue her army career.

Another child-shadow constellation is explored in the character of Eleven/Jane (Bobbi Millie Brown) from *Stranger Things*. Eleven, named after a number she is given at a secret government laboratory where child prodigies are turned into weapons, is a tortured individual whose special gift (telekinetic powers) both drive her on her journey and impair her connection with others. Her broken childhood creates a significant shadow which Jane/Eleven keeps resisting while also inspiring her to find herself in a colourful consumer society which is alien to her. The shadow is also the driving force behind Jane's creativity and individuation process as she keeps going back to the tiled rooms of the laboratory, either in flashbacks or physically, every time she reproaches herself or questions her abilities. In many ways, Eleven resembles Tim Burton's 'dark child' (best personified in Edward Scissorhands) – an umbrella character which defines the director's career. The child is wounded, creative, and longing for human connection – yet unable to touch for fear of hurting others (Bassil-Morozow, 2010). Possessing special powers that can hurt is a fairly new element in on-screen female individuation; it certainly adds complexity to characters such as Eleven or Princess Elsa from *Frozen*.

Ultimately, Jane succeeds in being useful to the capitalist society by quashing the evil coming from its collective unconscious, including rival ideologies and inconvenient truths – the shadow of capitalism – hiding underneath its aspirational lifestyle, personified by the Starcourt Mall. The shadow – the ability to cause harm to others – bestowed upon her by Dr. Brenner (Matthew Modine) also becomes the bridge to Jane's new community (an important part of the individuation process) as the ability to harvest frustration and anger into telekinetic harm proves to be invaluable when dealing with evil Russians, various demons from the parallel world called the Upside Down, and other baddies. Eleven's individuation happens along the boundary between the personal and the collective, her superhero abilities saving the capitalist regime from itself.

Importantly, the narrative of *Stranger Things* allows Eleven to get angry – *really* angry – without being pushed into the 'Carrie' territory (which is good news because horror representations of young women depict repressed anger as a point of no return). Eleven's anger binds the narrative together as it simultaneously offers an outlet for Eleven's frustrations and a salvation for her community. Whereas she regularly stumbles upon 'Carrie' moments (such as being rejected by her the classmates in her new school in Season 4, and lashing out), her energy is inevitably harvested for the common good and her identity is woven into society. Her individuation process is inherently social, the female anger being an integral (and constructive) part of it.

Other characters openly celebrate their shadow. Margot Robbie's recurring character, Harley Quinn, the fighter-trickster in *Birds of Prey* (2020) and the two (rather different!) *Suicide Squad* films, is forced to become a solo flyer after her break-up with Joker (the relationship tends to be shown in flashbacks so, technically, it is outside the present narrative frame). Despite her slim figure, Harley is a deadly and fearless assassin. Unlike Mulan and Rey, and like Wonder Woman, Harley openly wears her female persona: her outfits tend to be revealing and her behaviour is deceptively seductive. However, her persona is displayed in an ironic way, metaphorically as well as literally – a trickster's way of duping her enemies into a false feeling of safety.

In all three films, Robbie's character is sexually attractive albeit her seductiveness is openly theatrical, ironic and consciously referential: in *Suicide Squad* (2016) she performs an aerial acrobatic routine for the team who came to recruit her into the 'suicide squad'. The Harley of *Birds of Prey* (2020) is a roller girl, projecting silliness and playfulness. For much of the 2021 *Suicide Squad* remake, Robbie's trickster-fighter wears a red ball gown which she has to wear because her dictator 'fiancé', Silvio Luna, is attracted to dramatic, fragile, exaggerated femininity. In all three films, she wears full make-up which is often neglected and smudged.

Tricksters of all genders are semiotically confusing as their aim is to escape the system's desire to 'pin' the signifier and to build a meaning for each object. The trickster is pre-and-anti-systemic and therefore plays with signifiers, rejecting and mocking the system's push for a stable meaning. Tricksters cause semiotic chaos by transgressing boundaries and disobeying rules; by not having a name or having several; and by targeting the system's ability to be in control (Bassil-Morozow, 2015). The female trickster's dress code is bound to be based on the evasive, floating never-finalized signifier. The trickster's ever-changing, ever-chaotic presence reminds the system that permanence is not possible and that any reference is but a man-made, system-produced artifice. There are simply no 'genuine' objects. As Baudrillard notes, iconoclasts whom one accuses of disdaining and negating images, were those who accorded them their true value, in contrast to the iconolaters who only saw reflections in them and were content to venerate a filigree God' (Baudrillard, 1994: 5). The trickster is rejoicing at the loss of the sturdy and reliable meaning yet it is also the trickster who can recreate power and creativity as well as renew an ageing system. In this sense, Harley Quinn disrupts the chain of signification and reorders the images and objects in order to challenge the existing social order – the one in which women are expected to wear a rigid persona, be a nice wife, mother and daughter, and to serve their society by being placid and by surrendering their reproductive functions to the system.

Her hair styles, too, underscore the subversion of the 'dumb blonde' stereotype. Throughout the three films, her hair undergoes a range of transformations, mostly in the direction of 'ruining' the perfect shade of platinum blonde by various ombre tinges. For instance, in *Suicide Squad* and *Birds of Prey* she has pigtails dyed 'mermaid' blue and pink, and in *The Suicide Squad* strands of her long white hair are dyed red and black creating a messy, over- processed effect similar to Emma Stone's recent Cruella character. The two-toned hair, of course, has been a consistent trope in the horror genre since Whale's *Bride of Frankenstein*, standing for otherness and subversion of the female persona. The disruptive hair contrasts with the glamorous, coiffed locks of classic Hollywood stars. Appearance has always been a significant part of the Western social semiotics. Cultural visions of 'propriety' code black or brightly coloured hair, and certain hairstyles such as pigtails, as liminal and suitable for certain vocations – for instance, entertainment, but otherwise not fitting into the expectations of middle-class decency and professionalism. The same applies to tattoos and extreme piercings which are relegated to the margins and coded as inappropriate because of their emphasis on individualism and defiance of the bland, unifying forces of the systemic. An individual in the workplace is part of a larger machine, their will subjugated to its demands and needs.

It is important to remember, however, that rebellion sells and can be packaged as neatly and sold as brazenly as a product as the persona. Although Harley does use her dress sense to break boundaries and challenge norms, often by staging a clash between her appearance (a beautiful red ball gown) and her behaviour (being a ruthless killer), her rebellion is a recognizable trope in popular culture whereby a sexy, dangerous female vamp character (like Xenia Onatopp (Femke Janssen) in *GoldenEye* (1995)) attempts to challenge or disrupt the world dominated by men. The trope is attractive, does sell, and Harley Quinn is its worthy extension. Whether this neatly-packaged rebellion will result in any real change remains to be seen.

Conclusion

Agentic options for female on-screen characters have certainly been expanding, with more characters utilizing the full archetypal range, from motherhood to heroic deeds. Importantly, many contemporary narratives have been challenging this and other cultural prescriptions as to how a standard female journey should be structured. The female warrior characters in *Game of Thrones* – Arya Stark, Brienne of Tarth or the Wildling women – would not be happy in the role of providers of care and warmth to the suffering community. Many other heroic, seeking female characters are happy to perform heroic deeds alongside family duties, demonstrating a full archetypal and intellectual potential. Archetypal strands that had previously been out of reach for the female protagonist – looking, breaking through, finding, being creative, dealing with the shadow, etc – now add complexity to these characters' journeys. These new stories are exciting and providing important behavioural templates for future generations.

References

Bassil-Morozow, H. (2010) *Tim Burton: The Monster and the Crowd*, London: Routledge.

Bassil-Morozow, H. (2015) *The Trickster and the System: Identity and Agency in Contemporary Society*, Hove: Routledge.

Baudrillard, Jean (1981/2000) *Simulacra and Simulation*, London: Routledge.

Bennett, Eve (2021) '"I Can't Get Her to Wear a Dress for the Life of Me:" American Telefantasy Action Heroines, Utilitarian Style and the End (or Not) of Postfeminism', *Quarterly Review of Film and Video*, 40 (1), pp. *138–161*.

Buikema, R. and Van Der Tuin, I. (Eds.) (2009) *Doing Gender in Media, Art and Culture*, London: Routledge.

Clover, Carol J (1992) *Men, Women and Chainsaws, Gender in the Modern Horror Film*, Princeton, NJ: Princeton University Press.

Hendrey-Seabrook, Therie (2007) 'Reclassifying the Female Detective of the Fin de Siecle: Loveday Brooke, Vocation, and Vocality', *Clues: a Journal of Detection*, 26 (1) (Fall), pp. 75–88.

Jermyn, Deborah (2017) 'Silk Blouses and Fedoras: the Female Detective, Contemporary TV Crime Drama and the Predicaments of Feminism', *Crime Media Culture*, 13 (3), pp. 259–276.

Jung C.G. (n.d.) *The Collected Works*, Herbert Read, Michael Fordham and Gerhardt Adler, (eds.) R.F.C. Hull (trans.), London: Routledge. (Except where a different publication was used, all references are to this hardback edition.)

Marriott, Hannah (2019) 'The Fall finale: an anatomy of DSI Stella Gibson's best blouses', *The Guardian*, 19 December.

Mulvey, Laura (1995) 'Pandora: Topographies of the Mask and Curiosity', in Ada Testaferri and Laura Pietropaolo (eds.) *Feminisms in the Cinema*, Bloomington and Indianapolis: Indiana University Press, pp. 3–19.

Neumann, Erich (2002) *The Child: Structure and Dynamics of the Nascent Personality*, London: Karnac.

Testaferri, A. and Pietropaolo, L. (eds.) (1995) *Feminisms in the Cinema*, Bloomington and Indianapolis: Indiana University Press.

Radin, Paul (1956/1972) *The Trickster: A Study in American Indian Mythology*, New York: Schocken Books.

Rowland, Susan (2015) *The Sleuth and the Goddess: Hestia, Artemis, Athena and Aphrodite in Women's Detective Fiction*, London: Routledge.

Smelik, Anneke (2009) 'Lara Croft, Kill Bill and the Battle for Theory in Feminist Film Studies', in R. Buikema and I. Van Der Tuin (Eds.) *Doing Gender in Media, Art and Culture*, London: Routledge, pp. 178–192.

Taylor, Jessica and Glitsos, Laura (2021) 'Having it both ways: Containing the champions of feminism in female-led origin and solo superhero films', *Feminist Media Studies*, 21, pp. 1–15.

Whissel, Kristen (2022) 'Dial M for Murder: the Detective Thriller, the Postwar Uncanny, and 3D Cinema', *New Review of Film and Television Studies*, 20 (1), pp. 49–62.

Williams, Zoe (2017) 'Why Wonder Woman is a Masterpiece of Subversive Feminism', *The Guardian*, 5 June.

Chapter 7

The Female Trickster

The emergence of the rebellious, unruly, and chaotic female protagonist in recent television narratives, signals that the female trickster is quickly becoming a genre of its own. Shows such as *Crazy Ex-Girlfriend* (The CW/Netflix), *Disenchantment* (Netflix), *Killing Eve* (BBC), and *Fleabag* (BBC) deconstruct the female spectacle, make fun of it, and suggest discourses alternative from the vision of the female as a blank slate for male projections. This signals a social shift, and shows that there is a demand for a new type of female character, the one who does not conform to the traditional vision of what it means to be a woman; a character who is not afraid to challenge the norms and to make change happen.

Both in traditional and contemporary narratives the trickster serves as a metaphor for system renewal; for the necessity to shake things up a little (or a lot) every time they feel stagnant. The trickster arrives to disturb the system; to shock it. The trickster is often a funny man, a fool, or a rebel, breaking taboos and expectations thus delivering bouts of freedom and renewal into otherwise ordered and stringent structures.

Predictably, this fool or clown is usually male. A quick glance at the headlines concerning the lack of female comedians across the world says it all: 'Have Things Improved for Female Comedians?' (*The Independent*, 2017), 'Why Aren't There More Women On The Top-Earning Comedians List?' (*Forbes*, 2013), 'Where are All the Female Standups?' (*The Guardian*, 2012) and 'Men are Funnier than Women, Study Claims' (BBC, 2019) although the situation is slowly improving, not least thanks to on-demand services such as Netflix. Needless to say that the same goes for the rebel, the creator or the risk-taker: women in power positions face everyday struggle of proving that they are capable of doing the 'tough' job of running the company or making difficult decisions.

As O'Neill notes, 'society has normative prescriptions for behaviour, dress, and placement in the social hierarchy depending on whether one is categorized as male or female' (O'Neill, 2001: 52). Mythology and folklore, which are full of male tricksters of all shapes and sizes, are not so keen on female ones. The tasks of building, challenging, and renewing systems are seen as almost

DOI: 10.4324/9781003253044-8

exclusively male. The woman, on the other hand, is regarded as a supporter or – at best – as a subtle contributor to the system. Women are not supposed to rock the boat. The trickster is a figure that lacks nuance and is not delicate. Women are not allowed to swear, to be rough, or to wear mismatched clothes. The female persona is not compatible with tricksterish behaviour.

The trickster canon is rich and comprises a whole variety of cunning creatures: human, animal, half-human and half-animal; divine, partially divine, or not divine at all; capable of taking the form of a spider, raven, coyote, badger, salmon, bird, rabbit, fox, monkey and many other animals. However, none of these tricksters is female by default. Women are 'written out' of trickster narratives because their prescribed performative functions do not include unruly elements; or these elements have been labelled excessive - as signs of mania, hysteria or madness. The trickster is grotesque, but the female grotesque evokes the wrong kinds of excess: uncanny rather than carnivalesque, to use Mary Russo's terminology, and the uncanny woman is not entertaining but scary (Russo, 1994: 1). The trickster also inhabits the limen, the boundary, and pushing the boundaries of the existing social order by introducing change – in other words, being proactive – is traditionally seen as being in breach of the female persona.

Bodily fluids, the focus of so many a joke in trickster narratives, stop being funny and become abject when applied to female characters. For an on-screen female character to indulge in toilet humour or openly discuss her sex life is unusual. It would mean crossing the boundary into the realm of the uncanny and risking to appear as abject rather than funny. The combination of femaleness and abject used to be relegated to the horror genre. Russo notes that 'as bodily metaphor, the grotesque [grotto-esque] cave tends to look like … the cavernous anatomical female body' and

> it is an easy and perilous slide from these archaic tropes to the misogyny which identifies this hidden inner space with the visceral. Blood, tears, vomit, excrement – all the detritus of the body that is separated out and placed with terror and revulsion … on the side of the feminine – are down there in the cave of abjection.
>
> (Russo, 1994: 1)

Brian De Palma's rendition of Stephen King's *Carrie* (1976) is a good example of the fear associated with the female body. A menstruating woman is subject to taboo and stigma in many societies while in the West the subject of menstruation has traditionally been surrounded by mystery and 'dignified silence'. Coded as abject, relegated to the cultural limen, some natural functions of the female body, to use Kristeva's expression, challenge the master from their place of banishment (Kristeva, 1982: 2).

The abject woman is traditionally presented as at war with herself, her own body and its natural functions (Polanski's *Rosemary's Baby*, 1975, for example) because such characters are reflections of the male (and male writers' and directors') fear of the female grotesque although, ironically, this fear represents the distortion of the female psyche, female body, and its functions. Menstruating, sexual, pregnant women become terrifying, bewitching, angry and threatening because, when not owned by men and not mirroring them, they are immediately classed as 'foreign bodies'. Creed emphasizes that maternal semiotic authority is repressed by the symbolic law lest it becomes uncontrollable (Creed, 2007: 14). In order words, a disorder caused by a woman is not at all funny – it exists only along the mother/shadow axis. There is no female trickster – only the horrifying 'vagina dentata'.

By contrast, when the bourgeois propriety in cinematic or literary narratives is challenged by a male trickster, the result is rethinking of some of the restrictive societal norms (such as table manners or dress code). In this sense, while the male trickster, despite being an agent of chaos, is tolerated as a creature living on the margins and occasionally used to refresh the structure, the female trickster is too powerful a force to be ever invited to participate in structural change. Compared to an unruly female, a male representative of disorder is not seen as repulsive. We laugh at his antiques while women are coded an unfunny because, to cite Kristeva again, 'what represses... borrows its strength from language' (Kristeva, 1982: 14). The structure keeps culturally coding women as 'unfunny' to ensure that they accidentally do not start 'Ragnarok', that they do not trigger the collapse of the structure; they are 'put in a position of passive object in relation to defilement and the margin' (Kristeva, 1982: 70).

Luckily, a number of recent television narratives challenge this association of the female grotesque with abjection. The female grotesque is explored in them as a normal part of the individuation process; as necessary for the very existence of a functional human agency. The shows challenge the female persona as a concept as it has always fed into the notion of normality which, in the words of Russo, concedes to the misogyny permeating '"the fear of losing one's femininity", "making a spectacle of oneself", "alienating men" (meaning powerful men) or otherwise making "errors"' (Russo, 1994: 12). Trickster protagonists and other female characters in these shows make mistakes and look silly in the process just like any male comedic or dramatic character would. They are allowed to mature, progress and learn without looking like victims, damsels in distress or final girl type of survivalists whose agency and personality are defined entirely by their trauma as they cannot evolve past it.

They follow their individuation process, often blundering, doubting themselves and their decision-making. Their path is never perfectly straight, but that is the idea; the trickster is all about change, both personal and social, it is about challenging stagnation and social perceptions. The female individuation is inseparable from the trickster and its adventures, silliness and bravery. For the first time, these women are not judged or relegated to the realm of the abject: monsters, freaks or mutants.

Trickster: Definitions

The trickster is probably the most intriguing archetype. It has attracted serious attention from specialists outside the field of Analytical Psychology: sociologists, anthropologists and folklorists. Most mythological canons have a trickster character: a fool, a clown, a rebel, a prankster, or a village idiot who does the opposite of what the other residents of the village consider normal, and is therefore everyone's laughing stock.

The trickster's dislike for what we humans call 'the norm' is ingrained in the guises he takes (for it is often a male): animals, birds, creatures that lack a stable human form. The trickster is an agent of chaos so it is not surprising that there have been numerous attempts at defining its nature. Scholars from all branches of the humanities have been trying the capture the essence of the stubborn psychosocial phenomenon and, to a degree, they were successful. Many of them agree that the trickster has a dual nature and is a sort of oxymoron combining opposing qualities.

For Carl Jung, the trickster is an archetype – that is, an archaic, universal image regularly occurring in myth, folk tales and dreams. In his seminal essay 'On the Psychology of the Trickster Figure', Jung defines him as a creature of the unconscious, the wise fool, the clown, the delight-maker who has a dual nature: half-animal, half divine. Tricksters reverse the hierarchic order, are capable of changing shape and are famous for their malicious tricks and pranks. Jung also mentions the strong link between the Trickster figure and the tradition of carnival, where the Devil appeared as simia dei – the ape of God (Jung, CW9/I: paras. 465–472). The trickster is both 'subhuman and superhuman, a bestial and divine being, whose chief and most alarming characteristic is his unconsciousness' (Jung, CW 9/I: para. 472). Phylogenetically and anthropologically, it designates the dawn of civilization and the origins of human consciousness; ontogenetically he symbolizes a pre-conscious child, a creature who cannot be responsible for what he does because he is unaware of his actions. As such, it 'is a faithful reflection of an absolutely undifferentiated human consciousness, corresponding to a psyche that has hardly left the animal level' (Jung, CW9/I: para. 471).

The duality of the trickster's nature and its mutability are also emphasized by several cultural anthropologists. Paul Radin writes in the preface to *The Trickster: A Study in American Indian Mythology* (1956) that the trickster 'knows neither good nor evil yet he is responsible for both. He possesses no values, moral or social, is at the mercy of his passions and appetites, yet through his actions all values come into being' (Radin, 1972: xxiii). He also foreshadows 'the shape of man' (Radin, 1972: xxiv).

Like Radin, Karl Kerenyi calls attention to that paradoxical 'creation through destruction' quality of the trickster. Mythological tricksters are silly and irresponsible; they may walk into an existing order of things and thoughtlessly ruin it – yet out of their careless actions a new life is born. As Kerenyi notes in his analysis of tricksters in Greek mythology, often the folk prankster 'approximates to the figure of a beneficent creator and becomes what the ethnologists call 'a culture hero' (Radin, 1972: 180–181). Greek tricksters combine the sly and the stupid in them; in their behaviour we can discern both intention and lack of it. They symbolize the twilight of human consciousness:

> Prometheus, the benefactor of mankind, lacks self-interest and playfulness. Hermes has both, when he discovers fire and sacrifice before Prometheus did – without, however, bothering about mankind. In the playful cruelties which the little god practiced on the tortoise and the sacrificial cows at his first theft, and which conferred no benefit on mankind, ... we see the sly face of the trickster grinning at us, whereas in the deeds of Prometheus we see the sly and the stupid at once...
>
> (Radin, 1972: 181)

The French anthropologist Laura Makarius seeks to explain the trickster's contradictory nature by linking it to the sphere of ritual magic. According to her, the trickster is a taboo-breaker and violator of prohibitions, and 'can only retain the contradictions inherent in the violation itself' (Hynes and Doty, 1993: 73).

Apart from the promethean (and oxymoronic) role as an inadvertent culture hero, the mythological trickster has other functions in society. Most scholars agree that the trickster figure serves as a chaos-inducing element intent on challenging the existing order of things. As such, it is neither good nor bad but is a weapon which can be used to modify a rotten order or to destroy a good one. Dealing with the trickster is like a balancing act. For instance, the folklorist Barbara Babcock-Abrahams argues that the trickster is responsible for 'the tolerated margin of mess'; it is the kind of creature who does not respect rules, restrictions and regulations: 'Although we laugh at him for his troubles and his foolishness and are embarrassed by his promiscuity, his creative cleverness amazes us and keeps alive the possibility of transcending the social restrictions we regularly encounter' (Babcock-Abrahams, 1975: 147). Likewise, Andrew Samuels calls attention to the trickster's ability to revive the 'civilizing forces' of society by shaking them up (either in a positive or a negative sense). As such, this figure 'acts as a yardstick and spur to consciousness' (Samuels, 1993: 83).

An interesting point is brought forth by Mac Linscott Ricketts who writes that the trickster figure is 'the symbol of the self-transcending mind of humankind and of the human quest for knowledge and the power that knowledge brings' (Hynes and Doty, 1993: 88). Ricketts also calls the trickster 'a primitive humanist' whose structure-challenging antics are psychosocially equal to the democratic attitude characteristic of modernity:

> Unlike the shaman, the priest, and the devotee of supernaturalistic religion, the trickster looks to no 'power' outside himself, but sets out to subdue the

world by his wits and his wit. In other words, as I see him, the trickster is a symbolic embodiment of the attitude today represented by the humanist.

(Hynes and Doty, 1993: 88–89)

Other scholars recognize the trickster's role in identity formation: by challenging the structure, by rejecting it and by laughing at it, we find out own unique way of living and of doing things. For instance, Robert Pelton emphasizes the positive outcomes of the trickster's ability to challenge dominant structures which can be destructive and oppressive. He notes in the Trickster of West Africa (Pelton, 1980) that the trickster can be regarded as a 'process designed to combat darkness by bringing to light the causes of disorder' (Pelton, 1980: 286). Pelton brings together the creative and destructive traits of the trickster when he states that this figure represents the human race both phylogenetically and ontogenetically. Moreover – more than anything it is also an all-encompassing metaphor of human development and learning. Both individually and communally, the trickster seizes the fragments of his experience and discovers in them 'an order sacred by its very wholeness' (Pelton, 1980: 21).

Thus, the trickster describes the process of individual development and meaning-making in relation to a socializing and civilizing structure. As a psycho-anthropological phenomenon, it is of paramount importance for the balance between the social and the personal in the individual's life. In her book The Female Trickster: the Mask that Reveals (2007), Ricki Stephanie Tannen links this figure to Jung's idea of 'individuation' – the process 'by which individual beings are formed and differentiated' (Jung, CW6: para. 757). In particular, it is 'the development of the psychological individual as a being distinct from the general, collective psychology. Individuation, therefore, is a process of differentiation, having for its goal the development of the individual personality' (Jung, CW6: para. 757). Tannen writes that 'Trickster energy is the archetypal energy of individuation – for a culture as well as an individual' (Tannen, 2007: 3).

In *Wild/Lives: Trickster, Place and Liminality on Screen* (2010) Terrie Waddell expresses a similar view when she argues that the trickster is 'an archetypal agent of change with the potential to guide us through each jolting shift in the process of growing up' (Waddell, 2009: 1). As such, it is an important narrative element because 'with its enthusiasm for peeling away outer facades and exposing emotional vulnerabilities, trickster, as a conductor of change, is a potent driver of stories dabbling in enforced self-examination' (Waddell, 2009: xi).

The highest meaning of this archetype is in the management of the relationship between personal and social elements in the life of the individual. Essentially, the trickster symbolizes human ability to manage and process change as well as to adapt to the environment. By showing the middle finger to the gods and kings, the trickster insists on the right of the individual to make decisions instead of being dependent on the system for guidance. All people are unique and yet they are also part of a whole hierarchy of communities, from basic (family, school, urban area) to the highest level involving culture and nation. The trickster is responsible for maintaining the balance between these two spheres of the individual's life. Because the individuation process also involves maintaining the balance between these two spheres, the trickster is one of the key elements of the individuation process. It is also one of the driving forces of this process, pushing the individual towards a better understanding of his or her place in society.

The Female Trickster: Rejecting the Female Persona

It is easy to see that almost all of the trickster attributes promote being creative, free, and proactive to the point of appearing 'uncivilized' and 'dangerous' to the social order. A proper woman is not supposed to break boundaries (this would not be decent), seek to escape entrapment (on the contrary – she should try to stay as confined as possible, both physically and psychologically), be out of control of her body (and there are many taboos around female physiology and hygiene) or express her sexuality openly (she will be branded a 'whore'). She should also stay away from creativity which is reserved to men, and of course, scatology is a big taboo for female characters.

Since certain functions of the female body are censored by cultural protocols (orgasm, menstruation, childbirth, menopause, or anything to do with excretion) or, alternatively, mystified or idealized, rude jokes have been reserved exclusively for men. At best the male trickster occasionally turns into a woman to achieve a goal or as a prank (like Loki when he turns into an old lady to gauge the secret of Balder's vulnerability, or when Wakdjunkaga turns into a woman to live with the chief's son). At the same time, many of the trickster tales emphasize the power of the penis and establish a correlation between its size and its owner's maturation.

The penis is thus seen as funny and ridiculous, but also a source of creativity and power. In trickster tales it also stands for the acquisition of human identity: the trickster's maturational trajectory in trickster cycles starts off with the trickster having a lot of fun (including sexual), and ending with him becoming an ordinary member of society (where the fun ends). The female reproductive system is not afforded this kind of duality; nor is it afforded a similar transformation: the vulva is not funny, and does not stand for identity, maturation or power. On the contrary, as Creed highlights in *Monstrous Feminine: Film, Feminism and Psychoanalysis*, far from celebrating female agency and stepping outside the boundaries of the female persona, culture and cinema have consistently linked it to the horror genre: 'Horror emerges from the fact that woman has broken with her proper feminine role – she has made a "spectacle of herself" – put her unsocialized body on display' (Creed, 2007: 42). By contrast the male trickster's 'body on display' is celebrated as transgressive; as a necessary evil, as an action which has the potential for awakening the stagnating system from its harmful slumber.

The Forgotten Female Trickster

Naomi Wolf mentions the Greek mythological figure Baubo as someone who 'echoes the powerful vagina symbolism' (Wolf, 2012: 172). Baubo lifts her skirts to make Demeter, who is mourning the disappearance of her daughter, laugh again. As Wolf puts it, 'Demeter's laughter helps restore fertility to a world threatened with barrenness by her grief' (Wolf, 2012: 172). This is Robert Graves' version of Baubo's performance:

> On the tenth day, after a disagreeable encounter with Poseidon among the herds of Oncus, Demeter came in disguise to Eleusis, where the king Celeus and his wife Metaneira entertained her hospitably; and she was invited to remain as a wet-nurse to Demophoon, the newly-born prince. Their lame daughter Iambe tried to console Demeter with comically las-civious verses, and the dry-nurse, old Baubo, persuaded her to drink barley-water by a jest: she groaned as if in travail and, unexpectedly, produced from beneath her skirt Demeter's own son Iacchus, who leaped into his mother's arms and kissed her.
>
> (Graves, 1992: 90)

Wolf goes back to the time when vagina and vulva still had its important status; when it still had the right to be represented as a symbol of power and as the ultimate symbol of transition which surpasses the penis in its ability to represent liminality. The grotto-esque is the originally tricksterish, the originally rebellious. In fact, the grotto-esque symbolizes the crossing of the boundary between non-existence and existence, corresponding to the psychopomp func-tion of the trickster. Yet, the female trickster, with her powerful liminality, was lost. Wolf writes:

> The vagina began as sacred. There are vagina symbols carved into the cave walls in the earliest historic settlements. The earliest artifacts of human prehistory featured vaginas. [...] Ffrom 25.000 to 15.000 BCE, 'Venus figurines' - fertility images with pronounced vulvas - made of stone or ivory were abundant in Europe, and similar images crafted from the mud of the Nile were common in Egypt. [...] Five thousand years ago in what is now Iraq, Inanna's vulva was worshipped as a sacred site; Sumerian hymns praised the goddess's 'lap of honey', compared her vulva to 'a boat of heaven', and celebrated the bounty that 'pours forth from her womb'.
>
> (Wolf, 2012: 166–168)

The elimination of vagina (and the female trickster) from the Western mythology and culture was gradual. The Greek antiquity, Wolf emphasizes, already saw women as psychologically unstable, their sexuality mysterious and in need of subordination (Wolf, 2012: 172–173). In *Powers of Horror: an Essay on Abjection* (1982) Kristeva explores the 'semiotics of biblical abomination', of which the attitude towards the feminine formed a large part (Kristeva, 1982: 99–100). Association of vagina with defilement rather than the tricksterish bringer of change in the Western tradition has since been a form of 'protection against the poorly controlled power of mothers' (Kristeva, 1982: 77). Importantly, 'the power of pollution [...] thus transposes on the symbolic level the permanent conflict resulting from an unsettled separation between masculine and feminine power at the level of social institutions' (Kristeva, 1982: 78).

It is important to note, however, that although Kristeva's work offers an explanation of the fear of defilement associated with vagina, as well as its metonymic cultural derivatives – horror films about victimization and menstruation, or the cultural coding of women as unfunny – its use of post-Freudian/Lacanian feminist theory makes it fairly limited in its understanding of the behavioural and cultural possibilities for women. Its mapping of gender and sexuality also remains linked to the original Oedipal framework according to which women have limited entry into the Symbolic order conditional on them desiring a family.

The Oedipal framework echoes Joseph Campbell's remark that women do not need to go on a journey because they are already there, already attained perfection. It emerges that women also don't need to rebel against a structure – they are already part of it; they are their stalwarts, the keepers on tradition, so to say. It is only men who seek innovation via imperfection, and express creativity via rebellious novelty, society insists, for rebellion can be full of hardship, roughness and ugliness.

However, females do mature, make mistakes, search for identity, transition, metamorphose, suffer from uncertainty, feel lost, and make decisions. The trickster – in its socio-anthropological rather than Jungian sense – is a good way of exploring viable life choices for women which go beyond the cage of the Oedipus complex. To keep adhering to the Oedipus metaphor to explore female narratives would be self-punishing, self-limiting and accepting the vision of the female body as veering between two extremes: disgust (active) and perfection (passive). Every act of female defiance on screen still looks fresh and even shocking as the female trickster becomes a breaker of taboos, an explorer of shame, and an innovator.

The New Generation of Female Tricksters

Most trickster narratives (mythological, literary or cinematic) share a number of stock themes and motifs that serve as the backbone for the plot. Usually, a trickster narrative starts with the cunning creature being or feeling restricted (often physically), goes on to describe the trickster's escape and his adventures, and ends with the dissolution/transformation of the trickster. The most common structural elements of trickster narratives are being trapped, boundary-breaking, shapeshifting, naming issues (no name or multiple names), shamelessness, creativity, obsession with sex, scatological references, loss of control over body and mind, animal motifs, and dissolution/death of the trickster at the end of the cycle (Bassil-Morozow, 2015: 12–31). Not all elements have to be present in a narrative, and they do not have to follow in any particular order although it is fairly common for an entrapment scene to open a trickster narrative (the trickster is stuck/locked in a bottle or a box), and for the dissolution motif to round it up (the trickster disappears).

Being Trapped

The absence of the female trickster in moving image narratives – or even of female characters associated with movement and change – has been symptomatic of the industry being dominated by male decision-makers. In moving image narratives the trickster entrapment motif has traditionally been featured in male individuation narratives (for instance, *The Mask* (1994), *Bruce Almighty* (2003), *Hector and the Search for Happiness* (2014)) as a way of emphasizing the struggles and victories of the protagonist. Yet, the entrapment motif corresponds to the woman's fight for agency, for the right to individuate. Ultimately, the theme of entrapment stands for the desire for growth, for progression, for change. A rare example of a female trickster narrative prominently featuring the entrapment motif is *Drop Dead Fred* (1991) in which Lizzie (Phoebe Cates) is oppressed and humiliated by her family members and finds respite in reviving the imaginary friend from her childhood – Drop Dead Fred (Rik Mayall).

Physical entrapment in narratives is an allegory of control and order. It symbolizes the structure's desire for being in charge. The trickster that is not controlled is a menace as, unrestrained and therefore unpredictable, it can damage or even destroy the system. Neither the systemic control nor the trickster's actions aimed at blocking it are intrinsically good or bad. In fact, the entrapment motif foregrounds the balance between stability and change. Tricksters can be imprisoned at any stage throughout the narrative, and when they are locked up, this is usually as a punishment for some misbehaviour such as theft, lying or murder. When a narrative starts with the trickster freeing itself from his prison, the rest of the narrative is devoted to the characters' efforts to regain control over the situation and to recapture or tame it.

Restrained tricksters can be presented as suffering and heroic, malevolent, and dangerous or playful and stupid – but their task is always to defy and dupe the system. Their transgressions are also of differing importance. For instance, Prometheus is an example of a heroic prisoner; Loki, who directly threatens to bring down the pantheon, is a malevolent one; and the Native American trickster Wakdjunkaga, who finds itself trapped inside a dead animal's skull, foolish and impudent. Imprisonment inside the belly of a monster, giant fish or whale, with subsequent escape, is one of the most popular versions of this motif.

Entrapment does not have to be physical – it can be mental, in which case it is often displayed by a protagonist prior to their turning into a trickster or plunging into chaos. The trickster feels trapped because its personality is larger than life (or 'overinflated', from the system's point of view): the assassin Villanelle (Jodie Comer) in *Killing Eve* is unhappy in 'normal' society, but even the company of murderers and outlaws is too constraining for her. She ends up rebelling against her employers, an international mafia organization called The Twelve.

The trickster often merges with the protagonist as an unrealized (and unconscious) portion of the protagonist's personality, prompting the desire for change, the impulse to escape the entrapment. For instance, Princess Teabeanie (aka Bean) in Matt Groening's animated series *Disenchantment* (created for Netflix) is a free spirit trapped both metaphorically in medieval traditions and rituals and physically – in the castle where she lives with her father, King Zog. Her mother, Queen Dagmar, supposedly died years ago, and her statue features prominently in one of the castle rooms. Towards the end of Season 1 it emerges, however, that Dagmar was poisoned and turned into stone, and a special elixir made from elf blood can bring her back to life. Her imprisonment in stone also reflects the motif of entrapment in the discussion of the female agency.

Right away Bean is shown as unwilling to conform to the roles prescribed to her by the pseudo-medieval society. Featuring humour that is often edgier than that of *The Simpsons*, the first season of Disenchantment maps out the journey from being stuck in a prescribed lifestyle to finding one's own voice, and plotting an escape.

The series start off on a note on which narratives involving princesses as either protagonists or love interests usually finish: a wedding. Bean is supposed to enter a marriage of political convenience to ensure peace between the kingdoms of Dreamland and Bentwood. However, instead of the 'happy ever after', she accidentally kills her future husband, Prince Guysbert, during the ceremony, and when offered a replacement husband in the form of his brother, Prince Merkimer, she and her friends proceed to turn him into a pig. Not to mention that she spends the night before the wedding drinking and fighting in a local pub.

Inspired (or rather spurred on) by her personal demon called Luci, the princess does a number of silly things, ranging from drinking and getting into fights at a local pub to trying to seduce a Viking named Sven who (along with his friends) came to rampage Dreamland. Bean's erratic behaviour provokes more attempts by her father and his advisors to keep her under control (and thus trap her even more): at one point she is locked in her room, another time she is sent to a monastery, and she is repeatedly told that her behaviour does not correspond to that of a proper princess. At some point she describes her future as a mother and wife to prince Merkimer as 'entering a state of semi-permanent pregnancy'. The externalized trickster (Luci) pretty much escapes by the end of the first episode; while its carrier – the princess – leaves the kingdom of Dreamland in the last episode of the season. The trickster's duty is to unsettle that what is stagnating, and Luci does its job well.

Women rattling their trickster cage (and being stereotyped by society as belonging to the shadow) is also the central theme of Netflix's original series, *Orange is the New Black*. The protagonist of the series is a middle-class woman, Piper Chapman (Taylor Schilling), who finds herself in prison after her drug-smuggling antics from a decade ago are discovered. Although the initial focus of the narrative is on Piper, throughout subsequent seasons the show moves on to explore the lives of other representatives of the diverse population of Litchfield: the Russian matriarch Galina 'Red' Reznikov (Kate Mulgrew), the volatile Suzanne 'Crazy Eyes' Warren (Uzo Aduba), the optimistic and grounded Tascha 'Taystee' Jefferson (Danielle Brooks), the intimidating and sarcastic Carrie 'Big Boo' Black (Lea DeLaria), the glamorous transgender inmate Sophia Burset (Laverne Cox) and many more.

The series is an exercise in exploration of the dynamics of human nature in a small and stifling environment. Most of the conflicts (as well as emotional connections) the inmates experience are caused by this trickster feeling of being stuck in a box with no escape. In season 4 the pressure becomes so unbearable that it results in several deaths and causes a prison riot which rages throughout season 5. A rebellion is a sign that trickster energy has been neglected and left to fester instead of being carefully released. It is hard to put the trickster that has escaped back into the box. Because of genre requirements, the trickster in *OINTB* is not split off into a separate character or characters such as a demon or a doppelganger. Yet, it can also be said that the entire prison is a trickster place as it is physically and metaphorically split off from society, pushed to the margins and left to fester.

Rebecca Bunch (Rachel Bloom) in *Crazy Ex-Girlfriend* also possesses an unstoppable, powerful energy of the trickster. In season 3 it is revealed that this energy is actually linked to a mental health illness – Borderline Personality Disorder. Her BPD, however, is not externalized into an allegorical figure, and Rebecca experiences all the madness of the trickster raging inside her. The narrative curve throughout the four seasons traces Rebecca's transformation as she struggles to contain the powerful energy, and to 'be normal' which she mistakes for a state of being permanently happy. However, her search for normality results in the opposite of being happy – in a suicide attempt. Having escaped from its cage, the trickster gains exposure and therefore has to be dealt with instead of being ignored. Rebecca has to face her issues instead of trying to escape from them into the world of projections and illusions.

In BBC's *Fleabag*, the entrapment motif is largely exemplified in the series by Fleabag's sister, Claire (Sian Clifford). Fleabag (Phoebe Waller-Bridge) is a twentysomething Londoner. Although she owns a small cafe (which is not doing too well), her life lacks direction, both personally and professionally. She is a promiscuous, pornography-watching sex-addict juggling a string of grotesque relationships and random encounters (including a Catholic priest, played by Andrew Scott) with managing a failing business. She is also trying to come to terms with the death of her best friend who committed suicide after her boyfriend cheated on her. Halfway through the first season, we learn that he cheated with Fleabag herself.

Whereas the protagonist acknowledges and attempts to process her shame at being a perceived failure (both personally and professionally), Claire epitomizes the constraining set of behaviours which a middle-class woman must display: decent, proper, demure, always observing the protocol in social situations, and never discussing uncomfortable or taboo subjects. Claire does not acknowledge that either shame of failure exist even though, deep down, she is as broken as her younger sibling – her marriage is a sham as her husband has a tendency to pro-position to other women (including Fleabag), she is unhappy and lacks con-fidence. Claire is neurotic, pale and thin, and obsessively hides her insecurity with elaborate cosmetic routines, uptight demeanour and middle-class rituals such as formal dinners and parties, all of which make things appear to be smooth and unproblematic. If having to stave off what Goffman calls 'situational improprieties' is bad enough if you are middle class, the task becomes monu-mental if you are a female (Goffman, 1966: 5).

Throughout the two seasons, up to the very last episode, Claire is the true bearer (and wearer) of the female persona: she has a well-paid office job, wears appropriate clothes for her gender and class (silk blouses, nice trousers), does not talk about her problems ('everything is totally fine' is the standard answer), does not say any 'bad' words (like 'penis') or discuss controversial or difficult subjects, particularly if they relate to female sexuality or anatomy (defecation, masturbation, miscarriage). Claire likes to ward off embarrassing moments by reminding herself that she has 'two degrees, a husband and a Burberry coat'. She is wary of physical touch or expressing emotions in any other way.

She also keeps reminding herself, her sister and her family that her rela-tionship with her husband Martin (Brett Gelman) is fine when this is far from the truth. In other words, she is trying to live up to the ideal of the middle-class female persona: outwardly nice, presentable, polite, wealthy, and suc-cessful – the kind of person who does not say what she really thinks; who announces to the waitress that the sauce is delicious when she really thinks it is disgusting. She wants to appear 'normal' in terms of what society requires from individuals, and particularly in terms of what her social circles expect from her. This kind of persona aspires to the 'economy of presentation' which allows the participant in a social situation to 'by-pass unresolved issues' and to instead 'proceed to the ones that might be resolved' (Goffman, 1966: 4). With this constraining mask on, she is struggling to individuate.

One of the key lessons of trickster narratives is that perfection is impossible, however hard one tries to bypass all the uneven bits and uncomfortable elements. The permanently embarrassed, passive-aggressive sister serves as a foil to the trickster role of Fleabag in that their difficult relationship shows the emotional strain a persona has on the individual required to wear it. Claire likes to be in complete control over her body and work schedule. However, her desire for perfection and her definitional claims are regularly wrecked by Fleabag's trickster spirit, particularly in formal situations guarded by strict behavioural protocols such as funerals, weddings, and dinners.

The grotesque woman and her split-off, repressed issues are no different from the trickster themes discussed in male narratives. The fresh element here is the very possibility of seeing female feelings of entrapment and the yearning for a change as valid, as something that is not alien to female nature and psychology. After all, male trickster narratives often depict women as the ones plotting to trap the man, limit his agency, and to curtail his freedom and creativity. One example of this is Meryl (Laura Linney) in *The Truman Show* (1998) who keeps telling Truman that he cannot go travelling because he has a mortgage and 'they are trying for a baby'. Similarly, Clara in *Hector and the Search for Happiness* attempts to make Hector commit to her while he is having doubts about whether he actually enjoys his safe, settled, bland lifestyle.

Importantly, this fresh examination of the 'caged trickster' theme links to narratives of self-development and exploration of one's identity instead of going back to the age-old story of what Jane M. Ussher sums up as 'beautiful but cruelly treated young woman' longing for 'rescue and salvation' and enduring 'hardship and misery whilst dreaming her impossible dreams' (Ussher, 2011: 10). Neither of the heroines discussed above are traditionally pretty, modest, passively masochistic, or waiting to be saved by a prince. Rebecca, Bean, and Fleabag are proactive and keen to go on a journey of exploring their inner trickster, even if this journey means taking risks, making difficult choices, and dealing with unpredictable results.

Boundary-Breaking

Society is propped up by boundaries, physical as well as psychological: rules of decency and propriety, property borders, psychological boundaries, etc. Tricksters are notorious boundary-breakers. In myth, folk tales, and literary and cinematic narratives, they cross all kinds of boundaries, from physical (such as property borders) to metaphysical (for instance, sacred cultural values and taboos). Metaphorically, this means that the trickster has no respect for the structural aspect of the social. Neither do they respect the structuring function of the system. They do not accept 'the way things are', and keep attempting to re-draw the map. Boundaries separate the unconscious, pre-civilized individual (or child) from an adult member of community, conscious of their actions and prepared to take responsibility for them.

In classical mythology, the trickster is often depicted as a psychopomp, a mythical conductor of souls to the nether regions. Greek Hermes and Roman Mercurius are both psychopomps; in many other trickster stories the right to cross the boundary between life and death is designated as immortality. The role of the psychopomp emphasizes the trickster's transcendent qualities, among which is the ability to transgress the frontier between consciousness and the unconscious. With her ability to physically create life, the female trickster is the original psychopomp, the original grotesque – the prototypical trickster.

Examples of male tricksters breaking boundaries are numerous and go back to various myths and fairy tales, such as the story of Prometheus stealing fire from the gods of Olympus, the wily Odysseus who came up with the idea of the Trojan horse which helped him and his comrades to infiltrate the besieged enemy city, or various African tricksters like the Zulu child trickster Uthlakayana who leaves the safety of his house and constantly walks into dangerous places such as the house of a people-eating monster.

Yet, risky and aggressive behaviours are reserved for men. What do female rebels and bringers of chaos add to the boundary-breaking aspect of the trickster? In the case of the female trickster, these boundaries become definitions of what it means to be a 'woman'. The female trickster is brave to ignore these boundaries and to appear 'unattractive', messy, or seen as having bad manners. Predictably, the genre that succeeds in this is comedy.

Princess Bean in *Disenchantment* strives to redefine her identity after being typecast as a wife and 'producer of royal babies'. This redefinition takes a variety of unexpected forms: Bean swears, is a drunk, is not sensitive or squeamish, is clumsy, does not look elegant in a beautiful dress, and is generally up to no good. Bean is also proud of her buck teeth (which come in handy when she needs to bite off a piece of rope, for instance), and wears boyish clothes instead of ladylike attire. When expected to look feminine, Bean rebels and invariably wreaks havoc. In episode 6 of the first series, she humiliates herself as an ambassador to Dankmire, the homeland of her stepmother, Queen Oona, when she swings upside down in a ballgown, revealing her underwear.

Fleabag's leading character is another example of a female boundary-breaker. Fleabag is particularly good at causing chaos – disrupting social situations with rude behaviour or comments, be it a family dinner with her father, sister, and stepmother, or her sister's birthday party at which she arrives with yet another accidental boyfriend, and ends up upsetting everyone. Rather shockingly, in series 2 she seduces a priest, smashing into a whole set of strict rules and traditions.

Waller-Bridge's characters also crosses the boundaries of the narrative, the so-called 'fourth wall', when she addresses her audience now and then as an aside. Occasionally she speaks directly to the camera, crossing the fourth wall and revealing the personality behind the persona. For instance, during the 'anal sex' scene in the first episode of Season 1, she communicates her feelings and sensations directly to the audience while her partner ('the Arsehole Guy' played by Ben Aldridge) is unaware of this internal-external dialogue. By contrast, her love interest in Season 2, the Hot Priest (Andrew Scott), notices these transcendental moments and starts asking her where she keeps disappearing (although, as a boundary-breaker himself, he does occasionally look into the camera as if he knows what lies behind the looking glass). Throughout the two seasons, Fleabag keeps revealing the true emotions and impulses – her own and others' – hiding underneath the veneer of propriety.

The protagonist of *Crazy Ex-Girlfriend*, Rebecca Bunch, also crosses a whole range of boundaries into lands previously out of reach for women: she can be loud and impulsive; she swears and says rude jokes, and she is completely uninhibited when it comes to discussing sex and the female anatomy. She also does not shy away from toilet humour. Importantly, the show's creators used the musical numbers to consistently mock the female persona – the image of a decent and dainty woman. Many of the songs in the series deal with these expectations, dismantling them one by one. The show exposes the cultural technologies behind the feminine persona. For instance, in 'I'm So Good at Yoga' (S1) and 'Research Me Obsessively' (S2) Rebecca and her friends examine society's obsession with women who are pretty, slim and popular, and explore their own feelings of jealousy and inadequacy upon encountering someone who looks seemingly perfect.

Rebecca and her friends often sing about taboo subjects that have been traditionally erased from female narratives: periods, period sex, excretion, and the messy side of childbirth. In film and television childbirth is traditionally montaged to look like a brief moment of pain followed by times of bliss, love and happy parenthood. *Crazy Ex-Girlfriend* changes this perception by exposing the messy side of the process. In the song titled 'The Miracle of Birth', Rebecca's friend Paula sings about explosive diarrhoea, vaginal tears, and the expelling of placenta that accompany the process.

Similarly, sex is normally shown as a beautiful culmination of a passionate evening, with none of the biological details. By contrast, in 'Period Sex' Rebecca sings about using a towel while having sex during her period, and in 'I Gave You a UTI', the subject of bladder infections as a result of having too much sex is explored. None of these topics are exactly romantic, sensual or alluring, and are certainly not something that would normally get any kind of representation on screen.

Amazon's *I Love Dick* breaks the taboos similar to those explored in *Crazy Ex-Girlfriend*. It is the story of an exhausted, failing female film director, Chris (Kathryn Hahn), who chases a famous academic and artist, Dick (Kevin Bacon), a very peculiar character – all double denim and cowboy boots. Despite being married, the female protagonist stalks her handsome and mysterious cowboy by following him around, breaking into his house and writing him endless letters bursting with highly embarrassing, obsessive sexual confessions and fantasies.

Dick initially appears to be unattainable and not at all impressed by Chris, either sexually or intellectually. The female protagonist with a gender-neutral name defies behavioural norms by pursuing a man in a manner that is traditionally perceived as masculine – by gradually breaking down his defences. The very first episode gives the viewer quite a shock, but not because of the abundance of sexual references, or nudity, or swear words – they have become so commonplace on screen that we have been pretty desensitized to them. The female character is presented in a candid way – not charming, delightful, polished or well-mannered, but awkward, clumsy, and raw. She has been divested of the mask of 'prettiness' or 'passivity' demanded by society, and falls in love with someone off limits, declaring her feelings for him openly and publicly. At one point she prints out the letters and sticks them to every building in town. Season 1 ends with Chris finally managing to seduce Dick, but still unable to have sex with him as her period arrives early. She walks away, bleeding into her clothes. Instead of hiding menstrual blood, or representing it as horrifying (as tradition demands), the makers of the show made it graphically grotesque, and turned it into a celebration of feminine desire and passion. This is not something to be concealed but displayed and celebrated.

Shamelessness

The taboo (the boundary) the female trickster protagonist breaks most often is menstruation. Period taboo has always been part of the female persona, and a source of shame. As Delaney et al note, in many cultures periods is a taboo of exclusion – a phenomenon so well described by Stephen King in *Carrie* (and in subsequent film adaptations). In many societies

> the menstruating woman is believed to emit a mana, a threatening supernatural power. The taboos of menstruation are practices that help others to avoid her dangerous influence and that enable her to get through the menstrual period without succumbing to her own deadly power.
>
> (Delaney et al., 1988: 7)

Simone de Beavour notes that menstruation, which is associated with the moon cycle, in the eyes of males must make woman part of the 'fearsome machinery which turns the planets and the sun in their courses' which also means that she is 'the prey of cosmic energies that rule the destiny of the stars and the tides' (De Beauvoir, 2011: 181). The projection of the fear, via the metonomy of 'natural rhythms', of the potentially unpredictable and tempestuous natural world onto women, results in the combustible combination of objectification, prohibition and fascination. Associated with the maternal and accompanied biological processes, the woman is seen as possessing a much-feared 'maternal authority' that in some cultural expressions such as horror films transforms into a negative authority, an irrational, abject power (Creed, 1993: 13).

Shame is a tool used by society to shape a compliant individual, to direct a child towards a socially-acceptable behaviour, to create a human being capable of co-existing with others in a civilized environment, capable of being juggling their own needs with the needs of others. Coincidentally, the pressure on women to conform has been skewed towards community while individualistic behaviour was controlled in them with the use of shame. Women as family people, as child bearers, as helpers and kind carers are 'decent' women while the ones enjoying themselves are selfish, irresponsible, or even dangerous. The female shame has been put into a box and repressed, hidden from view, for centuries.

A 'respectable woman' is the opposite of the trickster. In his study of sexual profanity and interpersonal judgement, Robert O'Neill notes that male respondents considered women who swear to be less attractive than women who do not. Conversely, women rated males who swear as more attractive than male non-swearers (O'Neill, 2001: 92). O'Neill further observes:

> ... it is not surprising that female targets would be rated more sociable and more attractive in the nonswearing condition than male targets, given the cultural emphasis on female beauty and female accommodation to others. [...] If ... conformity to norms of gender appropriate behaviour results in social approval by those of the opposite gender, then there are clear indications that such swearing is viewed as gender-appropriate for males and inappropriate for females.
>
> (O'Neill, 2001: 93–94)

The female persona, with its associations with perfection and cleanliness, stunts the agentic in its wearer while constantly absorbing cultural shame. Women are being seen as bearers of 'sin', and privy to terrifying mysteries of the female body such as periods and childbirth. That is why whenever a narrative explores a subject that had previously been a taboo, it looks fresh to the point of shocking. This kind of defiance is still rare on screen, and when it is present, it often takes the form of a comedic narrative.

Female tricksters in our examples have been defying the 'female shame' in a whole variety of ways; mainly by demanding to have the same right for self-expression as the men. A woman swearing or making lewd jokes would be labelled as 'unhinged' and undignified. Rebecca, the protagonist of *Crazy Ex-Girlfriend*, freely discusses urinary tract infections, thrush, and period sex. Rebecca swears and is not keen to fit into gender or class stereotypes. She is not ashamed to talk about the female body in ways that make that show unique in the entertainment industry. These discussions are neither censored nor meant to sound sexy; the writing is completely honest in ways in which it has not been before.

For instance, in season 1 Rebecca has a urinary tract infection as a result of having a lot of sex with Greg (Santino Fontana), and ends up in a hospital emergency room. The infection becomes the subject of a song in which Greg boasts of his sexual prowess which – he claims – is the cause of the bladder problems. In season 4 Rebecca has thrush, attempts to treat it with home remedies, and ends up with bacterial vaginosis. She is so embarrassed that she attempts to postpone a scheduled date. The extensive range of embarrassing health problems are part of Rebecca's individuation process but they are not veiled by the persona and are not 'written out' of the individuation narrative.

A middle-class character, a graduate of Harvard and Yale, and a real estate lawyer, a character like Rebecca has never been shown as having embarrassing problems like a fungal infection. Being middle class is actually a trickster position, stuck 'betwixt and between' (to use Victor Turner's expression) the upper and the working classes. As such, it finds itself in a precarious situation, never sure as to its status or the rules and definitions of what it actually means to be 'in the middle'. The middle-class woman is expected to possess a certain set of qualities; a set of attributes such as politeness, absence of strong emotions, and professionalism. None of our middle-class trickster heroines – Rebecca Bunch, Fleabag, Chris Kraus, or Piper Kerman – manage to keep their persona intact. All of them demonstrate that there are passions, problems, emotions, obsessions, frustrations, and deep-seated guilt underneath the cool demeanour.

Fleabag, too, rejects the notion of shame. She talks about anal sex in direct soliloquies to the camera and about miscarriage to her family in a restaurant. She takes the top off in front of the banker (Hugh Dennis) interviewing her for a loan. In season 2, she hits Martin for being rude about Claire's miscarriage (even though Martin does not know that Claire has just had it). Other females in her family cross boundaries and display a whole array of behavioural grotesqueries. Her family is firmly middle-class, yet her mother-in-law draws penises for her art exhibitions.

Mythological and folkloric tricksters are often thieves and liars (both Hermes and Prometheus steal from the gods), these two properties emphasizing their determination to break the social contract, to express their agency and to stick the middle finger to authority. Fleabag, too, betrays the (middle class, female) persona by committing a range of misdemeanours (and not being ashamed of it): in the first two episodes of season 1 she steals a bottle of wine from a corner shop, a £20 note from the wallet of her date, and takes an expensive artifact, belonging to Godmother, from her father's house. Even as a minor offender, Fleabag does not fit neatly into the box of societal expectations: a middle class woman, she enjoys recreational theft. Her moments of stealing can also be seen as flashes of inspiration, as impulses which she cannot control.

Creativity and Creationism

The trickster's creativity does not mean the ability to make beautiful, polished artistic works but rather the childish openness and acceptance of the world; the ability to see things in a different light, from a range of different viewpoints; the desire to change things; to revel in the flow of ideas. This kind of creativity is raw and playful. The trickster refuses to be institutionalized because it knows that being ingrained in one way of seeing things leads to the loss of the precious creative impulse.

Female trickster creativity can take many different forms, and is linked to her rebelliousness and willingness to cross boundaries: the way she dresses (often outrageously), the way she speaks (she is often foul-mouthed), and the ways she behaves (inappropriately for a woman). For instance, Villanelle in *Killing Eve* loves fashion, but uses it to subvert societal standards rather than conform to the gender norms. She dresses for her own enjoyment, and often wears bizarre outfits to serious events such as her 'assessment for fitness to work' meeting with her employers which she attends looking like a giant doll wearing oversized pink tulle dress.

A trickster's creativity is messy and unpredictable, born out of a wild desire to live, and to bring things to life. It is impulsive, often misplaced or even completely inappropriate, like Fleabag's 'Psycho' joke when she accosts Harry in the shower with a large kitchen knife. Harry panics badly and starts crying. A trickster's creativity is also linked to its shapeshifting qualities such as changing genders, and turning into other people and animals. By dressing as a (male) horror film character, Fleabag demonstrates exactly this kind of fluidity; even though her thoughtless shapeshifting is not appreciated by poor Harry.

Fleabag is impulsive and unpredictable – a sign of raw creativity – leaving her friends and relatives to deal with the fallout of her chaotic behaviour. A frustrating and rather useless navigator, she insists that she has a 'map in her head' and causes her sister Claire to miss a turn on a roundabout. Claire is frustrated, and to cheer her up, Fleabag makes a joke about 'a Tinder for lesbians'. This fails to work, as the sister breaks down out of sheer frustration. Yet, she also pushes her repressed and conservative sister to be more impulsive, and to break out the routine, which in Season 2 results in Claire leaving her shambolic marriage and narcissistic husband (Brett Gelman), and going out with a good-looking Swedish colleague (Christian Hillborg). The chaos Fleabag creates is simultaneously dangerous and healing.

Similarly, Rebecca's behaviour is unpredictable to the point of being random, but she has a positive effect on her friends and colleagues. This mad, creative unpredictability coupled with empathy and helpfulness change the world around her, and the lives of her friends. With Rebecca's support and encouragement, Paula (Donna Lynne Champlin) becomes a lawyer. The men in Rebecca's life both suffer from and appreciate the creative chaos that follows her – Josh Chan

(Vincent Rodriguez III) becomes more self-aware and starts going to therapy, Greg Serrano (Santino Fontana/Skylar Astin) seeks help for his drinking problem and overcomes his procrastination, and Nathaniel Plimpton III (Scott Michael Foster) becomes a 'nicer person' (or, at least, makes an attempt to be more empathic and considerate of others).

Loss of Control

The trickster's lack of control of its body invariably translates into chaos in their surroundings. Soon enough everyone in the trickster's vicinity starts losing control of their destinies and bodies. The female trickster's messiness takes on political overtones as women have traditionally lacked control over their lives while being expected to have mastery over their behaviour in public. The perception of women as being 'hysterical', as someone who is irrational and unable to manage their emotions, feeds into the trickster paradigm and into the vision of the trickster as a bedsit of everything that is repressed, forbidden, and prohibited.

The need to 'fit in', Goffman notes, means that 'the individual must be "good" and not cause a scene or a disturbance; he must not attract undue attention to himself, either by thrusting himself on the assembled company or by attempting to withdraw too much from their presence' (Goffman, 1966: 11). In other words, 'to fit in' means to navigate the trickster position of being 'betwixt and between'; it means trying not to be 'too much' or 'too little'. One needs to be right in the middle, which may lead to failure.

'Loss of control' is one of the staple themes of trickster narratives in that the trickster is not fully in charge of its body and mind, and causes everyone in its vicinity to also lose control over their minds and bodies. Fear of losing authority, of not managing the situation, is intimately connected with the feelings of shame, embarrassment, and inadequacy. When tricksters play their tricks on humans, they show the power of chance over rational frameworks and established orders.

Female trickster behaviour subverts the female persona as it has been traditionally defined, by taking stereotypes of femininity into the extreme, and by making the very notions of rationality and control sound absurd. Importantly, female tricksters show that the very dichotomy of control versus chaos is flawed as it is often used to justify inappropriate male behaviour, which, by the very virtue of it being male, is not regarded by cultural systems as irrational or strange.

Fleabag's entire life is a series of shameful mishaps, ranging from taking her top off at a bank interview to stealing the statuette of a naked woman, made by her infuriating stepmother (played by Olivia Colman). Fleabag is chaos personified, negating, breaking, or simply ignoring the rules of 'decent behaviour' all the time; but in its turn, this is caused by her inability to control her own life due to a series of traumas – her mother's death and her best friend's suicide.

One of the key lessons of trickster narratives is that perfection is impossible, however hard one tries to bypass all the uneven bits and uncomfortable elements. The permanently embarrassed, passive-aggressive sister serves as a foil to the trickster role of Fleabag in that their difficult relationship shows the emotional strain a persona has on the individual required to wear it. Claire likes to be in complete control over her body and work schedule. However, her desire for perfection and her definitional claims are regularly wrecked by Fleabag's trickster spirit, particularly in formal situations guarded by strict behavioural protocols such as funerals, weddings and dinners. Ignoring the reality of her own emotions makes Claire unhappy, yet she projects her inner turmoil onto Fleabag and blames her for the chaos erupting wherever she goes.

Claire is horrified when the trickster spirit takes over her seemingly perfect middle class life. Fleabag's creative chaos is highly contagious. In the opening scene of season 2, Fleabag 'hijacks' Claire's miscarriage, causing a stir and attracting attention – not least because she ends up hitting Martin who then hits her back. At the Women's Awards Ceremony organized by Claire's firm (S2, E3), Fleabag breaks the glass trophy and then replaces it with the stolen naked woman figurine. When announcing the winner, Claire, against her will, repeats the sexual harassment joke Fleabag had just told her. When awkwardly flirting with her lover and co-worker Klare, she keeps inadvertently hinting at sex. The 'fitting in' process, which is supposed to result in outward perfection, is continuously disrupted by the trickster's external/internal spirit.

Even though Fleabag is blamed for the ruined social occasions and everyone's loss of control, the actual location of shame and embarrassment is internal, hidden behind the persona, and smoothed over by polite demeanour. For instance, the restaurant scene opening Season 2 is full of awkward, explosive, funny tension. The sisters' father (Bill Paterson) is about to marry a narcissist (hilariously played by Olivia Colman) who keeps interrupting him and inventing new ways of attracting attention to herself. Claire is married to a selfish, needy man who had tried to kiss her sister, and then denied it. She is also cheating on him with a colleague in Finland. The priest is fighting his demons. The people at the table cannot face these issues so the pressure escapes, suddenly, in a very embarrassing situation. Fleabag's erratic behaviour is a litmus test for hidden vulnerabilities, wounds, emotions, and desires. All she does is expose the tension between ego-consciousness and persona; the tension that her relatives and friends, as social beings, are either unaware or keen to avoid because facing the demons would involve the pain of self-realization, and not everyone is ready for it. By contrast, wearing the mask is an easier solution both for the individual and society as it supposedly protects the surface of social interaction. When Fleabag is involved, the mask disappears, and the situation implodes, exposing the ultimate failure of persona to prevent social tensions.

Similarly, in *I Love Dick,* the protagonist's obsession is a manifestation of the dysfunctionality and narcissism of patriarchal structures, with their institutionalization of subjugation and objectification of women. Dick sees himself as a leading expert on art, surrounded by women who catch his every word, and soak in the admiration. However, when the admiration turns into a weapon of objectification – when it slips from under his control – Dick loses his power as a man, an alarming moment, and becomes an empty slate for female projections.

In film the trickster has often been used as a narrative device shaping and guiding the (male) protagonist's transformation like it does in *The Mask, Yes Man* or *Hector and the Search for Happiness*. In a trickster-based plot, the trickster is a chaotic phenomenon arriving into the protagonist's life and dragging (usually him but there are exceptions such as *Drop Dead Fred*) into the liminal zone and through messy and chaotic change. At the end of the narrative the protagonist emerges out of the liminal zone with a different view on life and his place in it. With his new status and self-awareness he no longer needs the trickster who then disappears (until next time). In this sense, being out of control while simultaneously causing chaos is an unpleasant but ulti- mately positive phase that leads to transformation and personal advancement.

The lack of female protagonists in trickster-transformation narratives, until now, can be explained by the lack of interest, on part of the decision- makers, in female individuation process. Luckily, we increasingly see more of them, including Disney's *Turning Red* which opens with an overview of Mei's deceptively perfect life and seemingly effortless balancing of studies, friendship and family relations. This balance is revealed to be fragile when the trickster – Red Panda, an apt metaphor for puberty – arrives and makes Mei question her identity and her relationships. Panda's clumsy disruption lasts for the duration of the narrative until Mei makes the decision to inte- grate it – unlike her other female relatives who lock their trickster-shadows, in the form of variously sized and tempered pandas, in pendants and other objects. In refusing to ritualistically part with the panda, Mei makes peace with the imperfect side of herself. She now owns and appreciates the disruption (including that of the female persona). Disruption, as trickster narratives show, means progress.

The Problem of the Name

Lack of a permanent name is a common trait in trickster narratives. It shows a refusal to conform and to belong to a civilization, to a particular set of norms. Princess Teabeanie whose full name is Teabenie Mariabeanie de la Rochambeau calls herself Bean – a word describing a very prosaic food, which stands in contrast with her official, aristocratic name. Similarly, like many tricksters, Fleabag does not appear to have a human name, but calls herself Fleabag – not the most flattering nickname, and definitely not the most 'feminine' one either. Fleabag feels strange, subnormal, different, but there is also a strong political subtext to this – she rebels against the image of a decent middle-class woman, a particularly tenacious social projection. She refuses to be named as the name is linked to having a definitive identity. Cruella/Estella in Disney's *Cruella* has two names because she lives as a 'decent' human being by day and as the shadowy version of herself by night. When the shadow starts to spread and takes over more aspects of her personality, she chooses Cruella as her main name.

The protagonist of *Killing Eve* uses two names: Villanelle (which is her codename) and Oksana Astankova (her real name). As an assassin, she operates simultaneously in several countries and constantly assumes new identities. She is fluid, uncatchable, always 'betwixt and between', refusing to be defined and to have a stable, identifiable social role. She despises the system and, in spite of being part of one (she works for 'The Twelve'), is always ready to kill her bosses and to escape. Ultimately, she kills for her own enjoyment, even though the mafia as a system offers her a lavish lifestyle and an opportunity to vent her anger. Villanelle/Oksana is not attached to any of her names as this would mean having a place in a social structure, which is precisely what she is trying to avoid.

Dissolution

In many trickster tales – and this is particularly noticeable in large cycles containing a series of trickster transformations – the trickster spirit is dissolved at the end of the narrative. After the creative, chaotic unconscious energy has been woken up for the purpose of disrupting the stale (personal or social) order, it must go back to its dark wellspring. The trickster impulse does not die but is absorbed by the personality structure, and becomes an essential part of the individuating forces which would later closely guard the balance between the personal and the social in the individual's life. The trickster energy is still alive underneath the structuring forces of the social order. The 'taming of the trickster', or its dissolution, signifies the victory of the civilizing forces over the dark powers of the unconscious. It also shows that the trickster impulse can be dangerous, needs to be used sparingly – and only for the purposes of regeneration and renewal.

This particular aspect of the trickster has been successfully utilized in trickster films as a part of the framing mechanism, alongside 'lack of control' and entrapment motifs. For instance, having undergone a personality overhaul, the protagonist of *The Mask* Stanley Ipkiss no longer needs the green-faced alter-ego and discards the mask at the end of the film. Other tricksters die (Jack Nicholson's Randle Patrick McMurphy in *One Flew Over the Cuckoo's Nest*), disappear or transform into a manageable creature. Still, this does not mean that the trickster spirit is gone forever – it just disappears temporarily until it is needed to cause chaos when the system stagnates again.

Interestingly enough, the female trickster tends to be more persistent mostly because it usually inhabits longer-running formats. In shorter formats, it dissolves at the end of the narrative, having taught the protagonist the value of conflict, chaos and imperfection, like it does in *Drop Dead Fred, Brave* and *Turning Red*. In formats with multiple seasons, remakes and sequels, the trickster lives on and refuses to go away for a long time, or even at all. The little cat-demon Luci in *Disenchantment,* Villanelle's murderous impulse (which she does try to 'cure' with therapy and religion in Season 4 of the show) and Rebecca's antics in *Crazy Ex-Girlfriend* keep disturbing systems of all shapes and sizes.

The durability and persistence of the female trickster can also be explained by the fact that the female trickster impulse has a lot more work to do in terms of challenging societal norms and expectations: the female persona is thicker than a male social mask. The female trickster lingers on as the protagonist's return to 'normality', having obtained a new status, should not mean the return to the constraints of the female persona. The female trickster remains on guard, emphasizing the importance of looking silly and behaving in a ridiculous way for any woman who wants to individuate.

The Animal Connection

Animals are frequent guests in trickster myths. In fact, they symbolize the trickster's connection with the 'underworld' of instincts and animal behaviour. Many mythological and folkloric tricksters are animals, and even when they are not, some association with the animal kingdom is often present. African trickster club boasts a spider (Kwaku Anansi), a hare, and a tortoise; Northern American group includes a raven, a coyote, a rabbit and Wakdjunkaga's numerous animal transformations. The fox is the principal trickster of Russian fairy tales; India has the monkey called Hanuman (one of the heroes of Ramayana); the most-known Chinese trickster is also a monkey – the hero of the novel *The Journey To the West* (1590); in Peruvian fairy tales the trickster's role is played by a guinea pig; Argentinean folklore has Tokwah who is neither human nor animal; Japanese folktales mention Hare and Badger as cunning transformers.

There is a range of animal associations in female trickster narratives. They emphasize the shapeshifting, cunning, and deceptive aspect of the trickster; its unwillingness to become 'civilized' (with 'civilized' meaning 'joining a particular system and accepting its rules'). They also show sexual confidence and rebellion neither of which 'decent' women are expected to display unless they are part of the masquerade acted out for the male gaze.

Princess Teabeanie has her personal demon Luci who is often confused with a cat. Luci is considered to be a bad influence on Bean because it makes her do outrageous things, but primarily because it pushes her to break with tradition. Luci is obviously a trickster and an escape artist – it frees itself (alongside other trapped demons) from a cage where it is locked by an exorcist called Big Jo, and manages to escape from pretty much any other entrapment set up by its enemies. Animals in female trickster narratives often represent the protagonist's frustration with life, social expectations or are a reaction to injustice. For instance, Estella/Cruella in Disney's *Cruella* steals Baroness's ferocious Dalmatian dogs in retaliation for her mother's death.

In Russian fairy tales, the fox (Kuma Lisa) is a trickster character; the 'wily one', who lies and cheats, often to trap and eat other animals, or to con them out of their possessions. Fleabag's fox who keeps scaring the Hot Priest (who believes the animal stalks him) is a projection of his mixed feelings about Fleabag: he is both fascinated by her and afraid of his own emotions, of the power and destructive potential of sexual attraction. The fox appears at the moment when Fleabag and the Priest are discussing the subject of celibacy (S2, E4) and the Priest looks spooked. The haunting effect of the failure to be in control of one's emotions becomes apparent every time the priest unexpectedly bumps into Fleabag: 'I thought you were a fox' he says to her before the wedding ceremony. Unsurprisingly, the final scene of season 2 ends with the fox turning up at the bus stop after the priest and Fleabag have just parted, and Fleabag, knowing that the priest will be terrified, sends the animal after her lover. In a similar fashion, Fleabag's father is using the imaginary mouse, supposedly stuck in a mouse trap in the attic, to express doubts about his forthcoming wedding. The animal trickster stands for rule transgressions, for agency, for the escaped (if selfish) individuality in the face of societal structures (including religion and marriage).

Similarly, Rebecca often associates herself with animals, mostly with cats (one such metonymic/allegorical cat, for instance, stands for Rebecca's vagina demanding sex), and once with a triceratops, a stocky dinosaur resembling a rhinoceros. This association is played out in a song called 'Triceratops Ballet', a drug-induced fantasy experienced by Rebecca and Valencia (Gabrielle Ruiz) about their former boyfriend Josh Chan. While Valencia hallucinates about being a ballerina engaged in a dramatic dance of passion and betrayal with Josh, Rebecca is a triceratops sitting on top of Josh and eating his heart. This image shatters the female persona - the image of a pretty, elegant woman designed by society to be admired and consumed – and replaces it with a woman who is clumsy to the point of horror.

Like Rebecca's triceratops, Mei's red panda in *Turning Red* is a big and clumsy animal, an image openly defying the expectations associated with the female persona. This does not mean, however, that Mei is asexual; on the contrary, she cannot stop thinking of various boys, including members of the boyband *4Town* and a (unlucky, it turns out) cashier of the nearby convenience store. Compared to her elegant mother dressed in an unmissable combination of turquoise and jade green, Mei does not use the female persona to be attractive or interesting. Mother's coiffed beauty means submission to the female persona whereas the daughter keeps her animal alive and relies on her personality to form relationships and make decisions.

Shapeshifting

Tricksters are notorious shapeshifters. They frequently change their appearance, transform into various animals and objects – even change their sex. Parts of their bodies fall off, but they grow back or can be reattached onto the body. The trickster's hands, legs, penis and anus all have minds of their own and 'do what they want'. Tricksters' bodies are fluid and malleable, and it is hard to damage them 'permanently'.

Following Radin's and Joseph Henderson's argument, the trickster is an incomplete individual, a fluid transitory path from animal to human (Jung, 1964: 103–104). A creature steeped in 'primary omnipotence', it thinks that it is part of the world, and therefore can hardly be expected to be fully responsible for its body's actions. While a fully-fledged individual (ideally) feels psychologically complete, the trickster is not entirely aware of its physical and psychological fragmentedness. A cultural blank slate, an emerging individual, the trickster does not yet definitely know its identity, including sex or gender, and it is the patriarchal thinking that turned it into a primarily male creature.

The default mythological and folkloric trickster is male, although he occasionally transforms into a woman. Yet, shapeshifting, or psychological pliability, is a quality that is traditionally ascribed to women. The woman is 'mysterious' and 'enigmatic', expected to be malleable as in 'free of content', merely a mirror ready to absorb and reflect male projections. Laura Mulvey and Mary Ann Doane emphasize that the expectation to masquerade, to play a role, to perform, to be on display, to pretend to be something that she is not, are expected both of the actress and the female spectator. The actress plays a character who is merely an element of the male narrative (Mulvey, 1975) while the female spectator has to manage her psychological proximity with the characters on screen by imagining to be a man, or pretending to be a hyperbolic woman (Doane, 1982). This is a boundaried, controlled masquerade, not accounting for female agency because the roles played and the costumes worn are determined by the male pleasure. Masquerade belongs to the female persona, not to the trickster.

The female trickster rejects this conservative vision of female masquerade and turns it into a spectacle without boundaries – energetic, sparkling, and subversive. *Killing Eve*'s Villanelle/Oksana loves dressing up, and speaks multiple languages. She is ethnically Russian, but lacks any cultural markers. She could transform into anyone, anywhere, and still retain her individuality and eccentricity. Similarly, Fleabag makes a range of impulsive decisions, from kissing a businesswoman (played by Kristin Scott Thomas) she met at Claire's party to lying about having a miscarriage to save her sister from public embarrassment. Fleabag avoids definitive life goals, and certainly does not have plans to have a family, or even to find a perfect partner. She blunders through life, learning through trial and error – something that previously only male protagonists were allowed to do.

The female trickster protagonist genuinely does not know what she wants to do in life, and even though she may be searching for meaning, this meaning does not necessarily lie in having a family, being submissive, or using her sexuality to trap a male partner. Fleabag has multiple partners, Villanelle mostly chases older women, and Rebecca cannot decide whether she actually wants to have a serious relationship with any of the three men chasing her.

In trickster tales, shapeshifting symbolizes the trickster's lack of maturity as well unwillingness to squeeze into the limits prescribed by the system. It is refreshing to see the female protagonist try on different guises, but not for the male gaze to enjoy. She does this to find out who she is, or what she wants. This is a big step from Campbell's woman who does not need to go on a journey because 'she is already there'.

Licentiousness

Male trickster characters are associated with sex, and are notoriously virile. Trickster myths and tales from all over the world contain some spectacular, shocking and hilarious examples of trickster sexual escapades. In film and TV, Ace Ventura, the Mask, Cuckoo (*Cuckoo*, BBC, 2012–2018), Randle Patrick McMurphy and many others unashamedly parade their sexual prowess and eagerly get naked pretty much in front of everyone.

Similarly, sexuality in female trickster narratives is neither pretty nor dainty. On the contrary, it is voracious, passionate, aggressive; sometimes born out of anger and frustration. It is grotesque and carnivalesque but not abject as it lacks the necessary shame to accept and absorb societal projections. This is female sexuality in its non-projected, often shocking and embarrassing trickster incarnation. For instance, Fleabag is sexually voracious with a compulsive habit to sleep with random people. Possessed by the trickster spirit, Fleabag is also obsessed with sex which she sees everywhere. Even a therapist's scarf reminds her of it (S2 E2). In the first episode of Season 1 Fleabag confesses to her audience (while sitting on the toilet – traditionally a taboo setting for female characters) that she loves sex because it makes her feel needed and desired. She is omnivorous and insatiable: she masturbates a lot (at one point, to an Obama speech with her boyfriend Harry (Hugh Skinner) next to her in bed), picks up a random guy on public transport, and propositions to Belinda (Kristin Scott Thomas) whom she meets at a business awards ceremony. Fleabag turns everyday situations into something to do with sex, often bordering on harassment, from a bank loan interview to a breast examination. Usually the prerogative of the male version of the trickster, sex obsession flies in the face of decorum and modesty – the shame-forming requirements for being a decent member of a civilized society.

Chris Kraus, naturally, is obsessed with Dick and makes her sexual fantasies public by writing them into a narrative, printing them off, and sticking them onto surfaces all over town. The entire show is based around unleashed, unedited, uncensored female sexuality which floods into a man's life and turns upside down his position in society and his confident, rigid vision of himself.

Sexual and romantic escapades are important milestones on the path of the female protagonist led by a trickster or performing a trickster's function. Bean of *Disenchantment* is also not hesitant or demure when it comes to approaching men, be it the Viking leader Sven (who actually came to capture Dreamland), or commoners who all flee from her because going out with king Zog's daughter may result in trouble. In season 3 it is revealed that Bean may be queer as she falls with love with Mora the Mermaid who unceremoniously disappears as Bean and her friends escape Steamland on board a ship. In any case, Bean's romantic and sexual escapades are not shaped or guided by tradition or society, but are part of her bumbling, blundering individuation path full of awkward, persona-defying moments.

Scatological References and Other Taboos

Displayed by a woman, sex obsession or toilet humour make the transgression look more formidable because culturally defined behavioural limitations – the gendered persona – are tighter for females. When a woman pushes the boundary, she moves to the limen where she is judged and stigmatized. The female trickster and those influenced by it, however, are prepared to deal with the consequences.

None of the trickster-influenced characters and protagonists suffer from shyness when it comes to toilet humour. Trickster tales, myths, and films all show tricksters behaving badly and defying the norms of society by joking about inappropriate subjects. Jim Carrey's protagonists do this particularly well, from Ace Ventura's 'talking arse' and being born out of a rubber rhino's backside, to Lloyd Christmas feeding laxatives to his best friend.

Until now, this kind of humour has been off limits for the female protagonist, and it is good to see it present in female trickster narratives. Fleabag farts in a lift while carrying a box full of cakes to an important business function, terribly embarrassing her prim and proper sister. Chris Kraus walks into the desert, blood streaming down her legs. A far cry from male creators' representation of menstrual blood as something scary to the extent that it warrants a horror-style representation (Carrie), this is simultaneously a frank and life-affirming depiction of menstruation.

Rebecca also freely discusses her trips to the toilet as well as sensitive issues such as a bladder infection. For instance, in Season 1 episode 6 of the show Rebecca rushes to the bathroom plagued by bowel issues and ends up inadvertently listening to the man of her dreams, Josh Chan, having sex with Rebecca's arch-rival, Valencia, next door. Meanwhile, in Season 3 Valencia who, unlike Rebecca, is not a big fan of toilet jokes, sings a thinly veiled 'ode to poop' in a song titled 'This is My Movement'. The number uses doublespeak: on the surface of it, Valencia is talking about social media, with the real topic being the fact that she has not 'pooped' for a month. The number's parodic, neat mis-en-scène (piano, candles, beige walls, and columns), Valencia's perfect outfit (black trousers, frilled blue blouse), editing and camera angles clash with the song's scatological lyrics. Valencia refers to 'rumbling inside' which 'cannot be contained'. She loves her persona and keeps it pristine by relegating the trickster to the doublespeak, while the external pastel perfection of her outfit and surroundings remains intact.

Reclaiming Fashion and Make-Up

The mask of femininity consists of many aspects, including visual, behavioural, biological and psychological. At least several female trickster characters chose to keep the visual elements of the persona, repurposing 'prettiness' as a form of rebellion. It is a deliberate display of 'otherness', fully acknowledged, recognized and appreciated by the proprietor, akin to Joker accentuating his clown face as a metaphor for a set of qualities disowned by the capitalist society. It is an acknowledgement, creatively re-structured, that the woman is the target of the 'voyeuristic and fetishistic gaze in the cinema' who reverses the relation and appropriates 'the gaze for her own pleasure' (Doane, 1982: 77). While 'male subjectivity' is traditionally matched with 'the agency of the look', the female trickster confuses the owner of the gaze by her re-aligning her appearance with her agency (Doane, 1982: 77).

For instance, Villanelle, Cruella and Fleabag enjoy fashion as a genuine trickster quality: it promotes change, it is a shapeshifter's true weapon. Although all TV and film tricksters are different in their re-appropriation of the mask, their intention is the same: reclaiming the agency, and re-asserting the right to control their appearance. Cruella is a designer, Villanalle a fashionista, and Fleabag uses her appearance as a means of seduction. As Monica Titton notes, fashion can be a site of resistance; moreover, 'not only has fashion embraced feminism – feminist has become fashionable' (Titton, 2019: 749). Interestingly, this juxtaposition exists across all archetypes female characters try on, including the shadow, the trickster and the hero. Many new female characters, across different genres, whatever roles they embody, tend to tone down or not pay attention to their femininity or appearance. They include, for instance, Rey (hero/ine) in the *Star Wars* franchise whose dressing style is gender neutral, Merida (child/hero/ine) in *Brave*, Bean in *Disenchantment* (child/trickster) and the numerous female detectives priding themselves on their lack of interest in clothes, including sweater-wearing Sarah Lund and Catherine Cawood who does not give a damn about clothes or make-up.

Equally, others – Fleabag (the trickster), Wonder Woman (hero/ine), Mulan (hero/ine, 2020), Cruella (the shadow) – are depicted, depending on genre conventions, as attractive or paying attention to their appearance. Narratives such as *Red Panda* embody the split, which is also generational, with the

daughter Mei choosing not to repress her nature to fit in with the requirements of the persona while the mother and other female relatives lock their
emotions (together with the trickster and shadow aspects of their nature) in
small objects such as amulets.

The female trickster's interest in fashion and make-up taps into the debates
about whether the third-wave feminism's embracing of beauty and sexuality is
a concession to patriarchy and a sign that women gave up on achieving
structural change (Shugart et al., 2010; McRobbie, 2007). Yet the trickster's
goal when she dresses up is to shapeshift and to cross boundaries, it is to
destabilize the system and to mock its structures. While not immune to critique, the goal is nevertheless different from reclaiming sexuality: it is more
about reclaiming chaos via agency, and agency via chaos; it is also about
showing the system how bizarre its views on femininity are.

For instance, the creators of *Crazy Ex-Girlfriend* mock the visual aspect of
the female persona in many of the show's songs, including 'The Sexy Getting
Ready Song' (S1) or 'The Math of Love Triangles' (S2). In 'The Sexy Getting
Ready Song' Rebecca dismantles the mystery behind feminine perfection on a
night out by showing the grotesqueness of some of the procedures women
undergo to look good, including trying to squeeze into shapewear and burning one's neck with curlers. Similarly, in 'The Math of Love Triangles'
Rebecca dons a shiny blue strapless dress and rather fake-looking diamonds,
and performs a Marilyn-style number extolling the wonders of being silly and
pretty in order to prey on men. In musical numbers throughout the series,
Rebecca zooms in on the grotesqueness and hyperbole of traditional femininity. By masquerading as different characters, she explores media and societal projections women unquestioningly transplant as parts of their
personality. In this sense, dressing up means liberation through laughter.

Conclusion

Liberation and laughter is what tricksters do best. This chapter has brought
together the concepts of trickster and persona to illustrate the continuous
dynamic between individual agency and the rigidity of social rules; as well as
between change and progress on the one hand, and the established social
order on the other. Both in cinema and television the trickster as an element
of the narrative refers to the presence of chaos in an otherwise organized
system. It has a range of standard attributes such as the impulse to express
one's personality in a uniquely creative way as well as the rejection of
embarrassment, shame, conformity, and refusal to belong to a structure.

Meanwhile, the concept of persona has been examined using a combination
of Erving Goffman's presentation of self theory and Jung's persona concept.
It has been argued that the female persona – the artificial vision of socially
acceptable femininity – is a particularly rigid psycho-social structure, com-
prising repressive and unrealistic expectations for women's looks, bodies and

conduct in public situations. It has showed how the female trickster can challenge these prescribed attributes and expectations while defying the individual-controlling techniques: shame, social embarrassment, social rejection, and ostracism.

Female trickster characters seek out, to use Russo's expression, 'affirmative models of risk and deviance in the high registers of modernism' (Russo, 2017: 25). Not only do they seek them out, but also explore them, and fearlessly demonstrate them to the viewer. No longer are they afraid of their body, they explore the bodily functions previously not associated with stereotypical female behaviour. Scatological humour defies the high expectations of the female persona – the veneer of perfection, decency and prettiness projected onto women as objects, not as real people.

The female trickster reclaims performativity and creativity – both carnivalesque – by separating them from the female persona, and thus from the requirements of the male pleasure. She engages in activities that may be aesthetically unpleasant, bizarre, or classified as taboo subjects. Importantly, these subjects (including sexual behaviour, menstruation, etc) are not portrayed as abject as they would have been by horror narratives, but are normalized, centralized (as opposed to pushed to the limen, the margins) and treated with humour.

The female trickster protagonist paves the way for the entertainment industry to start portraying women as realistic rather than unnaturally attractive, and to start exploring the beauty of the grotesque - the attraction of the imperfect; to start reflecting the human variability that applies to women as well as to men. Like any trickster, she reveals the precarious balance between external demands and individual needs in the individuation process: the people she embarrasses on a regular basis (friends, relatives, lovers and random acquaintances) often end up questioning their own life journeys. After all, the trickster's ability to dissolve self-control over minds, bodies, and destinies is not just a source of comic effect in narratives. It provides a narrative impetus for characters to get on the path of self-discovery. Ultimately, the female trickster represents the agentic breaking through layers of passivity and cultivating chaos for the purpose of renewing the system.

References

Abrahams, Roger (1983) *African Folktales*, New York: Pantheon Books.
Babcock-Abrahams, B. (1975) 'A Tolerated Margin of the Mess: the Trickster and his Tales Reconsidered', *Journal of the Folklore Institute*, 11, pp. 147–186.
Bassil-Morozow, H. (2012). *The Trickster in Contemporary Film*. London: Routledge.
Bassil-Morozow, H. (2015) *The Trickster and the System: Identity and Agency in Contemporary Society*, Hove: Routledge.
Bassil-Morozow, H. (2018) *Jungian Theory for Storytellers: A Toolkit*, London: Routledge.

Beauvour, Simonede (1949/2011) *The Second Sex*, London: Vintage Books.
Creed, Barbara (2007) *The Monstrous Feminine: Film, Feminism, Psychoanalysis*, London: Routledge.
Crossley-Holland, Kevin (1980/1993) *The Penguin Book of Norse Myths: The Gods of the Vikings*, London: Penguin.
Delaney, J., Lupton, M. J., and Toth, E. (1988) *The Curse: A Cultural History of Menstruation*, Urbana and Chicago: University of Illinois Press.
Doane, Mary Ann (1982) 'Film and Masquerade: Theorizing the Female Spectator', *Screen*, 23 (3–4), pp. 74–87.
Doty, W (1993) 'A Lifetime of Trouble-Making: Hermes as a Trickster', in W. J. Hynes and W. Doty (eds.) *Mythical Trickster Figures: Contours, Contexts*, Tuscaloosa and London: University of Alabama Press, pp. 46–65.
Doueihi, A (1993) 'Inhabiting the Space Between Discourse and Story in Trickster Narratives', in W. J. Hynes and W. Doty (eds.) *Mythical Trickster Figures: Contours, Contexts*, Tuscaloosa and London: University of Alabama Press, pp. 193–202.
Douglas, Mary (1968/1996) *Purity and Danger: An Analysis of the Concepts of Pollution and Taboo*, London: Routledge.
Erdoes, Richard and Ortiz, Alfonso (1999) *American Indian Trickster Tales*, London: Penguin.
Estes, Clarissa Pincola (2007) *Women Who Run With the Wolves: Myths and Stories of the Wild Woman Archetype*, London: Rider.
Goffman, Erving (1966), *Behaviour in Public Places: Notes on Social Organization of Gatherings*, New York: The Free Press.
Graves, Robert (1992) *The Greek Myths*, London: Penguin.
Hynes, W.J. and Doty, W. (eds.) (1993) *Mythical Trickster Figures: Contours, Contexts*, Tuscaloosa and London: University of Alabama Press.
Hynes, William (1993) 'Mapping the Characteristics of Mythic Tricksters: A Heuristic Guide', in W. J. Hynes and W. Doty (eds.) *Mythical Trickster Figures: Contours, Contexts*, Tuscaloosa and London: University of Alabama Press.
Hynes, William (1993) 'Inclusive Conclusions: Tricksters – Metaplayers and Revealers', in W. J. Hynes and W. Doty (eds.) *Mythical Trickster Figures: Contours, Contexts*, Tuscaloosa and London: University of Alabama Press, pp. 202–219.
Jung C.G. (n.d.) *The Collected Works*, Herbert Read, Michael Fordham and Gerhardt Adler, (eds.) R.F.C. Hull (trans.), London: Routledge. (Except where a different publication was used, all references are to this hardback edition.)
Kerényi, Karl (1956) 'The Trickster in Relation to Greek Mythology', in Paul Radin, *The Trickster: A Study in American Indian Mythology*, New York: Schocken Books.
Kristeva, Julia (1982) *Powers of Horror: an Essay on Abjection*, New York: Columbia University Press.
Makarius, Laura (1993) 'The Myth of the Trickster: the Necessary Breaker of Taboos', in W. J. Hynes and W. Doty (eds.) *Mythical Trickster Figures: Contours, Contexts*, Tuscaloosa and London: University of Alabama Press, pp. 66–87.
McRobbie, Angela (2007) 'TOP GIRLS? Young women and the post-feminist sexual contract', *Cultural Studies*, 21 (4–5), pp. 718–737.
Mulvey, Laura (1975) 'Visual Pleasure and Narrative Cinema', *Screen*, Autumn, 16 (3), pp. 6–18.
O'Neill, Robert (2001) *Sexual Profanity and Interpersonal Judgement*, LSU Historical Dissertations and Theses.

Pelton, Robert D. (1980) *The Trickster in West Africa: A Study of Mythic Irony and Sacred Delight*, Berkeley: University of California Press.

Radin, Paul (1956/1972) *The Trickster: A Study in American Indian Mythology*, New York: Schocken Books.

Ricketts, Mac Linscott (1966) 'The North American Trickster', *History of Religion* 5 (2), 327–350.

Ricketts, Mac Linscott (1993) 'The Shaman and the Trickster', in W. J. Hynes and W. Doty (eds.) *Mythical Trickster Figures: Contours, Contexts*, Tuscaloosa and London: University of Alabama Press, pp. 90–106.

Russo, Mary (1994) *The Female Grotesque: Risk, Excess, and Modernity*, London: Routledge.

Samuels, Andrew (1993) *The Political Psyche*, London: Routledge.

Shugart, E., Waggoner, C. E., Hallstein, D. and Lynn O'Brien (2010) 'Mediating third-wave feminism: appropriation as postmodern media practice', *Critical Studies in Media Communication*, 18 (2), pp. 194–210.

Tannen, Ricki Staphanie (2007) *The Female Trickster: the Mask that Reveals*, London: Routledge.

Titton, Monica (2019) 'Afterthought: Fashion, Feminism and Radical Protest', *Fashion Theory*, 23 (6), pp. 747–756.

Ussher, Jane M (2011) *The Madness of Women: Myth and Experience*, London: Routledge.

Velie, Alan R. (1979/1991) *American Indian Literature: an Anthology of Traditional and Contemporary Indian Literature*, Oklahoma: University of Oklahoma Press.

Waddell, Terry (2006) *Mis/takes: Archetype, Myth and Identity in Screen Fiction*, London and New-York: Routledge.

Waddell, Terry (2009) *Wild/Lives: Trickster, Place and Liminality on Screen*, London: Routledge.

Westervelt, W.D. (n.d.) *Legends of Maui, a Demi God of Polynesia, and of His Mother Hina*, Amazon (print on demand).

Wolf, Naomi (2012) *Vagina: a New Biography*, London: Virago Press.

Conclusion

Although representation of women in moving image narratives has been slowly improving since the 1970s, the real change began to happen fairly recently, perhaps as a result of social media highlighting the need for better, and more varied, representations, and spreading awareness of issues such as sexual harassment, violence against women, gynaecological issues, pregnancy and childcare, motherhood and career, and many more. Another factor has undoubtedly been the growing influence of on-demand television competing for audiences and increasingly hiring new talent: little-known screenwriters, directors, actors, and producers.

Alongside the ruthless warriors, aloof and unemotional characters like Queen Elsa in Disney's franchise *Frozen*, confident survivors like Beth Harmon in *Queen's Gambit* and shameless rule-breaking tricksters such as nameless protagonist of *Fleabag*, the new generation of heroines have been proving that there is no one way of doing the journey. Locking female role models within the opulent and attractive, yet still very limited and narrow-minded 'Goddess feminism' would be a mistake in terms of the scope of the woman's journey. It would mean to stereotype women (and female characters) yet again, to trap them in one role when it is time to move on and to acknowledge the complex, varied and creative nature of the protagonist, the journey and all its constituents.

The new generation of female characters is now breaking through the constraints of the female persona and taking on the entire archetypal range, including the hero/ine, the child and the self which had previously had little use in female-driven narratives, and the shadow/trickster axis which had traditionally had even more limited applicability to female characters. Now the audiences are finally seeing women battling with moral issues (the shadow), misbehaving, innovating and breaking social rules (the trickster), searching, exploring, investigating and fighting (the hero/ine), growing up and discovering her identity (the child), and trying to achieve balance between the different part of her personality (the self).

This does not mean that the heroine is no longer interested in relationships and has completely rejected the relational in favour of action. The new

DOI: 10.4324/9781003253044-9

heroines can still be mothers, wives and lovers, of course, but, crucially, their character arcs go beyond Theme 2 which contains 'family' archetypes. They often combine themes, and using relationships as elements of their journey where previously falling in love, attracting a partner, or having a child would have been the main goal of the narrative. Now parents, partners and children, forming the communal and the familial milieu of the narrative, are built in, sometimes highlighted, sometimes obscured and sidelined, like it does in crime dramas in which the female detective's affairs or her relationship with her children are woven into the journey of self-discovery.

The rethinking of the female persona in moving image narratives has also been uneven. Whereas the behavioural constituents of the persona (passivity, heteronormativity, exclusive relatedness and family orientation etc) are the first to be rejected, and replaced or, at least, complemented, by elements of agentic behaviour, the appearance aspect of the female persona is still very much here, sometimes residually so but often displayed blatantly in slim figures, revealing outfits, perfect make-up or nice hair. The necessity of this element is much debated in both feminist circles and within screen studies, its longevity surprising more so that many of its satellites are now gone. Even the most decisive of princesses like Elsa from *Frozen*, and deadliest of trickster-fighters like Harley Quinn are still portrayed as good-looking even though they are not trying to secure a partner. Of course, appearance can be used as a weapon or as part of self-expression, as a sign of creativity and an element of one's identity. In any case, this part of the female persona does not seem to be going anywhere and may remain an essential element of female creativity.

The tension between the individual and society is inevitable as argued by many disciplines, including sociology and various branches of depth psychology. Masks are part of our social nature, we all need to wear them. However, we need to campaign for a better, flexible persona for women, and for better gender balance. We need to rethink the concept of the female persona. Even if we cannot get rid of the concept of the social mask altogether, we still need better masks for women.

Index

For Product Safety Concerns and Information please contact our EU
representative GPSR@taylorandfrancis.com
Taylor & Francis Verlag GmbH, Kaufingerstraße 24, 80331 München, Germany

www.ingramcontent.com/pod-product-compliance
Lightning Source LLC
Chambersburg PA
CBHW050649280326
41932CB00015B/2838